MW00623672

Dirty books

Manchester University Press

Dirty books

Erotic fiction and the avant-garde in mid-century Paris and New York

Barry Reay and Nina Attwood

MANCHESTER UNIVERSITY PRESS

Copyright © Barry Reay and Nina Attwood 2023

The right of Barry Reay and Nina Attwood to be identified as the authors of this work has been asserted in accordance with the Copyright, Designs and Patents Act 1988.

Published by Manchester University Press
Oxford Road, Manchester M13 9PL

www.manchesteruniversitypress.co.uk

British Library Cataloguing-in-Publication Data
A catalogue record for this book is available from the British Library

ISBN 978 1 5261 5924 3 hardback

First published 2023

The publisher has no responsibility for the persistence or accuracy of URLs for any external or third-party internet websites referred to in this book, and does not guarantee that any content on such websites is, or will remain, accurate or appropriate.

Typeset
by Cheshire Typesetting Ltd, Cuddington, Cheshire
Printed in Great Britain
by TJ Books Ltd, Padstow

Contents

Acknowledgements   *page* vi

Introduction   1
1 Beginnings: Jack Kahane and Obelisk Press   4
2 The syndicate: pornography for the private collector   35
3 Olympia, Paris   62
4 Repurposed pornography: the role of erotic classics   97
5 Dirty books   121
6 Sexual revolution: Olympia, New York   153
7 Literature or pornography?   187
Conclusion   221

Notes   227
Index   290

Acknowledgements

Like the books and writers discussed in what follows, our collaboration has been a transnational one, working between Australia and New Zealand, and then New Zealand and Greece. *Dirty Books* was partly written and researched during COVID-19 times; it has been a demanding process.

We would like to thank the editors of *Porn Studies*, Feona Attwood and Clarissa Smith, for publishing our 2021 article, 'The syndicates: writing pornography before the sexual revolution', which became, in effect, the blueprint for this book.

The debts to archivists are many. Barry Reay managed a visit to the library of the Kinsey Institute at Indiana University before the COVID travel restrictions and is, as always, appreciative of the assistance of Liana Zhou, Director, Library and Special Collections, and Shawn Wilson, Associate Director of Collections. But much of the archival research was done from a distance, perusing catalogues, targeting potentially fruitful collections, and arranging massive copying. The kind archivists and other staff at the following repositories (in no particular order) were unfailingly helpful, often at times of severe institutional and personal stress: Yale Collection of American Literature, Beinecke Rare Book and Manuscript

Library; Manuscripts and Archives Division, New York Public Library; Harry Ransom Humanities Research Center, University of Texas at Austin; Department of Special Collections, Charles E. Young Research Library, UCLA; University Museums and Special Collections Service, University of Reading; Special Collections Research Center, Syracuse University Libraries; Rare Book and Manuscript Library, Columbia University Library; the National Archives, Kew; the State Library, Victoria; and Baillieu Library, University of Melbourne. The interloans staff at the University of Auckland Library have been constantly accommodating.

The archival copying of items that we would normally visit on site was carried out by extremely efficient and professional proxy researchers (again, in no particular order): Kelli Leigh Fisher, Ann Leifeste, Erica Ivins and Susan Moore. We really could not have finished the book without their help.

Finally, we would like to acknowledge Emma Brennan, our commissioning editor at Manchester University Press, for her support, enthusiasm – and our book's title.

Introduction

Pornography is a gauge of the social and cultural temperature of an era. Today we live in an environment where ubiquitous sexual explicitness and easily accessible erotic material exist alongside cancel culture, where (for perfectly understandable reasons) the sexual behaviour of a creative can trigger the death of their work. But not so long ago, during the period covered by this book, the sexually explicit was hidden. Censorship determined – or attempted to determine – what could or could not be written and published.

We first came across the story of writing pornography to order when we were researching Gershon Legman, a fascinating maverick in the history of sex.[1] Legman, who seemed to know everyone involved in the realms of sexual folklore, literature and medical research, referred both to a 1940s New York syndicate of struggling artists, poets and writers (some destined for fame) providing pornography to a wealthy US collector, and to what Legman termed a 1950s combine of young hack writers churning out English-language pornographic books, dirty books, for a Parisian publisher. We were hooked, not least because some of those involved were, or became, well known: the writer Henry Miller was involved in each enterprise. We researched more. We consulted the archives. We read the dirty books. The story grew. It turned out that the Paris publisher used his dirty books to subsidise important works of modernist literature, serious stuff. It transpired that he had a father who had earlier published censorable material, using lighter literature (much of it written by himself) to support more high-quality writing. We discovered that the Paris publisher later moved to New York, where he was involved in the publishing milieu of the 1960s sexual revolution. We also realised that the boundary between the dirty books and the modernist literature – the 'serious stuff' – could be hard to discern.

In New York and Paris from the late 1930s until 1970, daring publishers produced banned English-language literature, and young writers, poets and some artists wrote pornography to order, many anonymously. The names of some of those involved may already be familiar to the reader (Miller, Anaïs Nin), others less so (Legman, Iris Owens). In New York in the earlier period, they wrote for a broker for a mysterious oil magnate who sought pornography for his own sexual gratification, though some of the product would later go on to be published more widely. In Paris, the publication of English-language erotic writing was generated by two innovative publishers. Jack Kahane, with Obelisk Press in the 1930s, published work banned or impossible to publish in England or America (Radclyffe Hall, Charles Henri Ford and Parker Tyler, Miller, Lawrence Durrell and Nin). In the 1950s and 1960s, Kahane's son, the publisher Maurice Girodias, and his Olympia Press, produced avant-garde, modernist literature (Samuel Beckett, William Burroughs, J. P. Donleavy, Lawrence Durrell, Jean Genet, Miller, Vladimir Nabokov and Alexander Trocchi) as well as unadulterated porn – dirty books, or 'dbs'. Many of the pornographers mobilised by the New York syndicate and by Girodias wrote to survive, but some also relished the freedom to experiment that anonymity provided. Men wrote as women; women wrote as men.

Themes emerged from this story. Anonymity and fake authorship clouded gender and provided freedom of sexual expression. Women, we discovered, played a central role in the production of erotic literature, exploring and challenging the relationship between feminism and pornography. Writers in exile felt the freedom to experiment; Paris was central to English-language pornography, aided by legal loopholes and French liberalism, although, as Girodias found out, that situation changed. It is debatable whether this pornography undermined 'heteronormativity', as one commentator has claimed, but it certainly 'reflected a wide variety of tastes and sexual proclivities'.[2] That modernism and pornography were linked is unsurprising. Modernism employed the sexually graphic in the service of literary innovation in what has been called 'aestheticized obscenity'.[3] Pornography produced the sexually explicit for the sake of arousal, sex for the sake of sex. But the relationship between modernism and pornography was ambivalent. When, as we will see, both pornography and avant-garde texts were being produced by the same publisher, or when the former was written to support the latter, the relationship could become somewhat blurred.

This book is literary history rather than literary criticism or literary analysis (though the latter approaches will inform our work). It examines some of the themes of twentieth-century English-language written erotica by focusing on moments in pornographic history that produced avant-garde literature and what arguably became a literary wing of the sexual revolution of the 1960s.

1

Beginnings: Jack Kahane and Obelisk Press

Our story begins with an English publisher in Paris in the 1920s and 1930s. Jack Kahane, formerly an exporter of velvet in Manchester, set up in 1929 what would become his publishing business, the Obelisk Press. He began with a partnership with Henri Babou, but then went out on his own in 1931, using the proceeds of what Neil Pearson, his bibliographer, calls the 'mildly titillating' novels that he wrote under the pseudonym Cecil Barr.[1] Kahane, who referred to his life as moving from 'dealing in cotton to dealing with the products of some of the finest brains in existence', established a formula that would be employed to great effect: the use of Paris as a site for evading English and American censorship; and the publication of 'dirty books' to support far more serious works of avant-garde literature.[2]

Kahane's son, Maurice Girodias, more of whom later, said that Obelisk became known internationally: 'For anyone who wanted to write freely, outside of any censorship parameters, there was now at least a technical hope of publication.'[3] Henry Miller was certainly aware of Kahane's reputation. As he wrote to Lawrence Durrell in 1936, 'He won't publish a thing unless it has a sensational quality, unless it might be banned in England or America. That's his strategy for the present.'[4] When Miller read the typescript for what became Durrell's *Black Book* (1938), he knew that Kahane was the only choice to publish it: 'The whole thing is a poem, a colossal poem ... *This is the poem*. It's like the black death, by Jesus. I'm stunned ... It seems to me, at the moment, that Kahane would be the only man to do it.'[5]

Pearson has over fifty writers on his list of Obelisk authors, but the press's more notable output would include some modernist classics: Charles Henri Ford and Parker Tyler's *The Young and Evil* (1933), Henry Miller's *Tropic of Cancer* (1934), *Black Spring* (1936), and *Tropic of Capricorn* (1939), Lawrence Durrell's *The Black Book* (1938) and Anaïs Nin's *The Winter of Artifice* (1939).[6] The press also published D. H. Lawrence's *Lady Chatterley's Lover* (1936), but there were at least six editions before it reached Kahane.[7] Similarly, Radclyffe Hall's *The Well of Loneliness* (1933) was not initially published by Obelisk and came at the end of productions by other presses. Its publishing history, and censorship tribulations ('I would rather give a healthy boy or a healthy girl a phial of prussic acid than this novel'), began in 1928; it came to Kahane after numerous copies of the book had already been published in France (by Pegasus Press, as a strategy to circumvent English censorship) and in America (where an attempted curb failed).[8] *Time and Tide* magazine wrote in 1928 that the attempts to censor *The Well* had created an international best-seller, and the book had sold 150,000 copies well before Kahane got his hands on it.[9] Given their pre-Obelisk history of multiple publications, we will not include *Lady Chatterley* and *The Well* in our discussion, though Kahane's interest in the controversial books demonstrates a willingness to back important projects. Alec Craig must have had Obelisk in mind in 1938 when he wrote of the irony that anyone who wanted access to 'some of the most distinguished writers' in English had to travel to Paris.[10]

Kahane stumbled onto his formula. He and Babou published Norah James's book *Sleeveless Errand* in 1929, after it had been seized in Britain as an obscene book, and it sold well – 'like mitigated wildfire'.[11] 'My object grew clearer every day', Kahane wrote in his autobiography. 'I would start a publishing business that would exist for the convenience of those English writers, English and American, who had something to say that they could not conveniently say in their own countries.'[12] From early on, Kahane used lighter fiction (much of it written pseudonymously by him) to enable more elevated literary endeavours. Kahane's son Maurice Girodias, with his own career fresh in his mind, later summarised his father's programme:

> No one had thought of producing light erotica for the Anglo-Saxon tourist visiting the continent, spicy enough to attract those timid souls, and yet not too much so as to avoid trouble with the French authorities. The easy profits one could make in that way could help finance a more speculative activity; for instance, each time an important book would be banned in the United Kingdom or in America, it would be one more *cause célèbre* to be added to the publisher's list … And as to the run-of-the-mill novels for the tourists, my father felt confident that he could turn out one or two a year himself, and find more elsewhere without too much trouble.[13]

Maurice would continue his father's formula but with far more explicit erotica supporting the significant fiction.

Kahane was envious of the Parisian bookseller Sylvia Beach's discovery of James Joyce's *Ulysses* (1922). He would visit her and ask, '"How's God?" (meaning Joyce). He admired me "no end" for my discovery of such an "obscene" book, as he termed it, as *Ulysses*, and never relinquished the hope of persuading me one day to let the Obelisk Press take it over.'[14] Kahane managed to publish both Joyce's *Haveth Childers Everywhere* (1930), an extract from what would become *Finnegan's Wake*, and his short collection of poems, *Pomes Penyeach* (1932), published first by Beach and Shakespeare and Company. Kahane would have been pleased with *Haveth Childers Everywhere*, with its handmade Japan paper and impossible prose: 'Round the musky moved a murmel, but mewses whinninared and belluas zoomed'.[15] But the editor was on the lookout for 'the book of his life', 'the great work he had been waiting for since the beginning'.[16] Then, along came Henry Miller and *Tropic of Cancer*. He read the manuscript in his garden, through into the night:

> 'At last!' I murmured to myself. I had read the most terrible, the most sordid, the most magnificent manuscript that had ever fallen into my hands; nothing I had yet received was comparable to it for the splendour of its writing, the fathomless depth of its despair, the savour of its portraiture, the boisterousness of its humour. Walking into the house I was exalted by the triumphant sensation of all explorers who have at last fallen upon the object of their years of search. I had in my hands a work of genius and it had been offered to me for publication.[17]

Miller told Anaïs Nin in 1932 that the editor at the French publishing house Hachette had told Kahane that *Tropic of Cancer* was 'magnificent, overwhelming (épouvantable [appalling] *etc. etc. etc.*) beside which *Lady Chatterley* and *Ulysses* is *lemonade*. He says I'm a powerful, formidable writer – and he has never seen a book like it. (I thin[k] they're all going mildly crazy – losing their perspective, etc.)'.[18] Kahane had found his *Ulysses*.

The foundation to Kahane's enterprise was the money made from his light best-sellers. Although Miller was unkind when he referred to them as 'vile[,] vile crap', they were never intended as anything else.[19] Miller's friend Alfred Perlès called them 'light, entertaining, risqué, hovering on the thin borderline dividing the erotic from the downright pornographic'.[20] *Daffodil*, written by Kahane under the name Cecil Barr, is a comedy of manners, 'a light amoral trifle, amusing and swiftmoving', as its author described it.[21] The main character, Daffodil, is a strong-minded, independent virgin (a status supposed to add to her allure), an illegitimate child who has forged a living as an artist and artist's model. Much of the novel consists of attempts on her virginity – including an attempted rape – and she almost ends up (unknowingly) in a sexual relation-ship with her father, a notorious philanderer, a man who 'knows the inside of more bedrooms than any other man in Europe'.[22] The book is slightly risqué. 'Gradually, imperceptibly, I became aware of another feeling', writes Kahane, as Barr, as Daffodil, 'one I had never experienced before, but which I knew existed. A damp delight. A misty, yearning feeling. A surge of excitement. Sexual excitement.'[23] *Daffodil* is witty: 'His technique was perfect; he did not make love to women; he allowed his fascination slowly to assert itself, and then they made love to him.'[24] Kahane bragged that it sold 'like the tastiest and hottest of hot cakes'.[25]

Kahane's *Lady Take Heed!* (1937) – the last of the Barr novels, of which he wrote six – has the same uneasy, first-person, ven-triloquised, male descriptions of female pleasure. But it is rather more explicit: 'he thrust his hands between my thighs, his fingers penetrating me and clawing horribly inside me'.[26] It has lesbian scenes: 'I felt her lips hot against the skin above my stockings, here, there, clinging, searching, insisting, until they found their goal, and clung and clung, until my whole body burst into a flame of ecstasy, unimaginable, and the consciousness went out of me, sobbing, to the accompaniment of her muffled sighs.'[27] The book's main char-acter, Primrose (another floral-inspired name), is a young woman embarking on a sexual life ('I felt his bare body against mine and his strong sex entering into me').[28] She is pursued relentlessly by her stepfather, moving to Paris to escape his attentions after he has assaulted her. There she embarks on a same-sex affair ('I was excited and disturbed, but deliciously disturbed') and a relationship with a young French aristocrat who teaches her the pleasures of BDSM ('thanks to him I had at last discovered the full meaning of the word pleasure'), and she works for a wealthy banker whose intentions become immediately clear.[29] In other words, *Lady Take Heed!* pursues the familiar Barr theme of the besieged woman who survives her adversities: Primrose's father catches up with her in Paris and dies from the strain of raping her; she inherits a bordello and marries her first love. Such was the kind of material which provided the bedrock for Kahane's far more significant literature.

Several historians of twentieth-century pornographic film have drawn a distinction between films where sexual representation was covert, connoted, deferred and off-stage, and those where it became far more explicit, denoted, on-stage and overt.[30] Obelisk's Cecil Barr novels are comparable to the sexually connoted films. Kahane's son Maurice Girodias's Olympia Press would represent a shift from connotation to denotation, from the covert to the overt.

What of Obelisk's more serious literature? It is a varied and impressive list, with collective themes that include male and female homosexuality, decadence, adultery, sex work and sexual promiscuity. 'All those books', Girodias has noted, 'had offended the censor's sensibilities in some unforgivable manner. Each one had added a bit of prestige to the Obelisk imprint.'[31] We will consider Miller and Durrell later in the book, but it is worth discussing some of Obelisk's other writers here.

Norah James's *Sleeveless Errand*, published first by Babou and Kahane in Paris, saw Kahane on his way in the publishing world.

9

Suppressed in Britain by the Home Office – made much of in the book's preface – it deals with sexual promiscuity and marital infidelity, but without any really explicit sex. James, who worked as a publicist at the publisher Jonathan Cape (she attended the trial of Radclyffe Hall's *The Well of Loneliness*), was totally perplexed by the outcry:

> I could not understand why. The book had been read by a number of well-known literary people in manuscript, and no one had suggested that I should make any cuts in it. But, apparently, it was called an obscene book – simply because of the words used in it. I would have cut them out willingly if I'd been told it was necessary. But I'd never been told that. It never occurred to me that it would be considered obscene to let the characters in it use the language they used in real life.[32]

The book, seized and destroyed in England, was promptly published by Kahane in France and, as James noted in her autobiography, would go on to sell more than twenty thousand copies in America.[33]

A description on page 6 is about as graphic as it gets in *Sleeveless Errand*: 'she would not remember that he had ceased to be her lover; that she would never sleep with him again; never feel his weight upon her eager limbs; or his lips moving from her mouth to her breasts'.[34] Nonetheless, it scandalised some readers ('degrading muck' was one condemnation quoted in the book's preface).[35] There are encounters with sex workers, alcoholics and the patrons of late-night London clubs and bars. There is copious drinking, gossip and loose sex: 'God, it's all bloody! Always the same thing – the Red Lion, the Café, the Haunt, home, copulation, sleep, the Red Lion, the Café, the Haunt, home, copulation, sleep. It's the hell of a lovely life!'[36] It is a book about ennui, a study of post-war boredom (the word recurs in the novel). 'I believe my generation's damned', Paula tells Bill before her suicide, 'and it's quite likely that the generation of war-time children is damned too ... We're bored with people who aren't bawdy. We call them prigs and prudes if they don't want to talk about copulation at lunchtime and buggery at dinner.'[37] Although the sex is suggested rather than explicit, it is certainly present: 'What's wrong with us? All sex-mad – sex, sex, sex.'[38]

When it was prosecuted for obscenity in 1929, it was its subject matter and language that was considered to be at fault:

> The story concerns a period of about two days, and is told in the form of conversations by persons entirely devoid of decency and morality, who for the most part are under the influence of drink, and not only tolerated, but definitely tolerated, promiscuity. Blasphemy is freely indulged in by virtually all the characters, and filthy language and indecent situations appear to be the keynote.[39]

The offence was compounded by the fact that it was written by a woman – 'I may be forgiven if I am surprised that this terrible book should have been attributed to a woman', the prosecutor told the magistrate. For it was womankind who had to be protected from such obscenity: 'Can you imagine any other than a degrading effect upon the minds of one's own womenkind in one's own house?'[40] As Chris Forster has discovered, the Home Office drew up a list of objectionable passages in the book, twenty in all, including some of those quoted above.[41] The danger was, according to their legal brief, that readers would be exposed to 'filthy language, unnatural practices and immoral incidents'. They imagined a daughter 'in a respectable English household' alighting upon the passage about buggery at dinner, quoted earlier, and asking 'Father, what is buggery?'[42]

Peter Neagoe's *Storm* (1932), another banned title, was also one of Kahane's foundational titles. Its prohibition – 'Banned in America', emblazoned on its cover – was a major aspect of its marketing appeal, providing what Kahane referred to as 'the halo that banning inevitably reflects'.[43] *Storm* is a series of stories about peasant existence: 'Lina was a big girl with good round calves tapering to the ankles. When she walked her rump danced, her thighs swelling under the pleats of her s[k]irt. Her pink face, toppled with yellow hair, looked like a ripe peach because there was fine down on it.'[44] There is a story, 'Gavrila's Confession', about a man who witnessed his wife's infidelity but was persuaded that the devil had deceived him: 'this is my house and that there naked woman on the bed is Reveca, but the long carcass of a man with her is not myself'.[45] There is another, 'The Village Saint', about a goat-herd who impregnates all the local women. The book is full of hirsute men ('a thick fur on his belly and on his chest'), buxom women, longing lovers ('Her body ached with yearning ... Her mountain blood was mad'), priests with large appetites ('My thoughts are rooted in the flesh. I have many sins. They are all of one kind though. So maybe I've just one great sin'), wooing, trickery, pine fragrances, hay stacks and rural similes ('It is easier to watch a flock of rabbits than a woman in love').[46] Kahane considered *Storm* 'a considerable success', helping to make his name and to 'consolidate the Obelisk Press'. 'The first duty of American tourists of a literary turn of mind, when in France', Kahane wrote in his autobiography, 'was to buy *Storm*, and thanks to my unremitting efforts to ensure that the book should be prominent in every appropriate shop window, the appropriate tourist could not miss it.' He was not exactly glowing in his praise of the quality of his author, considering Neagoe indicative of the type of work that the inferior *Daffodil* would subsidise but not 'anything like a great writer'.[47] For his part, Miller thought Neagoe's work 'feeble shit'.[48]

There were several significant publications. Cyril Connolly claimed that Kahane told him that his book, *The Rock Pool* (1936), was not 'salacious' enough; 'he used to tell me it was "a disgrace to his list"'.[49] It was not Connolly's first choice of placement: 'Alas my little novel The Rock Pool is smut bound', he wrote to Sylvia Beach after he had completed his 'very short, lyrical, and seedy novel'; 'I think that I must try and have it done in America, or else it will have to appear in an under the counter way, like the Obelisks.'[50] Connolly is best known as a literary critic, a long-time book reviewer for the *New Statesman* and *Sunday Times* and as the co-founder and editor of the journal *Horizon*. He wrote *The Rock Pool* when he was thirty years old.

It is a memorable piece of literature, and the novel accepts what to some contemporaries was behaviour beyond the pale – the poet Philip Larkin, who was profoundly influenced by the book, was convinced that its casual recognition of 'sexual inversion' was responsible for the book's delayed publication in England.[51] *The Rock Pool* is set in the early 1930s, during the Great Slump, in a decaying artists' colony in the south of France, 'Montparnasse-by-the-sea'. The main protagonist, Edgar Naylor, an anti-hero, a stockbroker and amateur historical biographer, based on someone whom Connolly knew, compares the community to a 'buried site, a mound where an archaeologist delves for evidence of a vanished civilization'.[52] His creator was aware that people might want to know 'why I chose such unpleasant, unimportant and hopeless people to write about, and why I have shown no moral condemnation of their vices'.[53] But that is the charm of the book.

Naylor's friends and sexual partners are not especially agreeable either, and even less successful. There are lesbians, and Naylor falls for one, Toni: 'I can't bear to have a man so near me – always puffing and panting. I can't bear it. I can't bear it.'[54] 'I have been like that since I was five', Toni elaborates later in the book. 'Why, even in Skye they asked me to leave because I was interfering with the wives of the fishermen!'[55] There are male homosexuals: 'Why, it's you, you charming creature ... don't think you took me in with that he-man role. Not with those long, bisexual ears – Let's go and have a drink at my place.'[56] There are those of ambivalent or undecided sexuality: 'I don't care if you do like women – you're queer – one part, if you can call it a part of you – is normal – but all the rest of you is queer. You're just a pansy that's gone wrong. You can't even be a proper pansy.'[57] They are all in and out of one another's beds.

The Rock Pool is a significant Obelisk publication. In 1963 the British poet Gavin Ewart explained to younger readers of the *London Magazine* 'how cramped and inhibited literary activities were in the thirties, particularly with regard to the novel', and listed *The Rock Pool* alongside another Obelisk publication, *Tropic of Cancer*, as 'pattern breakers. They exploded like delayed-action bombs under the fortress of Book Society respectability.'[58]

James Hanley's *Boy* (1935) was another bomb. It was first published in 1931 but achieved notoriety in 1934 when a new edition (ironically an expurgated version) was prosecuted as an obscene publication, and both the publishers and a Manchester lending librarian pleaded guilty and paid the fines.[59] Kahane saw an opportunity and published the book in Paris the following year, without the initial knowledge or consent of its author. He published it unexpurgated, apart from some minor modifications which we will note shortly. Hanley forwarded the unwelcome news to a future publisher at Chatto & Windus: 'Boy will appear on the pornography barrows after all. I can do nothing ... I have a certain amount of respect for certain presses, but none for the Obelisk Press.'[60]

Anthony Burgess would later compare Hanley to Joyce in his 'cultivation of strange rhythms' in his prose, hinting at his modernism.[61] Indeed the most comprehensive modern study of Hanley's writing has described his style as floating between realism and modernism.[62] In truth, *Boy* is more realist than modernist. It is a disturbing social novel about a young boy, Arthur Fearon, brutalised by his father, forced from school to earn a living for his family, who works briefly at the dockyards, and then runs away to sea at the age of thirteen. After surviving the sexual predations of his shipmates, he contracts syphilis on shore leave in Alexandria, becomes ill, and, as Burgess expresses it, 'is put down like a sick dog by the ship's captain' and thrown overboard.[63]

The book unsettles with its violence. There are chilling descriptions of his father's brutality: 'The man felled him with a blow. As the boy dropped, he dropped too. Without asking any more questions, he commenced to punch his son, all the while breathing deeply like a horse, the hands ascending and descending, though never a sound came from the boy himself.'[64] When Arthur escapes to sea, the violence (sexual) comes from his older shipmates. The steward 'noted that he was a nice-looking boy. He liked his wine-dark skin, the fine eyes, the delicateness of the features, the slight down upon his face, the slender white hands like those of a girl. Suddenly he leaned over and said: "Boy! Kiss me."'[65] There are knowing descriptions of shipboard sexual life (Hanley himself ran away to sea), and the threat of sodomy pervades the novel. The dangers of shore leave (and of Orientalist prejudice) are revealed in gossip about a dead boy found with a bottle in his anus: 'These Arabs are real dead nuts on [buggers for] boys. But this poor soft stupid little son of a bitch didn't have enough spunk [a hole big enough] … Same thing'll happen to you.'[66] 'God almighty', T. E. Lawrence wrote to Hanley in 1931, 'you leave nothing unsaid or undone, do you? I can't understand how you find brave men to publish you.'[67] One publisher's reader had been horrified when she saw his typescript: 'the whole book is nothing but buggery and brothels and filth and horror piled upon each other in endless repetition'.[68]

Hanley does not shy away from descriptions of early hetero-sexual passion. When Fearon visits an Egyptian sex worker, he feels 'as though somebody had drugged him ... His blood tingled. It was like having swan's down drawn gently up and down his body. It tickled him. It was delirious ... He had a great desire to expand, to open and blossom like a flower.'[69] The descriptions are sexually explicit without being pornographic:

> one long arm glided down his body until it reached the harbour of all his feeling and desire. There it remained. The boy was kissing her body. He was rather like a dog. [He was like a form of lapdog.] She felt his tongue licking her skin. [She felt his hot tongue licking.] She looked down at the tiny hands that had cupped themselves to hold one of her breasts. She crushed him to her. And heard him murmur: 'Oh Jesus Christ! Oh! Oh! Oh!'[70]

Frank Harris's *My Life and Loves* (1934), a mixture of self-promotion and pornography, was one of the more sexually explicit of the Obelisk books. Bernard Shaw's wife, Charlotte, burned Volume I, page by page, 'so that not a comma should escape the flames' (Shaw's description), in order that the servants did not read it.[71] Either Samuel Roth, the American pornographer, or his ghost-writer Clement Wood, both of whom knew a thing or two about the subject, have Harris confiding to a friend, 'One of my ideas is simply to sprinkle in, every few pages or so, a racy anecdote from anywhere, pretending it happened to me and some woman – anything will do ... have an affair with a luscious young widow, with a couple of daughters, say ten and eleven; have her insist I take the daughters too'.[72] The motive for writing *My Life and Loves*, according to Roth/Wood, was to make Harris's fortune from writing 'smut'.[73]

'[J]ournalist and rogue' is Harris's headline descriptor in the *Oxford Dictionary of National Biography*.[74] At one time or another he was the editor of the *Evening News*, the *Fortnightly Review*, *Vanity Fair*, *Saturday Review*, *Hearth and Home*, *Modern Society* and (in the US) *Pearson's Magazine*; he wrote novels, biographies, short stories and plays. He seemed to know everyone of any importance. But Harris also had the reputation, especially after *My Life and Loves*, of being a liar and fabulist, with his earliest biographers referring to his 'brazen indifference' to reality and his 'empty fabrications'.[75] The man himself considered Volume 2 of *My Life and Loves* 'the most remarkable "memoirs" ever written and I'm pitting myself not against poor Casanova, but against St. Simon and the dialogues of Plato on Socrates'.[76]

Our concern here is principally with his sexual descriptions. The Paris bookseller Sylvia Beach recalled that after she had published Joyce, would-be authors brought her 'their most erotic efforts' and that Harris was one such visitor, telling her that 'he was really the only English writer who had got "under a woman's skin"' in his erotica. She claimed that she recommended Kahane to Harris because she knew that the publisher 'was always looking for "hot books"'.[77] (Before Harris agreed a contract with Kahane, Beach had effectively been publishing him by distributing his privately printed volumes with a commission of from 40–50 per cent of sales.[78]) By 'under a woman's skin', Harris presumably was referring to writing from the woman's point of view, for *My Life and Loves* has many passages where women describe their feelings of heightened desire. A married mistress told him, 'when I heard your voice, or imagined I did, I felt the lips of my sex open and shut and then it began to burn and itch intolerably ... at one moment I am hot and dry with desire, the next wet with passion, bathed in love'.[79]

The quotations of female pleasure appear in the context of the 1870s when Harris was seventeen or eighteen years old and living in Kansas; yet they were written in the 1920s when the author was in his sixties. Could he really recall this dialogue of passion in such detail? '"You darling lover!" she cried, her eyes wide as if in wonder, "my sex throbs and itches and oh! I feel prickings on the inside of my thighs: I want you dreadfully, Frank", and she stretched out as she spoke, drawing up her knees.'[80] Harris bragged of a prodigious memory: 'in Athens I learned Demosthenes' Oration, *On the Crown*, in the original Greek from beginning to end'.[81] It was these powers of recall, his 'exact remembrance' as he puts it, that he asserted enabled him to sketch out his interactions.[82] Yet he was also aware of the difficulty of writing about sex, the trickiness of capturing the intensity and subtlety involved in sexual relationships, how the pace of description can flatten the more protracted pursuit and neglect the rejections, and that the memory can 'colour incidents dramatically'.[83] By Volume 2 of *My Life and Loves* he was admitting that he was 'no longer a trustworthy witness'. 'To write one's life truthfully', he elaborated, 'one should keep a complete diary and record not only of facts, but motives – fears, hopes and imaginings – day by day at very considerable length.' He vowed to keep such a record 'from today on (November 22nd 1923)', but that was far too late for his readers.[84]

Without embracing Roth's claims about Harris's cynicism, it seems clear that he knew exactly what he was doing. He thought that sex would sell. But Harris wrote justified pornography, pornography with a stated purpose. He began the first volume of his memoirs by stressing the 'perfect freedom' of expression of what followed, aiming to counter the silence about sex in English novels and emulating what he took to be the 'license' of French writers: 'Our literary characters are lop-sided because their ordinary traits are fully portrayed while their sex life is cloaked, minimized or left out.'[85] His was 'the first book ever written to glorify the body and its passionate desires and the soul as well and its sacred, climbing sympathies'.[86]

Harris had also claimed that the book's purpose was to educate. Hence, one assumes, the numerous references to the use of the syringe after intercourse ('get up immediately and syringe yourself thoroughly: water kills my seed as soon as it touches it') and the not-always-accurate reproductive advice about the rhythm method of birth control and the employment of withdrawal ('Get me to withdraw before I come the first time').[87] One woman asks, 'But how will that help if you go on half a dozen times more?' He, or rather his young self, replies, 'Doctors say … that what comes from me afterwards is not virile enough to impregnate a woman'.[88] The worldly author – 'I have read lascivious books in half a dozen languages' – intervened in memories of his sexually precocious seventeen-year-old self to proclaim that pornography invariably misrepresented female sexuality: 'The truth is hardly one married woman in a thousand is ever brought to her highest pitch of feeling; usually, just when she begins to feel, her husband goes to sleep.'[89] He gave rather worrying guidance for 'success with women'. Flattery and persistence are the keys to attainment: 'taking the girl's "No" for consent, her reproofs for endearments and even a little crossness for a new charm. Above all, it is necessary to push forward after every refusal, for, as soon as a girl refuses, she is apt to regret and may grant then what she expressly denied the moment before.'[90]

My Life and Loves catered for a variety of sexual tastes. Harris claimed to have discovered cunnilingus in Greece when a woman asked him to do to her 'what the girl did to Nana' in Emile Zola's 'latest book'.[91] Harris prided himself on these skills. 'I found several unlooked-for and unimaginable benefits in this mouth-worship', he writes. 'First of all, I could give pleasure to any extent without exhausting or even tiring myself … Secondly, I discovered that by teaching me the most sensitive parts of the woman, I was able even in the ordinary way to give my mistresses more and more keener pleasure than ever before.'[92]

He also liked his sexual contacts young. There are descriptions involving twelve- and fourteen-year-olds that would outrage modern sensibilities. 'Even now', he wrote when he was in his sixties, 'a well-made girl's legs of fourteen make the pulses beat in my forehead and bring water into my mouth.'[93] It seems that this predilection was more widely known. Sylvia Beach wrote amusingly that when Harris asked her to recommend a book for a rail trip to Nice, she sold him *Little Women*, which, to Harris's disappointment, was not at all what he had anticipated: 'He jumped at the title, which to someone with an obsession like his could have only the French meaning of *petites femmes*. He grabbed the two volumes of Louisa Alcott's "hot book" and off he dashed to the station.'[94]

Kahane produced a compelling piece of anti-war fiction. Richard Aldington's *Death of a Hero* (1930) was one of Kahane's more superior products; the critic George Orwell thought its two volumes 'much the best of the English war books'.[95] It has modernist elements, experimenting with its prose, including narratorial asides ('Isabel and George Augustus depress me so much that I am anxious to get rid of them'[96]), but especially with its sexual candour. Aldington was uncertain whether his writing was realist or expressionist but settled on calling it 'a jazz novel'.[97] The author's original uncut manuscript, not published until the 1960s, is sexually explicit (using words such as 'cunt' and 'fuck') whereas the expurgated publications of 1929 – two slightly different versions, published in London and New York, respectively – prefer 'muck' and 'mucking' to 'fuck' and 'fucking' and use swathes of asterisks in place of potentially offending words and passages of prose.[98] Those who encountered all those asterisks must have pondered the obscenities that they concealed. Aldington wrote later: 'If the English are such babies, give them asterisks, I said, and let them see how absurd this cutting and slashing is.'[99]

Kahane and Babou's uncensored edition is closer to the unabridged than it is to the abridged. In the abridged versions, nearly twenty lines in total were removed concerning a couple's lovemaking and replaced in two instances by asterisks. In the excised sections they tongue kiss ('He put the tip of his tongue between her moist lips, and she touched it with hers') and he is puzzled when she asks him for 'something else'. These descriptions are all intact in the Kahane and Babou edition.[100] However, the Kahane and Babou edition was not without his own modifications. There are many examples, but a few may suffice. In the description of wedding bells, Aldington's original manuscript had: 'What said the bells? "Come and see the fucking. Come and see the fucking."' The abridged edition writes, 'What said the bells? "Come and see the ******. Come and see the ******."' The Kahane and Babou edition substitutes 'Come and see the bedding'.[101] The phrase 'Bloody old cunt!' appears unapologetically in Kahane and Babou's publication, instead of the expurgated 'Bloody old ***'.[102] But it uses 'muck' and 'mucking' as in the censored volumes; thus, '"Fuckin' old fool", "Silly old fucker"' become 'Muckin'' and 'mucker'.[103] The logic of these editorial decisions is far from clear.

Death of a Hero is a powerful, angry novel about a man, George Winterbourne, who moved in pre-war artistic, intellectual and free-thinking circles, who died in the First World War, along with hundreds of thousands of others, and who was not really mourned, even by his parents and his wife and mistress. This is indicated at the beginning of the novel, which intensifies the pathos as the narrative unfolds. There are also suggestions that he aided his own death by standing up into machine-gun fire. Aldington described his work as a lament, 'a threnody, a memorial in its ineffective way to a generation which hoped much, strove honestly, and suffered deeply'.[104] 'Atonement – how can we atone? How can we atone for the lost millions and millions of years of life, how atone for those lakes and seas of blood?'[105]

Because it dealt both with liberated living and thinking on the home front and with life in the trenches and the language of men in combat, there were ample opportunities to offend. Aldington writes of Winterbourne's wife and mistress (they were friends):

> They both had that rather hard efficiency of the war and post-war female, veiling the ancient predatory and possessive instincts of the sex under a skilful smoke-barrage of Freudian and Havelock Ellis theories. To hear them talk theoretically was most impressive. They were terribly at ease upon the Zion of sex, abounding in inhibitions, dream symbolism, complexes, sadism, repressions, masochism, Lesbianism, sodomy, etcetera … They knew all about the sexual problem, and how to settle it. There was the physical relationship and the emotional relationship and the intellectual relationship; and they knew how to manage all three, as easily as a pilot with twenty years' experience brings a handy ship to anchor in the Pool of London. They knew that freedom, complete freedom, was the only solution. The man had his lovers, and the woman had hers.[106]

Death and sex were linked: 'The war did that to lots of women. All the dying and wounds and mud and bloodiness – at a safe distance – gave them a great kick, and excited them to an almost unbearable pitch of amorousness.'[107]

It is not generally acknowledged that Obelisk was responsible for some central works of queer fiction (apart from *The Well of Loneliness*). Charles Henri Ford and Parker Tyler's New York-based *The Young and Evil* was one of Obelisk's most innovative books, a groundbreaking blend of modernist literary experimentation and queer sexual expression. They were young writers. Ford was the twenty-year-old editor of a literary magazine, *Blues*, and Tyler was a twenty-nine-year-old poet. When Kahane's son Maurice Girodias brought out an Olympia Press edition of *The Young and Evil* in the 1960s, Ford would claim principal authorship: 'the whole conception was mine', he reminded Tyler, 'you were *guest* collaborator remember'.[108] Both Djuna Barnes and Gertrude Stein were impressed with the novel. According to Ford, Barnes thought it 'unique she said and strange strange [*sic*] not life and like a dream'; Stein said 'it was the most important book she had seen by anyone of our generation'.[109] Ford and Tyler's typescript was rejected by publishers in the US: 'I read with infinite pleasure your brilliant novel but I could not think of publishing it as a book – life is too short and the jails unsanitary. But it was a pleasure to read.'[110] However, Sylvia Beach and the literary agent William Bradley recommended Obelisk and that was how Kahane landed *The Young and Evil*.

The people of *The Young and Evil* have sex, including multiple-partnered sex in varied combinations, and present themselves in an array of masculinities and femininities: 'The Lesbian said yes your face is so exquisite we thought you were a Lesbian in drag when we first saw you and for two long hours they insisted that he would do better for himself as a girl.'[111] Karel (Parker Tyler) in *The Young and Evil* is (in the terminology of the book and its time) a fairy with long black hair, plucked eyebrows and makeup – used 'achingly but unobtrusively. His eyebrows ... might cause an Italian laborer to turn completely around.'[112] His eyelashes are 'long enough now to catch in the boughs (should he go for a walk in Washington Square)'.[113] Their New York of the late 1920s and the 1930s is characterised by its 'polymorphous' and 'labile' sexuality.[114] Identities (though the word scarcely seems sufficient) shift: 'But Karel was thinking of Louis turning queer so beautifully gradually and beautifully like a chameleon like a chameleon beautifully and gradually turning.'[115] The inhabitants of Ford and Tyler's New York include masculine homosexuals, fairies (especially fairies), lesbians, cross-dressers, queens, prize-fighters and their girls, dancers, models, gangsters, sailors, trade (homosexually available heterosexuals), writers and poets, and the hustlers of Broadway and 72nd Street: 'And here *o murderpiss beautiful boys grow out of dung* ... They push flesh into eternity and sidestep automobiles. I bemoan them most under sheets at night when their eyes rimmed with masculinity see nothing and their lymphlips are smothered by the irondomed sky. Poor things, their genitals only peaceful when without visiting cards.'[116]

As Joseph Boone has observed, '*everything* is in transit: bodies, identities, desires'.[117] The text's lack of punctuation heightens this 'polymorphous fluidity'.[118] It combines linguistic delicacy (of the sort already quoted) with patent explicitness: 'do they grasp it with their five-fingered wrinkled cunts'; 'I want to wish you a forest of pricks with an *ocean of glue* because you'll never be able to hold them any other way'; 'thissailorsaidhefuckedhiminthemouth'.[119] *The Young and Evil* is truly experimental, then, in terms of its narrative structure (what Sam See called 'montage-like'[120]), its language (the language of the streets), its surrealistic imagery, its displayed sexualities and avant-garde literary style (word composition, punctuation, fractured sentences, layout). Juan Suárez has referred to the book's 'constant oscillation between modernist experimentalism and camp'.[121] Ford complained to Stein in 1933 that his book was not in the window at Brentano's (a major bookshop outlet for Obelisk): 'they said they were doing well by it to handle it *at* all, people pick it up and "complain" they said; "there *are* limits" they said. There are, but they're always changing'.[122] It is not surprising that recent critics have reclaimed Ford and Tyler as textual pioneers in the creation of a queer modernism.[123] Kahane deserves recognition as their publisher.

Obelisk did not shy away from controversy. Two of the press's books were about sex work. Wallace Smith's *Bessie Cotter* (1936) was published originally in the US in 1934 and in England in 1935. Kahane became interested in the book when its English publishers were prosecuted for indecency after some six thousand copies had been sold. The publishers William Heinemann pleaded guilty, paid a £100 fine and 100 guineas costs, and claimed that they had already attempted to locate, buy back and destroy the sold copies. The Attorney General seemed relieved at the guilty plea: 'it would not be necessary for him to refer in detail to the book', *The Times* summarised. 'The subject dealt with was an unsavoury one. The sole topic of the book was the gratification of sexual appetite.'[124]

The subject referred to was sex work. Bessie Cotter works in a Chicago brothel and is rather matter-of-fact about her profession: 'Let me put you straight. I told you I'm in this business, hustling, because I like it. And that's on the level.'[125] There is a refreshing candour and lack of moralising, which presumably annoyed the book's critics. As Elisabeth Ladenson has pointed out, 'Bessie Cotter was offensive both because of its subject and because that subject was not treated censoriously, or at least not censoriously enough.'[126] Smith was a journalist as well as a writer (and artist) and the style of reportage permeates his prose: 'Slowly and cheerlessly, dawn shifted through the window. It picked out the design of the wall paper, which it might more decently have left unrevealed. The bed in which Bessie Cotter slept was a contortion of white enamel, badly chipped, and tarnished brass. The bed-spring sagged wearily.'[127] However, most of the book consists of dialogue (Smith was also a screenwriter) as details of Cotter's world accumulate slowly, without sensation, in the interactions of a parade of characters: 'ten guys a night' at 'five bucks a throw'; 'That guy never gave you nothing but a habit'; 'I been hustling since I was fifteen'; 'Dames come in this business because they get a better break than they do working in a factory or in some office or even being married'; 'I suppose a butcher gets tired, now and then, of seeing his customers. Imagine how tired he'd be if they'd all ask for one thing all the time, like veal-chops'.[128] *Bessie Cotter* became a steady seller for Obelisk, with editions in 1936, 1938, 1946 and 1953.[129]

Like his son after him, Kahane had a good eye for the main chance. He published a book that had been suppressed before it was even published, condemned (in a news lull, just after Hitler's invasion of Austria in 1938) by elements of the popular press as 'A Disgraceful Book', 'A Vile Book'.[130] The headline in the *Daily Mirror* was 'Ban this book *to-day*' and the headlined article began: 'Before me lies the vilest book that has ever left the modern printing press.'[131] *To Beg I Am Ashamed* (1938), by Sheila Cousins (ghost-written by Ronald Matthews), was another book about sex work, or prostitution as it was then known. Kahane moved quickly: the book was condemned in March and Obelisk had it out by June, with another edition in August (further printings occurred in 1946 and 1951).[132] As Kahane himself remembered, 'The book was a great success, and in consequence of the maladroit (but to me invaluable) publicity that the press attacks gave it, I got large orders for it from all over the world.'[133]

Like *Bessie Cotter* it was the subject matter itself rather than the book's actual treatment of it that so exercised its critics. George Walter Stonier, the writer, critic and literary editor of the *New Statesman and Nation*, thought that the book's problems may have resulted from it being a woman's honest (though ghost-written) account of her life as a sex worker, with a rather 'unflattering view of men'.[134] The famous Graham Greene, who knew the book's ghost-writer and who had met 'Sheila Cousins' (not her real name), vouched for the book's veracity, praising some of its descriptive vignettes (the unkind have said that they were ones penned by Greene himself) and general insightfulness, quoting a passage that must strike every reader: 'The thought that chills me, as I leave my flat at seven, is that once more I must hear tonight, once, twice, three times maybe, the same unending gramophone record of male plaintiveness and pity and boastfulness and desire.'[135]

Much of the book is a depressing story of lodging-house life in interwar London, with its 'odour of decay and futureless despair', and where the horsehair sofa figures both in a group rape and a fumbling seduction.[136] There are moments of pure heartbreak: the death of Sheila's baby son in a workhouse infirmary is truly unbearable. But *To Beg I Am Ashamed* is far from sensationalistic. Sheila Cousins is Bessie Cotter-like in her acceptance of her way of making a living: 'What I am doing is a job like any other, a way of keeping alive. It is neither much more nor much less secure than most women's jobs.'[137] She is scathing about her clients, those who romanticise their paid sex – 'That greasy pretence of sentiment I found more repulsive even than the most hungry caresses' – and those who talked about the tragedy of her life one minute while 'minutes before, in bed ... had been using the grossest language to me and begging me to use it too'.[138] She is realistic about her trade: 'It was a good week: thirty pounds of receipts. But how much tolerant weariness went to earn it.'[139]

Kahane's versatility is clear. He published Marika Norden's (Mirjam Vogt's) *The Gentle Men* (1935), a pseudonymous novel consisting of letters to four Englishmen (one is actually Irish, but she considers him English), with whom the Norwegian protagonist had been romantically involved. There is no explicit language, and Pearson dismisses the author as 'a self-absorbed non-writer',[140] but she deserves some recognition for her portrayal of a married woman's love affairs with four married men and her merciless examination of them: 'Well, my dear superman, I shall now make it my onerous pleasure to dissect you', Norden writes to the unfortunate Tony.[141] 'Subconsciously I must have thought you very stupid, even then, for I was always unduly impressed when you said something sensible'.[142] Tony, she quips, was more interested in ducks than women. The various wives, and her own husband, are critically assessed in the course of the narrative. Arne, the husband, is 'at his happiest' when she is 'crushed, beaten, mad with unhappiness'.[143] The book is mildly daring, with repeated mentions of the letter-writer's menstrual periods, which must be unusual in 1930s literature, and a brief section on the advantages of lesbianism: 'Ah, you don't know how different life with a woman is! Love between women is so tender and beautiful. You ought to try it.'[144] The book is somewhat adventurous, though certainly not obscene.

Pearson is also dismissive of Richard Thoma's *Tragedy in Blue* (1936), an account of the medieval child-murderer Gilles de Rais, describing it as 'unreadable'.[145] But there is far more to the novel than that. Thoma is Aubrey Beardsley-like in his prose:

In July Gilles painted his white face white. Today his eyes were blue so he dyed his beard till in matched the Brittany sea when the angels are massed above it. His hair was long and curled. He wrapped himself in sea-green motley and wore gold-leather boots and gloves. His collar was of blue emeralds and an enamelled wreath circled his head. The green leaves did not meet on his brow but curled about it like a ram's horns. It was noon.[146]

Thoma's poesy lures the reader into the horrors that await the kidnapped children. Hence, 'His eyes are poppy flowers polished in the rain. His mouth is ecstasy running down the wind. His mouth is ichor cascading in the sky. His mouth is liquid sex ... Ah, the opiate of his hands!' rapidly becomes 'The tiger that was Giles was waiting. When he purred the children were hanged but when he rutted he fractured their skulls with knotted sticks or inflicted long deep wounds that made the wide-eyed, uncomprehending children suffer more.'[147]

The poet Thoma was a friend of Charles Henri Ford; Ford stayed with him when he first visited Paris. '[A]nd so it seems', Ford wrote to Parker Tyler, 'r. [Richard Thoma] has been out for less than two years and is just a highschool girl as far as affairs are concerned'.[148] Thoma was a Parisian contemporary of Henry Miller and associate editor and contributor to the literary journal the *New Review*. Miller and another Obelisk author, Neagoe, also wrote for the journal, which renders Obelisk's publication of Thoma's work less 'baffling' than Pearson thought.[149] Miller's friend Wambly Bald, columnist for the Paris edition of the *Chicago Tribune* and another inhabitant of Montparnasse, pronounced Thoma's prose story in the third number of the *New Review*, an extract from what would become *Tragedy in Blue*, as the best contribution to the issue: 'Thoma's mastery of form, his ability to finger brocades of words and squirt perfumes, reveals a decadence that is curiously redolent of Flaubert and reminiscent of Huysmans. His metaphors are bizarre and pulling. They smell of musk and other content.'[150] Miller later referred to *Tragedy in Blue*'s 'power' and 'splendor'.[151] Thoma has an intermittent presence in Bald's insider's guide. His poems in *Green Chaos* (1931) are 'exquisite blasphemies'; Baudelaire is 'dull as a policeman' in comparison to some of Thoma's verse.[152] 'There is something strangely dangerous, Machiavellian, about Thoma and his poetry', Bald wrote in 1933. 'Thoma is an able Montparnasse poet and will bear watching.'[153] Kahane was more perceptive than he has been given credit for.

Anaïs Nin's *The Winter of Artifice* was the last of the Obelisk books. Nin recorded its arrival in October 1939: 'My beautiful *Winter of Artifice*, dressed in ardent blue, somber, like the priests of Saturn in ancient Egypt, with the design of the obelisk on an Atlantean sky, stifled by the war, and Kahane's death.'[154] *Winter* consists of three novelettes, 'Djuna', 'Lilith' and 'The Voice', all based on Nin's relationships and all utilising material outlined in her diaries. In 'Djuna', which was omitted from later editions of the book – possibly as she tried to shed the influences of Henry Miller, perhaps because it is weaker than the other two – the narrator, Djuna (Nin), is involved both with Hans (Miller), a struggling writer, and with his wife Johanna (June Miller).[155] 'Lilith' (called variously 'The Double', 'The Father Story' and 'Don Juan and his daughter' when it was in draft) concerns the troubled relationship between Lilith (Nin) and her musician father (Joaquín Nin y Castellanos), who, she felt, abandoned her when she was young. They are reunited but Nin discovers that she no longer loves him. The third novelette, 'The Voice', deals with an analyst (Otto Rank) and his patients, including Djuna and Lilith, the narrators of the preceding novelettes (double-Nin, in effect). When Nin was writing 'The Voice', she was undergoing analysis with Rank, with whom she had an affair.[156] The story also drew on her own analytical patients; it was originally called 'Chaotica', after 'Hotel Chaotica', her name for her analytic workspace.[157]

These discrete pieces were touted separately to various publishers, without success, until they were combined in Kahane's publication.[158] The book is a literary version of Nin's extensive and complex love life, charted in her diaries but expressed more poetically in her novel. The contrast between the two accounts of her relationships (diary, novel) is a recurring theme. As she wrote several months earlier, 'In the book ['Djuna'], restraint, indirectness, trickeries! But I need a place [her diaries] where I can shout and weep … The overflow of an undisciplined extravagance. To hell with taste and art, with all contradictions and polishings … it will keep me sane for the world and for art.'[159]

Both the diaries and her novel had fictive elements but were based on real lives. Nin's cousin, and early love, Eduardo Sánchez, told her in 1941, 'In *Winter of Artifice*, we get the second transformation of a reality already once transformed in the diary. This twice transformed reality being wonderful but not accessible to all.'[160] The inaccessibility, of course, depended on knowledge of the crafted life stories. The literary agent Bradley said to Nin that he thought that his identifying Miller interfered with his appreciation of Nin's literary portrayal: 'overdrawn, overwritten, overintense, exaggerated, inhuman' – it is Nin's account but those words must have been seared into her memory – 'I think you overestimate him, that you have invented him.'[161]

Sharon Spencer has lauded *Winter* as a 'symphonic *tour de force*', a masterpiece with 'lyrical exposition', sophistication, 'a sustained prose poem'.[162] We have already noted Nin's own characterisation of restraint and subtlety. But the prose was not always moderate. 'I've never fucked a woman with a mind, you know', Hans tells Djuna in *Winter*. 'A woman who has written books. They always scared me away. But *you* … well, you don't look like a writer at all! You have the loveliest, the loveliest ass.'[163] There is a moment when Hans and Djuna have sex: '[I] felt myself dissolving, ripping open to his descent. I felt myself yielding up to his dark hunger … *I am being fucked by a cannibal.*'[164] Actually, 'Djuna' is rather flat, one-dimensional in comparison to the diary accounts of the Nin–Miller–Miller *ménage à trois*.[165] Perhaps its insipidness is because it provides muted access to Miller's narrative (the words of the fictional Hans) when we can have closer contact with his prose itself in the effervescence of *Tropic of Cancer*. 'Djuna' does not have the poetic flights of 'Lilith', nor the vertiginous power of 'The Voice'.

'Lilith' is more perfectly formed. It is inventive. The narrator describes the geography of her father's sexual conquests, as the Don Juan brags to his daughter:

> I not only played the piano in every city of the world … sometimes when I look at the map, it seems to me that even the tiniest villages could be replaced by the names of women. Wouldn't it be funny if I had a map of women, of all the women I have known before you, of all the women I have had? Fortunately I am a musician, and my women remain incognito. When I do think about them it comes out as a *do* or a *la*, and who could recognize them in a sonata?[166]

There's a long musical metaphorical description of the sexual tension between daughter and father, with 'heavy poundings on the drum like the heavy pounding of sex, the throb of blood, the beat of desire which drowned all the vibrations'.[167] It goes on, ten pages written in a frenzy according to Nin's diary, 'I passing the violin bow gently between my legs, drawing music out of my body, my body foaming … the drum beating, beating sex, and pollen inside

32

of the violin cases, the curves of the violin case and the curves of women's buttocks'.[168]

The dreamlike 'The Voice' concerns psychoanalysis. There are shrewd little descriptions. The hotel of the analyst is 'this convent of adulteries'.[169] The analyst is a 'soul detective'.[170] The Voice is an analyst, we are told early in the novelette: 'The man listening to confessions is strapped to his armchair and he sees them all struggling, defeated, wounded, crippled. They are laying themselves open before him, demanding to be condoned, absolved, forgiven, justified. They want this Voice coming from a dark armchair, a substitute for god, for the confessor of old.'[171] 'The Voice' also contains some of Nin's most surrealistic prose: 'She awakened with eyes at the end of long arms that floated everywhere', is one such description, 'and with eyes on the soles of her feet. She awakened in strands of angel hair with lungs of cocoon milk.'[172] There are many similar passages. And this despite Nin's insistence that it was Miller rather than her who was the surrealist.[173]

Nin wrote the moving ending of her book earlier on in the novelette's construction, in a moment of heightened emotion, drawing on the trauma of her aborted/stillborn child, and then added the rest later: 'The last time I had come out of the ether it was to look at my dead child, a little girl with long eyelashes and slender hands. She was dead. The little girl in me was dead too. The woman had been saved. And with the little girl died the need of a father.'[174] This said, it remains true that the novel does not have the force and the sexual drive of its author's diaries. The diary account of her daughter's demise is certainly stronger than in the novel – absolutely devastating.[175] Likewise, Nin's relationship with her father is metaphorically incestuous in the novel but explicitly detailed in her diary: 'His spasm was tremendous, of his whole being. He emptied all of himself in me … and my yielding was immense'.[176] The diaries highlight the novel's missed opportunities.

Jack Kahane was responsible for publishing some of the twentieth century's most innovative, and controversial literary works, using lighter erotic fiction to subsidise his more ambitious enterprise. His portfolio was remarkably varied, containing innovative modernism (queer, trans, anti-war, socially and sexually critical) as well as Harris's more pornographic *My Life and Loves*. As we will see, his publishing strategy was extraordinarily like that of his son in the 1950s and 1960s. In 1938 Kahane had even negotiated with Samuel Beckett to translate Sade's *The 120 Days of Sodom* into English.[177] Though in the end it did not eventuate, it shows that Kahane had an innovative pulse; the Englishing of Sade would be completed by Girodias two decades later and by Barney Rosset's Grove Press in the 1960s.[178]

Nin's *The Winter of Artifice* was Kahane's last publication. When the American publisher James Laughlin (publisher of Miller) told the playwright and writer Tennessee Williams that one of his stories was impossible to print in 'this country', it was to Paris that he looked: 'If you wanted to have it appear, it could be arranged to do it in Paris with the man who publishes Henry Miller there.'[179] This was in 1948, when Kahane was long departed, so Laughlin must have had in mind Maurice Girodias, Kahane's son. We will return to Girodias in a later chapter.

2

The syndicate: pornography for the private collector

Gershon Legman – a bibliographer, folklorist, sexual researcher and amateur pornographer – was involved in a pornography-writing group in New York in the late 1930s and early 1940s.[1] He had intimate knowledge of US and European booksellers, collectors and publishers, and knew many of those involved in the world of erotic literature during those years. He was aware, as he said of a French publisher, of where all the bodies were buried.[2] In particular, he was involved, through an intermediary, with the private collector Roy Melisander Johnson, an oil millionaire from Oklahoma who paid for regular, unpublished erotic manuscripts.[3]

Legman, and then his friend Robert Sewall, contributed at $50 a story; it should have been $100 but the intermediary, the bookseller Barnet Ruder, kept half.[4] Legman and Sewall were inventive, taking pseudonyms from the phone directory, modelling their stories on popular works of fiction such as *BUtterfield 8* (1935) and *The Postman Always Rings Twice* (1934), and parodying writers like Dennis Wheatley and Nathanael West. They included material aids for their private reader: supposed pubic hair, a used condom, a fragment of a silk stocking. Legman said that despite Sewall's aliases, his typewritten pages always physically looked the same, which undermined his anonymity somewhat.[5] One of Sewall's stories, a parody of Dashiell Hammett, was published later as both *The Sign of the Scorpion* and *The Devil's Advocate*, described by one connoisseur as the 'finest' American erotic novel ever written.[6]

But Legman said that their patron was alienated by Sewall's 'excessive' literary sadism so ended their relationship.[7] Legman soon tired of the erotica for hire: 'I wrote any number of these manuscripts, but eventually found it impossible to continue, as it was making me just as impotent sexually as it was presumably making the customer super-virile. I felt I was being cannibalized'.[8] One of Legman's efforts was *The Passionate Pedant*, reissued later by Grove Press in a volume called *The Oxford Professor Returns*, and containing some of the pornographic wit and humour discussed later: '"Well, gentlemen", said the professor, "we are gathered once again to discuss cunt in its socio-psychological and psycho-physiological significance in modern civilization."'[9]

Several notables in the literary and artistic scene in New York were involved in this erotic production line, though accounts differ on the details of precisely who initiated the project and it is likely that contacts were running in tandem. Legman was insistent that he introduced the former Obelisk Press authors Anaïs Nin and Henry Miller to the potentials of this private customer porn in a meeting with Nin at Frances Steloff's Gotham Book Mart in 1940, outlining how he gave her Ruder's contact details (which we will see she did not need), advised her on the mechanics of writing the erotic typescripts and said to keep carbon copies so that the stories could be repurposed.[10] This chapter will examine this syndicate, writing pornography for private consumption rather than publication, but involving writers, poets and others, as they tried to make a living while also honing their writing skills.

It is clear that there were other syndicates elsewhere and earlier; the artist Clara Tice, known as the 'Queen of Greenwich Village' and famous for her nude drawings in the 1910s and 1920s, but into her fifties by the early 1940s, illustrated books for Johnson, including, Legman claimed, the 1930s US reprint of three volumes from what became a famous pornographic text, *My Secret Life*.[11]

Legman knew of Chicago and Los Angeles agents and of typescripts produced in the early 1930s.[12] The poet Clement Wood and the writer Jack Hanley were involved initially.[13] It was Hanley who familiarised Legman with the 'pornography writing circuit', Legman claimed, after the erotica publisher Samuel Roth introduced the two men.[14] Peter Long's (Gene Fowler's) *The Demi-Wang* (1931) was a Hollywood product of that period, written for Johnson and then published later, a rather farcical – though witty – piece of porn featuring varied bestiality and a penis transplant among other topics.[15] Something of its male clubbishness can be discerned from the cornucopia of terms used for the penis, a virtual dictionary of slang, including 'roger-de-coverly', 'hasenpfeffer', 'ebenezer', 'haddock', 'pangolin', 'papiladoola', 'marcopolo', 'ferguson', 'alexander', 'prince-of-wales', 'hallelujah-stick', 'glorypole', 'super-richard', 'cherry-picker', 'flummer', 'harrower', 'hamburg', 'wallaby' and, of course, 'wang'.[16] The *Lord Roxboro* series, a supposed 'imitation' of the infamous Victorian text *My Secret Life*, was written for the millionaire 'about 1932', according to Legman.[17] It later emerged as *The Loves of Lord Roxboro* by Sir Walter Bone and claiming to have been written in 1898. At the time of writing it was available on Kindle as a piece of Victorian erotica, which, of course, it is not.[18]

The famous American writer Gore Vidal recalled a mysterious US-based pornography-writing collective in the 1940s:

just after the Second War when a number of New York writers were commissioned at so many cents a page to write pornographic stories for a United States Senator. The solon, as they say in smutland, never actually met the writers but through a go-between he guided their stories: a bit more flagellation here, a touch of necrophilia there … The subsequent nervous breakdown of one of the senator's pornographers, now a celebrated poet, was attributed to the strain of not knowing which of the ninety-six Senators he was writing for.[19]

This was a pornography syndicate serving the needs of an influential individual, later named by Vidal as David Ignatius Walsh, a Democrat from Massachusetts and former governor of that state. Given that Walsh was implicated (unjustly, it seems) in a famous sex scandal involving a male brothel near the Brooklyn Naval Yard (amid allegations of the activities of Nazi spies there), and Vidal's specific knowledge of the 'solon' (perhaps he wrote for the senator), this syndicate may have been homosexually focused.[20]

The detail of these various groups is vague. However, the point is that individuals and groups other than Legman's and Nin's were writing pornography for hire, whether or not for the oil millionaire.

Nin does not mention Legman's role. She tells the story at the beginning of her diary for 1940–41.[21] Miller was in need of money when he returned to America in 1940 and was therefore persuaded by the bookseller Barnet Ruder to write pornographic material for a mysterious stranger (Johnson). We are aware that Miller knew Ruder from a series of letters stretching from 1936 to 1941. Miller sent Ruder his *Tropic of Cancer* in sections by post in 1936 'to avoid the embarassments [*sic*] of the customs'.[22] He kept the bookseller up to date with his American tour in 1940–41 as he was writing his book *The Air-Conditioned Nightmare* (1945). Ruder sent Miller money over several years and did him a number of favours.

'Believe me, Ruder', Miller wrote in 1941, 'I have not forgotten all you did for me and all I owe you. Just one good break and I will clear off that balance at one stroke.'[23] So the Miller–Ruder link makes sense and he would not have needed Legman's claimed brokerage.

'This man became a legendary figure', Nin writes of Johnson, the mysterious stranger. 'In the first place we could not obtain any information about him, save that he was cultured, and that he lived through reading. That his life took place within books and manuscripts.' Nin states that Miller wrote the pornography: 'He wrote rapidly and richly.' He produced material that puzzled her: 'When I read it [it] made me both angry and excited.' 'What he wrote sounded to me like the revelation of a multitude of betrayals', and she wondered how he could have 'been carrying on all these experiences under my very eyes, as it were, while saying he loved me deeply'.[24] Miller said that he had made it all up.

But Miller quickly tired of the enterprise. He found it impossible writing for a faceless man: 'I cannot write for someone I don't know', Nin makes him say, 'I don't feel the human being present. It's ghostly. He never says anything. He is like some invisible ogre, merely swallows it all and says nothing. I am beginning to believe that he does not exist. In fact, I am sure that he does not exist.' Nin considered it tragic that Miller had always wanted appreciative patronage and had hoped that it might happen with the mysterious collector – but the man never said, 'I like your work. You write and I'll take care of you.'[25] Disenchanted, Miller handed the project to Nin and she decided to try the stranger with extracts from her diaries.

Under the guidance of Nin, others contributed erotica too: the artist Virginia Admiral (Robert De Niro's mother), the publisher Caresse Crosby, the writers Harvey Breit, James Cooney and Bernard Wolfe, the poet Robert Duncan and the Dadaist writer and poet Kenneth Patchen, author of *Memoirs of a Shy Pornographer* (1945), which, despite its promising title, is not an actual memoir of the enterprise, though it does feature a writer who suffers at the hands of an unscrupulous agent and publisher.[26] In an unpublished part of Nin's diary, she writes of Virginia Admiral and a female friend, 'one who looked like a diminutive Mae West [Admiral?], the other like a fragile Kay Francis'. 'Mae West and Kay Francis were eager to help with the typing because they were discovering new worlds.'[27] Nin became concerned that she was corrupting them. The poet George Barker was also involved, but his stories were too surrealistic for the collector, according to Nin; but Nin 'loved them. His scenes of lovemaking were dishevelled and fantastic. Love between trapezes.'[28] It was not an easy process, as the coordinator complained to her diary:

> To help those who needed money, I spread the writing of erotica recklessly and reached a point of danger to myself. I bear the responsibility of their writing, supplying paper, arranging meetings, interceding for advances, advising, correcting, and the brunt of the rejections and Ruder's complaints. The only moment of pleasure is when I carry in my pocket the money so eagerly, so desperately awaited by the hungry poets.[29]

Nin wrote that this collaboration of impecunious writers and artists prompted 'an epidemic' of erotic journals as the group recorded and recounted their sexual experiences or 'researched from Krafft-Ebing and medical books … Robert [Duncan] would offer to experiment, to test our inventions, to confirm or negate our fantasies. All of us need money, so we pool our stories.'[30] They drew on their experiences of psychoanalysis; Nin used her patient notes. Her cousin Eduardo Sánchez wrote her long accounts of his homosexual encounters – for him writing became akin to confession and absolution. 'Kay' and 'Mae' also confessed 'the contents of their analysis' and then the group discussed their sexual progress. 'Kay' was 'constantly tormented with the desire for being taken with violence. Her conversation was always about rapes, attacks, masochism'. 'We discovered', Nin writes, 'that psychoanalysis was really used by us to gain absolution and as such was a great liberating force.'[31] She said that the group saw itself as a sexual 'laboratory'; 'A wind of eroticism passed through all of us, tore down the last vestiges of timidities and secrets.'[32]

'I spent days in the library studying the *Kama Sutra*, listened to friends' most extreme adventures', Nin writes in her diary.[33] 'Gonzalo [Moré] told me the story of the Basque and Bijou and I wrote it down for the collector. "The Basque was a painter who was given the nickname because he never took off his beret even in bed."'[34] She included an abstract of the tale in her diary and the story was published later in her book *Delta of Venus* (1977) with other stories written for the collector.[35] Daniel Barnes has shown that some of the tales within tales in the book came from traditional folk pornographic narratives, a couple of which, interestingly enough, were collected by Gershon Legman (wearing his folklorist's hat).[36] Duncan kept notebooks recording his encounters: 'From the dark, forbidden, lower center of him, from the pit below his belly where the tabooed legs twisted came the penis that belonged to his magnificent body, a cock like a God's.'[37] Were the incidents real or were they invented?

Bernard Wolfe wrote amusingly of the agent Ruder, whom he called Barneybill Roster and suspected was keeping the typescripts for himself. 'I have encouraged certain young and aspiring talents to write along sexology lines', he made Roster/Ruder say. 'I'm after a *serious* literature of the genital flourishing, not dirt.'[38] In Wolfe's account, Ruder rather than Johnson guides the desired style and content, framing the enterprise as projecting more broadly than

41

the one man commissioning it: the creation of 'after-Lawrence and after-Freud sex-science fiction, conceived with depth and caliber and also, to be sure, though without descent to junkiness, a certain spirit, a dash, even some verve'.[39] In Wolfe's tendency for florid hyperbole, it becomes 'the field of New-Sexualism'.[40] Being paid by the page, Wolfe became adept at making that page contain fewer and fewer words. He ran out of ideas but then recalled that Ruder had observed 'what an infinitely better and more lasting work of art *Grapes of Wrath* would have become if expertly pornographized'.[41] So he began to pornographically appropriate similar works of literature, his last such victim being, he claimed, Herman Hesse's *Steppenwolf*.[42]

Nin wrote about their little coterie, describing herself as 'the Madame of an unusual house of literary prostitution'.[43] 'I gather poets about me and we all write beautiful erotica … The homosexuals write as if they were women … The timid ones write about orgies. The frigid ones about frenzied fulfillments. The most poetic ones indulge in pure bestiality and the purist ones in perversions.'[44] She recorded Miller's predicament as 'almost like in Dante's *Inferno* … condemned to write about sex'.[45] 'At the first opportunity I have to sit down and write that Don Juan thing for [the collector]', Miller wrote to Nin in early 1941. 'Then I'll feel done with him. I don't want to do that work any more for anything. I feel sorry you're involved – and urge you not to do a stroke more than you feel like. It's devastating. I feel as tho' I were getting rid of an incubus.'[46] (At the same time, he was reassuring Ruder that he would 'get down to the Don Juan complex etc. Believe me, I have ideas about it. I'm going to settle it once and for all.'[47]) In an unpublished section of her diary, Nin explained that Miller felt as though he was being punished 'for all the erotic appetites he had so violently awakened in human beings'. His heart had not been in the contracted writing: 'He did turn out a few lusty scenes, in which there was plenty of animality, but as soon as it was done, he was sick of it, as if he had gone with a whore and wanted to get out of the room as fast as he could.'[48]

Via Ruder, Nin also sent Johnson ('the old man') some of her diaries for $100 each, specifically inserting sexual scenes to cater for his requests. She was conflicted about the possibilities, knowing that her diary was expansive: 'Everything was included, mysticism, religion, psychoanalysis, portrait of the times, minor and major characters, the life of Paris, astrology, analysis, vivisection, passion-ate affairs, and all kinds of love, the whole complete range, from the maternal, protective to the sensual, mystical, fraternal, inces-tuous, erotic, pornographic loves.' But would he be interested in anything other than the erotic? Nin was tempted by the potential recompense for, as she writes, 'not only for years of courage and labour, but for years of sacrifices, and actual poverty voluntarily accepted'.[49]

She started with volume 32 of her 1931–32 diary, recounting the beginning of her relationships with Henry Miller and June Mansfield (later published, in unexpurgated but edited form, as *Henry and June*).[50] She waited for the collector's response and then Miller received an unpunctuated telegram from his agent: 'Dear Henry very much impressed have forwarded to my client making clear that he is under obligation to pay for this instalment I think he will be interested in others provided the material is similar. What do I do now greetings Barney.'[51]

Nin's diaries from that period record the constant sending of rewritten diary instalments to get the money used to support Miller in his own literary pursuits and to finance the needs of other friends and lovers:

The old man accepted the 33 volume! I was again given $100 which paid for the doctor for Helba [Huara] and Henry's [Miller's] trip. He asked me for expansions of the sexual scenes. I let myself go and wrote four descriptions of sexual scenes for 34. It was during the erotic madness days. I was powerfully excited by my own writing, had an orgasm while I wrote, then I went to Henry and was passionate – then to Gonzalo [Moré] who was passionate, responded to both.[52]

Then it was onto the next one – 'Virginia copied 35. I work on it. Ruder accepts 34.'[53] 'More realism! More realism!' Nin was told by Ruder.[54] '[L]eave out the poetry and descriptions of anything but sex. Concentrate on sex.'[55] Nin wearies, and questions herself: 'Will this writing prostitution I do change me, deteriorate me?' she confides in her diary in February 1941. 'Isn't this old man tired of pornography?'[56] Then, on 3 March, she is told that Ruder cannot send the latest volume to his client, as 'It is definitely lacking in the sexual elements (not exactly true there were 10 scenes in 100 pages)'.[57]

The supply of erotica was crucial to Nin's support of her lovers Miller and Moré during that time. An unpublished financial entry in her diary relates that her husband, Hugh (Hugo) Guiler, gave her $400 a month, out of which she gave $200 to Moré (and his wife Helba) and $200 to Miller. She calculates that she needs a further $137 a month for her housekeeper, food, laundry, medicine and other expenses. 'I have to earn this', she writes, 'Ruder's work supplied this.'[58] Entries in the diary for 8 March 1941 read: 'All my strength goes into Erotika', 'wrote 40 pages erotika for Ruder', 'typed 40 pages of Erotika for re-sale possibility'.[59] There is a quiet resentment that sometimes surfaces in the diaries: 'Look where I am! I am watching a play "Native Son" sitting by Mr Ruder who is ugly and vulgar and familiar. This is the prostitution I have entered into for Henry and Gonzalo.'[60] She heard that Miller had refused $200 a week to write Hollywood scripts: 'doesn't it make you angry?' asks Ruder: 'No, I said. I expect this. He does not want to sacrifice himself to free me.'[61] 'I have written 500 pages which I do not believe in – not my best writing', she observed several pages later, 'to take care of my children [Miller, Moré and others]. I have accepted many humiliating things – a kind of prostitution.'[62] And the pressure was unrelenting: 'gave Ruder 50 pages … Hugo says "I need money", so I wrote 50 more pages, then 50 again about Elena … and a seductive man who is Gonzalo with a will – Gonzalo not a child'.[63] Hugo required money to pay taxes, Gonzalo had a $50 medical bill and his wife needed a syphilis test: 'So I write for Ruder. A flowing, endless writing, like a cataract, welling from I don't know where. Eighty pages in one week!'[64]

Because of the demands of her collector, some of Nin's diaries became modified into pornographic copy. Strictly speaking, *Henry and June* may not be too far from *Delta of Venus* as examples of Nin's literary pornography. 'At night, in a fever', she writes in her diary, 'Henry's words press in on me. His violent, aggressive manhood pursues me. I taste that violence with my mouth, with my womb.'[65] What did the collector make of her dream about June where June's vagina opened and closed 'like the mouth of a goldfish' and where June had a penis: 'Yes, I have a little one, aren't you glad?'[66]

On occasion, the hundred pages for a hundred dollars was 'not erotic enough'.[67] 'Telephone from Ruder', she recorded in her diary on 9 November 1941. 'Old Man says none of the manuscripts you sent of Breit and the others came up to the standard you set.'[68] But generally the demand was there: 'The old man is begging me to write, to write *now*. He wants my erotica like a drug.'[69]

In Legman's words, Johnson wanted 'good hot fucking, and lots of it – plenty of sucking too – but no sadism, and not too much plot, background fill, or flowers of poetic diction in the erotic vein'.[70] 'I am sure the old man knows nothing about the beatitudes, ecstasies, dazzling reverberations of sexual encounters', Nin wrote in her journal in 1941. 'Cut out the poetry was his message. Clinical sex, deprived of all the warmth of love, the orchestration of all the senses – touch, hearing, sight, palate, all the euphoric accompaniments, background music, moods, atmosphere, variations – forced him to resort to literary aphrodisiacs.'[71] Nin was aware that she was creating under restrictive circumstances: 'When I gave sensuous or poetic-erotic descriptions, the client would complain, so I began to write tongue-in-cheek, to become outlandish, inventive, and so exaggerated that I thought he would realize I was caricaturing sexuality. But there was no protest.'[72]

Although some of Johnson's typescripts exist in the Special Collections Research Center at Southern Illinois University, it is difficult to discern any traces of the Legman–Nin–Miller production line in this collection; many items in the archive are copies of previously published stories by those other than the syndicate's contributors.[73] Legman recalled that the dealers had descended on Johnson's collection shortly after his death in 1960, so it is likely that the Special Collections Research Center was left with the remnants.[74] Legman claimed that he had seen over fifty of these manuscripts.[75] An American writer had created what Legman termed a 'supplement' to *My Secret Life*, almost as long as the original, he claimed, and produced volume-by-volume for the millionaire.[76] The current whereabouts of the original are unknown, but presumably it formed the basis for the previously mentioned *Lord Roxboro* series, which is certainly not as long as *My Secret Life*, though its short volumes seem a perfect length for the type of typescript provided for the millionaire.

John Ferrone, Nin's editor at Harcourt Brace Jovanovich, has even suggested that Johnson himself – 'the famous collector' – was a myth. He claimed that Nin was alerted to this around the time of the preparation of *Delta of Venus*, and that in reality 'Johnson' was an underground business, 'one of several operating in New York during the thirties and forties, that commissioned erotica and then sold copies of the manuscripts privately'.[77] Despite Ferrone receiving a letter 'from a man who had spent years of research on a group called "The Organisation"', this claim contrasts with other evidence about Johnson's existence, such as that of Legman who implied he had spoken directly with the reputed patron on a different matter (the above-mentioned Tice-illustrated copy of *My Secret Life*) and knew of him via a close dealer-friend of Johnson's.[78] It is strange too that Nin did not mention the myth in her postscript to her preface in *Delta of Venus*. In any case, it is clear that some of the material written for Johnson made its way into the hands of other collectors, by intermediaries like Ruder, or perhaps via the authors' own carbon copies.

Then there were the 'pornographic parodies' of Miller's *Tropic* books, passed off as by the man himself and causing confusion later, as we will see.[79] Some were by Legman's friend Sewall. Authorship was vague, even for the authors themselves, such was the speed and casualness of production. Legman seemed unsure whether he or Sewall were responsible for *The Oxford Professor* and *South of the Border*, written, like *Devil's Advocate*, in the early 1940s, and mimeographed, presumably for circulation beyond the intended recipient.[80] In fact, carbon copies of the texts proliferated as authors, procurers and dealers hoped later to capitalise on their pornographic product. Legman recalled selling his copies during times of hardship (most times) and then watching their dispersal, over the years, from dealer to dealer.[81] Clifford Scheiner has outlined the production of the Oxford Professor series, in which the *Oxford Professor* was merely one of eight instalments, mostly by Sewall and Legman.[82] But in fact there were many more versions of the *Professor* as volumes were split into smaller sections and run off independently. The elements of that varied series, in typescript, mimeographed and printed form, exist in copies in the library of the Kinsey Institute.[83]

The Oxford Professor imitations 'suited my own hifalutin' sexological style', said Legman, 'done tongue-in-cheek of course'.[84] Evidence of Legman's extensive knowledge of erotic literature was transmuted into the Oxford professor's, as he regaled his listeners with references to faux sexological publications like 'Bjokerhavn's splendid little monograph in the *Firth-o'-Forth Fuckological Fortnightly*, entitled "Australasiatic Types and the Relative Sparsity of Cunt-Hair Among Them"', or 'the sixth volume of Schurigius-Krimpenhuig's magnificent opus on *The Cunt and What Goes On in It*.[85] 'I suggest' – in an addition delivered in classic Legman style – 'the original Latin text of 1674, as all later editions and translations have been shamefully castrated, even the title being changed to *Woman, Inside and Outside*.'[86] It is thus possible to see in some of these stories a personal writing style Legman has described elsewhere as 'packing it all in too tight – all the digressions, discursions, the parenthetical divagations … with my brush overcharged to bulging, and dripping down my legs like a rutting goat'.[87] The professor comments on the best positioning 'in sixty-nine', of visiting 'peg houses', and of sexual positions like 'bagpiping', as 'the English call it' (using the breasts for the penis to 'thrust back and forth between them'), with one particular woman having 'all the skill and enthusiasm of the finest Highland bagpipe skirler'.[88]

The Oxford Professor Returns consists of six stories, five of roughly twenty pages each and one – 'South of the Border' – which was twice that length. Although Legman comments in his memoir that he was unsure who exactly wrote what (as we noted above), in another document he claimed Sewall's authorship of 'South of the Border',[89] and even making allowances for the different subject matter (the bulk of the book being the educated professor's tales of his sexual experiences with women of different ethnicities), it does have a different writing style and tone from Legman's. The penis is large and powerful in this longer text: a 'huge organ', 'bulging organ', 'his immense tool', 'so monstrous', 'a cock of such proportions … [it] plowed through the clinging, sensitive tissues like a great, destructive machine'.[90] The sadistic element (or in this case masochistic) that eventually resulted in Sewall's discharge from the syndicate was present too. One woman took her clothes off and put on 'a wide leather belt with the studs all over it; and she wouldn't screw him without it … her belly looked like somebody had been using her for a target with a bean blower when they were through'.[91]

As already suggested and evidenced above, some of the group's secret erotica emerged later in published form. Robert Sewall's *Sign of the Scorpion* was one, containing many passages of what the psychotherapists Eberhard and Phyllis Kronhausen have termed 'willing collaboration', where women come to enjoy their forced domination or degradation.[92] In *Sign of the Scorpion*, the virginal Clara Reeves is set upon in every conceivable way – orally, anally, vaginally, sometimes simultaneously – by both male and female partners, occasionally multiple, and with the whip now and again employed as a prelude to such activity: 'Clara gasped at the sudden thrill that went through her reluctant senses'.[93] Sewall was a master of the genre. Clara trembled with 'a sensation of mixed attraction and repulsion which she could scarcely define to herself'.[94] She was 'on fire with shame and excitement'.[95] 'She screamed again and again, but on a high note that rose from pain to pleasure as her sensations overcame her.'[96] 'How can you ... do that? Oh ... do that!'[97] The author assumes that the reader will be sexually aroused as they view characters who are sexually stimulated by watching others describing or engaging in various forms of congress: 'Clara was horrified as she watched the amorous scene, but she had a guilty realization that her own sex was dripping with excitement too.'[98]

The details and attributions of other possible publications are somewhat opaque. Legman thought that Miller's *Quiet Days in Clichy* and *Mara/Marignan Marinated* (and possibly also *Sexus*) were written for Johnson.[99] An affidavit in the back of Grove Press's edition of another book, *Opus Pistorum*, states that it was written (in parts) by Miller for another market, a Hollywood bookshop owner who supplied pornography to movie producers in the early 1940s.[100] Noël Riley Fitch, one of Nin's biographers, offers another scenario: 'When the "collector" offers double pay for pornography by Miller, they write fake Miller (perhaps at Miller's suggestion, for he does not want to get involved). Crosby offers (maybe with the aid of Anaïs) to write more fake Miller, entitles her two-hundred-page manuscript (in three parts) "Opus Pistorum," and shows it to him. The collector loves this "real" Miller.'[101] Jay Martin, an early biographer of Miller, concurred, certain that the real author was Caresse Crosby and that Miller colluded – indeed typed up part of the text for sale: 'What an irony: Henry had become Caresse's typist for a book parodying his work!'[102]

Alternatively, Legman was adamant that the text was a collection of writings by some of the group – Sewall, Crosby and/or Admiral, and himself – sometimes as a conscious parody of Miller.[103] Sewall was an adept literary mimic, using Miller and a range of contemporary writers to parody.[104] He started with the famous passage about Tania's clitoris in Miller's *Tropic of Cancer* ('I am fucking you, Tania, so that you'll stay fucked ... I will bite into your clitoris and spit out two franc pieces') and 'ran with it', according to Legman, 'lampooning it to a fare-thee-well'.[105] Legman knew Miller's style 'practically by heart'.[106] 'But then we never imagined', smirked Legman, 'that anyone would be so stupid as to believe, or to pretend, that these overblown parodies of his style were really by Henry Miller'.[107]

The confusion is understandable given that Legman led the subagents to believe that the Miller imitations were actually by Miller, and because Sewall's existence was unknown to the combine (Legman had him on a subcontract).[108] As Legman recalled proudly, 'My masterpiece of misdirection ... was when I told the agent ... that the manuscripts were as a matter of fact by Miller, *but imitating himself!* This seemed to allay all doubts.'[109] One of Sewall's first contributions, dashed off in Miller 'woman-hating fashion', was called 'France in My Pants'. There is a copy in the Kinsey Library and it is included in *Opus Pistorum* as the work of Miller. 'The French Way', another of Sewall's stories in *Opus Pistorum*, was inspired by Joris-Karl Huysmans rather than Miller, according to Legman. 'Sous les Toits de Paris' ('The Twats of Paris are Soused'), yet another chapter in *Opus Pistorum*, was a Legman/Sewall creation, Sewall writing the text and Legman inventing the title.[110] Legman claimed Sewall would lose momentum and inspiration with the writing, just as Legman had himself when writing his erotica. He said Sewall 'was beginning to repeat himself with a Second Black Mass, making love to a midget and so forth'.[111] After telling Sewall a story of a woman having brandy blown into her vagina, 'Bob worked it into one of his Miller parodies'.[112] Alexandra rubs 'a few drops of brandy into her fig' in 'A Black Mass and a Midget' from *Opus Pistorum* – another for Sewall's authorship list?[113] If this midget is a repeated theme, then was the one in 'La Rue de Screw' the original and yet another possible Sewall? Legman noted that Sewall's language differed quite markedly from Miller's and that this drew Ruder's suspicions.[114] Legman argued that Miller never used 'jism' or 'gism' for semen, *'Jean-Jeudi'* for penis, and would not use 'fig' for vagina – and it is true, he did not.[115] Each one of the six chapters in *Opus Pistorum* – albeit consisting of small, possibly variously authored sections – mentions figs, John Thursday (or nicknames like Johnny or John T) and Jean Jeudi. Figs are as common as John Thursday in *Opus Pistorum*: 'her naked figlet', 'her tiny split fig', the whore's 'ripe fig'.[116] Legman said Sewall did not understand a word of French so he provided Sewall with some erotic slang, 'some of which were already a bit out of date, like *Jean-Jeudi* for the penis, an abstruse allusion to the Greek god Jupiter that still lives on in English as "John Thursday," but hasn't been heard in French since the 16th century of Rabelais'. It is the use of such 'exotic French vocabulary', says Legman, that is the 'built-in proof that these were only parodies of Miller'.[117]

The merging of Miller and fake Miller was further abetted by the Kinsey Library's acquisition in the 1940s of many 'purportedly Miller manuscripts': 'Sous les Toits des Paris', 'The French Way', 'La Rue de Screw', 'Black Mass', 'France in My Pants', 'Cherchez le Toit' (all eventually chapters in *Opus Pistorum*); 'Paris de Luxe' (included in *Opus Pistorum* in the chapter 'The French Way'); and 'Mara-Marignan Marinated' and 'Quiet Days at Clichy' (genuine Miller works, accepted by him as such).[118] 'Some Paris Nights', another of the acquisitions, was probably also written by the syndicate and modelled on *Tropic of Cancer*, though its prose gives it away: 'I am staring openly at her breasts, stretching my neck like a crane in my efforts to look down her dress. They are crammed in there like grapefruit in a crate. They are white, round, and big, something for a man to hang onto with fingers and teeth and toes, like a monkey.'[119]

Miller denied authoring *Opus Pistorum*.[120] He told the diplomat collector of his works, J. Rives Childs, who had been informed by a contact that 'The French Way', 'Black Mass' and 'Rue de Screw' (all part of *Opus Pistorum*) were by Miller, that none of them were his. 'The titles of the three you mention I could never have invented! They are completely out of my "line". I abhor erotica – this sort – "smut for smut's sake" – as I suppose them to be.' 'And to think', he continued, 'poor Dr. Kinsey believes all this crap to be mine!'[121] He did admit that it was possible that others had provided those titles for work that he had previously produced but thought it unlikely. Miller recalled being shown some typescripts in the mid-1940s that a Hollywood bookseller had purchased 'to which my name was signed'. 'When I told him they were not mine, he seemed incredulous. I have a feeling they are the same scripts.'[122] Miller's careful bibliographer, Roger Jackson, has argued that his subject may have been the author of his own predicament because in California in 1941 he sold, under his own name, copies of typescripts provided by Nin, little thinking that this would come back to haunt him later in the form of *Opus Pistorum*.[123]

It is possible some of Nin's own erotica was temporarily misplaced amid this same system. Her diary for 1941 contains references to trying to 'resell' pornography that she had written for Ruder and the collector, and of Miller intending to sell her 'Erotika' in Hollywood.[124] In another interesting connection, both Nin's *Auletris* (rediscovered in 2016) and Miller's *Opus Pistorum* were typed up into five copies each by the Press of the Sunken Eye in 1950, by Milton Luboviski of the above-mentioned *Opus* affidavit.[125] Luboviski's affidavit says it was him that commissioned Miller's stories, but perhaps he was not the only bookseller to receive the material. George Howard – a bookseller based in Los Angeles – was also a friend of Miller's. Paul Herron cites letters by Nin to Howard to show that Miller had suggested to Nin that she send typescripts of her (and the combine's) erotica (written for Ruder/Bernays) to Howard (via Miller) to sell in California.[126] According to a contents list of Howard's archive, Howard had copies of the stories from *Opus Pistorum* and also Nin's stories published eventually as *Auletris*.[127] Herron cites a letter from Miller to Howard from January 1942, asking about a 'missing folder of erotica'.[128] Herron wonders if Nin's 'Life in Provincetown' (published for the first time in *Auletris*) was in that folder. Nin was, says Herron, a meticulous record keeper, so for material to go missing was unusual. This does not solve the authorship of *Opus Pistorum*, but it is further evidence that Miller was involved in passing on other authors' erotica for sale (perhaps as well as his own) and where issues of authorship were ripe for confusion – intentional or otherwise.

Either scenario – Miller or non-Miller – is intriguing. If any of *Opus Pistorum* is by Miller, it might give a rough idea of the material he would have written for Johnson, a pornographic cornucopia of priapic sex, where the penis (also known as 'John Thursday') reigns supreme, with rape, group sex, sex with animals, sex with a dwarf, urine play and much else. If not by the man himself, which seems the more likely ('Never even thought of writing about a black mass – beyond me!'[129]), it is still a guide to the writing provided by the syndicate, with the combine out-Millering Miller with what Legman described as 'wildcat pansexuality, and some nasty kid-porn exploitation stuff'.[130] 'I'll screw you … ass, mouth and cunt … until you have been marked forever by the passage of my prick', the narrator tells Toots in 'La Rue de Screw', surely the piece by Sewall referred to earlier, inspired by Miller; 'I'll fill your body with fucking, and your mind with fucking and your soul with fucking.'[131] 'Ah, Lotus', the narrator thinks to himself during sex with a Chinese woman in 'Sous les Toits de Paris', 'you'll soon find that you have a Chinese firecracker in your cunt ... I'll singe your ovaries with Roman candles and sky rockets will flash through your womb ... The spark is catching ... Lotus may fuck in Chinese, but she comes in Parisian French.'[132]

One of Miller's biographers, Robert Ferguson, has weighed up the possibilities of his subject's authorship. On the con side, there is Miller's denial of any ownership and the appearance of terms never used by the writer in other work – 'John Thursday' for the penis, is one such instance.[133] John Thursday 'hadn't a brain in his bald head, but left alone he can fend for himself';[134] 'if it's a sample of John Thursday she's after ... his head is already up';[135] 'She slobbers over the end like a kid with a juicy lollipop. John Thursday is a mess but at least he's having his beard shampooed'.[136] As discussed above, Legman said that he had provided Sewall with 'John Thursday', which would seem to clinch it for the cons, and we have already noted the chapters written by Sewall/Legman.[137] On the pro side, there are 'numerous Miller trademarks': the cunt as a clam, firework ejaculations, what seem to be instances of what Ferguson terms 'Miller's comic surrealism, like the description of a navel big enough to keep a horsechestnut in', and, finally, George Barker's dismissal of Miller's denials.[138] If nothing else, *Opus Pistorum* demonstrates the perils of anonymous porn. 'Both collectors and publishers since', says Fitch, 'have found it convenient to believe that Miller is the author.'[139]

With Nin, however, we are on firmer ground, for her contributions have survived in the form of *Little Birds* and *Delta of Venus*, published in the late 1970s, and *Auletris*.[140] 'His hand was moving, exploring, but so softly, it was tantalizing', she wrote in her story 'A Model'. 'I was wet, and I knew that if he moved just a little more he would feel this. The languor spread all through my body. Each time his tongue touched mine I felt as if there were another little tongue inside of me flicking out, wanting to be touched too.'[141] Her manuscripts survive both in the Kinsey Institute and in the archives at the University of California, Los Angeles.[142]

As we have noted, Nin's diaries illuminate the process of writing pornography for the collector: 'Every morning after breakfast I sit down to write my allotment of erotica';[143] 'A telephone call: "The old man is pleased"';[144] 'The collector accepted another hundred pages. I received another hundred dollars';[145] 'Isn't the old man tired of pornography? Won't a miracle take place? I begin to imagine him saying: "Give me everything she writes, I want it all, I like all of it. I will send her a big present, a check for all the writing she has done."' Nin tells Miller the collector is contradicting himself: 'He says he likes simple, unintellectual women – but he invites me to dinner.'[146] However, financial need trumps the aesthetics of personal style: 'we need money for taxes' and much else, writes Nin in 1941, 'So I write erotica. I have done in all five hundred pages. Eighty pages in one week.'[147] This contribution would increase further. When compiling *Delta of Venus* and *Little Birds* for publication in the 1970s, Ferrone was given 850 pages of erotica by Nin's second husband, Rupert Pole.[148]

Sometimes it is the pornography itself that reveals the process of its creation. In a monument to intertextuality, the short story 'Marianne' from *Delta of Venus* reveals – perhaps semi-autobiographically – the inspirations (textual and human), the financial imperatives and even the multi-faceted arousal of writing and reading erotica. The Marianne of the story is a painter who types erotica to support herself financially – given to her by the narrator (whom we cannot help but read as Nin herself). In terms we are familiar with from the diary, but here forming a preamble to the tale, Nin starts 'Marianne' by saying: 'I shall call myself the madam of a house of literary prostitution, the madam for a group of hungry writers who were turning out erotica for sale to a "collector". I was the first to write, and every day I gave my work to a young woman to type up neatly.'[149] (Marianne, we are told – again reminiscent of Nin's own research for her erotica – 'had read Proust, Krafft-Ebing, Marx, Freud'.[150]) Given the sexual content of the narrator's work, she 'could not help wondering, as I gave her my erotica to type, how it would affect her'. The narrator soon finds out, when, on visiting Marianne and finding her absent, she discovers different material on the typewriter: 'In the middle of her work, Marianne had been taken with the desire to write down her own experiences.'[151] The reader is then treated to what Marianne wrote. Nin's writing is thus the framework of this story within a story. The writing (and typing) of pornography arouses the desire not only to experience sex but to write down this experience in order that that sex can be re-experienced (which, of course, is the point of pornography).

Marianne's (autobiographical) story involves her arousal at the sight of a man who models for her painting. This man, Fred, it turns out, is aroused by her excitement. He was the one who commissioned the painting of himself (with erection). Sex does not initially take place as that is not the source of *his* satisfaction; he likes being watched. Meanwhile – outside her own erotic recounting – Marianne was 'affected by the continuous copying of other people's adventures, for now everyone in our group who wrote gave his manuscript to her because she could be trusted. Every night little Marianne with the rich, ripe breasts bent over her typewriter and typed fervid words about violent physical happenings.'[152] The restraint in the story, Marianne's unrequited longing – she 'was growing thin and perishing with unsatisfied desire' – was juxtaposed with her memories of past sexual imagery:

> Inwardly she was in a turmoil. Violent images passed before her eyes. She was remembering penny movies she had seen once in Paris, of figures rolling on the grass, hands fumbling, white pants being opened by eager hands, caresses, caresses, and pleasure making the bodies curl and undulate, pleasure running over their skins like water, causing them to undulate as the waves of pleasure caught their bellies or hips, or as it ran up their spines or down their legs.[153]

The repetition of 'caresses', the poetic flow and rhythm, the voyeuristic effect on the reader (or penny-movie viewer), gets transmuted again when 'It occurred' to Marianne – when oral sex and ejaculation for him does not end with penetration for her – 'to show him the manuscripts that she was typing. She thought this might incite him. They lay on the bed and read them together.'[154] The story within the story goes a step further when a sexually frustrated Marianne urges Fred to try to liberate himself by writing about his own experiences. In the penultimate act of circularity in this short story, a shy Fred takes his manuscript directly to 'the collector', offering it for sale and apologising for it being written by hand. 'The collector, finding it difficult to read, innocently gave it to Marianne to be typed.'[155] And, of course, she and the reader see it. This tale does not go well for Marianne. The 'secret of his passivity' is a history of arousal by being watched, and thus ends in her frustration: 'She wept a little, feeling betrayed as a woman.'[156]

'Marianne' is clearly a different sort of erotica. There is sex of a sort: 'All he would do was to place his hands between her legs. While she caressed him with her mouth his hand opened her sex like some flower and he sought for the pistil. When he felt its contractions, he willingly caressed the palpitating opening.'[157] Fred achieves his first ejaculation with a woman when Marianne performs oral sex on him: 'She licked it gently, with the delicacy of a cat, then she inserted a small portion of it in her mouth and closed her lips around it. It was quivering.'[158] But the overwhelming theme is one of repressed longing and sexual frustration: 'she yearned to be possessed by him more completely, to be penetrated'.[159] One cannot help but wonder what Johnson – the collector reading about the collector and with the final product in his hands – thought on reading this story.

Scheiner would include the writings republished as *White Stains* as the work of 'Anaïs Nin and friends', and possibly for Johnson, but we are sceptical of the attribution to Nin and the group. *White Stains*, which was first published by Samuel Roth in the 1930s (he stole the name from Aleister Crowley), has a very nineteenth-century feel about it (nursemaids, diseased prostitutes, maidenhead-taking and the sexual allure of women's calves) and was in any case published before Nin's group even existed. Legman dated the work at 1935.[160]

Scheiner describes *White Stains* as 'delicate fiction', 'extremely sensual, almost poetically so', characterised by 'lyrical expressions of complex erotic and sexual feelings', and with 'the language, syntax, perspective, cadence' of an undeniably Nin-like quality.[161] But the text does not bear out the 'extreme similarities' with Nin's 'self-acknowledged stories' that Scheiner claims.[162] While 'the lovely hillocks of her beautiful bosom' and her 'mossy fringe' may have led Scheiner to see parallels with Nin's botanical turns of phrase, 'full titties', 'the ugly red bandage of his lusty manhood', 'funny pussy' and 'her oily cavity' are decidedly un-Nin-like.[163] The first sentence in the story, 'Cunt' – another word not characteristically employed by Nin in her erotic writing – could not be any more non-poetic: 'Pretty young girls have nice tickly cunts between their legs for ardent young men to put stiff pricks into.'[164] Nin's refined style could not be further from the directness of the narrator of 'Cunts' who tells the female reader that once in the arms of a man 'you will think, "At last I am being fucked! I am a woman now, and a man is fucking me! His hard prick is actually in my cunt, and this delicious sensation which I feel as he pushes and thrusts is from his big, loving prick fucking my cunt."'[165] It is perhaps no great surprise that 'over the years this volume has become nearly forgotten. No one has openly claimed it for their own'.[166]

Despite the restrictions imposed by the client, Nin's work (that is, the books other than *White Stains*) contains those elements that she declared essential to true erotic writing, but which she was being forced to omit: 'The source of sexual power is curiosity, passion … Sex does not thrive on monotony … Sex must be mixed with tears, laughter, words, promises, scenes, jealousy, envy, all the spices of fear, foreign travel, new faces, novels, stories, dreams, fantasies, music, dancing, opium, wine.'[167] Nin's sexual interactions were much more delicate, lauded by Legman as 'the only possible pattern for the erotica of the future'.[168] On starting her work for the collector, Nin had thought America might have possessed a similar 'tradition of literary erotic writing' as that of France, but was wrong. 'All I have seen is badly written, shoddy, and by second-rate writers', she lamented. 'No fine writer seems ever to have tried his hand at erotica.'[169] Nin did not know it at the time of writing, but her erotica, published just months after her death in 1977, would gain more praise, revenue and reputation than any of her prior literary endeavours.[170]

Although she initially felt this material was 'a parody of masculine pornography' and told Ferrone it 'wasn't literary enough', she had agreed to its publication.[171] In the postscript to the preface in *Delta of Venus*, Nin says: 'I believed that my style was derived from a reading of men's works. For this reason I long felt that I had compromised my feminine self.' Despite the collector's directives, Nin saw, on reflection, 'that my own voice was not completely suppressed' and that 'I was intuitively using a woman's language, seeing sexual experience from a woman's point of view'.[172] Nin's style will be discussed further in a later chapter, but it was indeed clear that the erotica she produced and her unique style of expression were undeniably different from the other material sent to the collector. Whereas an act of oral sex in *The Oxford Professor Returns* involves a 'cock', 'glans', 'rod', 'shaft', 'prick' with 'jet after jet' of 'thick semen flooded into her throat', in Nin's 'Marianne' Fred's 'erect sex' is 'licked … neatly and vibrantly … kissed … enclosing it in her lips like some marvellous fruit'.[173] What starts, in Nin, as 'a tiny drop of a milky-white, salty substance dissolved in her mouth, the precursor of desire', ends less graphically as she 'caressed him and absorbed him until he came'.[174] In 'Elena', 'the semen would come' from Pierre 'like little waves breaking on the sand, one rolling upon another, little waves of salty foam unrolling on the beach of her hands'.[175] Although 'writing under pressure from a client who wanted me to "leave out the poetry"', Nin's 'dollar a page' erotica embodied a very unique tone and style of expression, described by her editor Ferrone as 'uniquely feminine, rich, beautifully written, literary and groundbreaking'.[176] When circulated outside Roy Melisander Johnson's infamous 'olive-green office filing drawers', it took on a life of its own.[177]

3

Olympia, Paris

In Paris from 1953 to 1966, Maurice Girodias, his Olympia Press and their collection of writers produced a steady stream of English-language erotic and pornographic literature, just under two hundred titles in all. This was a 'combine', wrote Gershon Legman, 'involving dozens of young hack writers ... churning out their 250-page manuscripts to feed Girodias' and his distributor Barney Rosset/Grove Press' almost weekly need for pornographic one-hand readers and paperbound fuck-books'.[1] Legman saw them as the 'true inheritors' of the syndicate discussed in Chapter 2.[2] The Parisian product was aimed at English and American tourists, the English-speaking colonial diaspora and the thousands of American soldiers and sailors in Europe at the time.[3]

These distinctive, green-covered paperbacks in Olympia's Traveller's Companion Series, with the alluring command on the back cover, 'NOT TO BE SOLD IN THE U.S.A. OR U.K.', were trafficked into those very countries. The cover, first chosen because it was 'drab', the colour of 'camouflage', soon became its distinctive feature.[4] As Girodias put it, 'fans were as fascinated by the ugly plain green covers as the addict by the white powder'.[5] The books were deliberately pocket-sized, Girodias said, to facilitate smuggling.[6] Austryn Wainhouse, who was involved with the Olympia project from the start, recalled a 'network of outlets, jobbers and depots stretching from Gibraltar to Macao. It was something to behold. Cartons, bales went out to booksellers in every conceivable latitude; whoever could read three words of English in Bombay, in Nairobi, in Barbados, there Girodias had a potential client'.[7] He said that the crew of American warships made money by offering their printed contraband to dealers in and around New York's Times Square, and that tourists financed their holidays by smuggling books back to England to sell: 'Dirty book clubs mushroomed in London: you rented *The 120 Days* [*of Sodom*] for ten guineas a week.'[8] In Paris, the dirty books' main outlets were the bookshop Librairie Anglaise, the English Bookshop, owned by a Frenchwoman called Gaït Frogé, George Whitman's Le Mistral, and Brentano's, the French bookshop that had been one of Obelisk's principal markets.[9]

Girodias had the right background. As we have seen, his father was Jack Kahane of the Obelisk Press (see Chapter 1). His venture did not appear out of thin air; rather it was built on the networks and publications discussed by Colette Colligan for an earlier period, including those of his own father, Kahane.[10] Girodias had served an apprenticeship at Obelisk, as he tells it, typing, proofing, packing, billing, shipping.[11] 'By now I've learned enough to become a professor of erotic technology', he wrote of his time there. 'My head is crammed with all this lurid information ... I hunt the typos in those endless sex scenes'.[12]

Perhaps the publisher with a pedigree had had in mind the success of the modernist pocket-sized books of the 1920s and 1930s, priced at 3s 6d to provide James Joyce and D. H. Lawrence to a wider (though still not mass) readership. One of these series was called the Travellers' Library (not far removed from the Traveller's

Companion); another, the New Adelphi Library, had trademark green covers (almost the same as Olympia's).[13] The young publisher started a new company, Le Éditions du Chêne, which absorbed Obelisk, but had lost control of both enterprises by the end of the 1940s, with the big publisher Hachette gaining the rights to Kahane's more lucrative publications (Miller, Harris).[14] Girodias had also been involved in a publishing venture with a friend of his father to 'print cheap European editions in English of some famous best sellers (I remember having bought the rights of "Grapes of Wrath")', but the Germans were approaching Paris and his associate, Kurt Enoch, fled to the US, where he co-founded the New American Library (1948) on exactly the same principles.[15] The point is, Girodias was no publishing neophyte.

Patrick Kearney has described the early Olympia Press as a kind of 'club' made up from an expatriate group of English and American writers and translators, principally from the staff of *Merlin*, an experimental periodical involving Alexander Trocchi, Richard Seaver, Austryn Wainhouse, Patrick Bowles, Christopher Logue and others, 'unified in a foreign land by a common language and by the sort of literary Bohemianism usually associated with the Paris of the 1920's and 30's'.[16] They were young: all were in their twenties. They were a self-confident collective, turning down in 1955 a piece of writing from what would become John Berger's *Ways of Seeing* (1972) as 'pedestrian' and 'weak'; *Merlin*, Wainhouse informed Berger, has 'very few aspirations in the direction of educating masses, either masses of intellectuals, to whom we seek to address ourselves, or to masses of persons who have a surely justifiable contempt for intellectuals' occupations'.[17]

Trocchi was clearly the Merlin collective's leader, described later by Seaver as 'as close to a definition of "life force" as I had ever encountered'.[18] Girodias was drawn by the young group's enthusiasm, naivety and affection for a Paris that no longer existed, and they became somewhat guilelessly absorbed into the Olympia ambit, providing authors, translators and editors for the press's list and various series.[19] Merlin was always on the point of implosion, as is clear from a letter that Wainhouse wrote to Seaver in 1955, referring to a crisis meeting and to a 'group ... truly lying in a god damned dustbin of cecity [blindness], indolence and murky confusion'.[20] Wainhouse complained that Jane Lougee, Trocchi's girlfriend, who financed the magazine, had too much influence on its content.[21] He confined to his diary that '*Merlin* existed on the strength of Alex'[s] phallus & the delight of Jane's vagina'.[22] Girodias arrived at the right time, then. The Merlin intellectuals were impressed by the publisher's suavity and apparent prosperity: Seaver remembered the 'shiny black Citroën, a sharp contrast to our seedy bicycles', but learned eventually that the car had not been paid for and that Girodias's 'financial fortunes were at an even lower ebb – if such were possible – than ours'.[23] 'I printed my first books on credit (Sade, Miller, Apollinaire), and was soon on my feet again', was the publisher's own short assessment of the situation.[24] Trocchi told the Merlinois, 'Let's face it, mon ... there are two virtues here: first, we can get our books published, and, second, we can eat.'[25] Girodias paid about £200, possibly more, per typescript, and £150 per translation.[26] The Scottish writer James Campbell has described the merger as 'a marriage made somewhere very far from Heaven'.[27]

Girodias's strategy was to use his pornography to subsidise the publication of more experimental literary works, the latter appearing under the Olympia Press and Collection Merlin imprints, and the former in Olympia's Atlantic Library, Ophelia Press, Ophir Books, Othello Books and Odyssey Library. Both genres were accommodated in the famous Traveller's Companion Series, the most substantial of the lists. The Collection Merlin imprints were serious but short-lived, with only six titles, two of them by members of the Merlin group: Samuel Beckett's *Watt* (1953); Jean Genet's *The Thief's Journal* (1954); the filmmaker James Broughton's poetry collection, *An Almanac for Amorists* (1953), which Broughton 'hounded' Trocchi to publish; Christopher Logue's poems, *Wand and Quadrant* (1953); and Austryn Wainhouse's novel, *Hedyphagetica* (1954), an inventive tale of militarism and authoritarianism.[28] The Merlinois were earnest young writers: 'These are the midtimes, the cleft twixt the good and the bad, the bad and the good times plentiful and lean, times when one is hard pressed to reckon how well or badly off one is, where the wind lies, if it blows, by what means to do the little sums, when to reap or eat or sleep or die'.[29] *Hedyphagetica*'s author once described himself as an 'American political thinker living in exile in Paris'.[30] Logue was privately critical about the coherence of the Merlin project, writing to Wainhouse in 1956:

> None of the collective had fundamental ideas in common and none were prepared to hammer any out. This state itself sprang from an inability to contain any central system of thought by any of the individuals concerned. So I acquired a thorough knowledge of Marxism, Bowles went to logical-positivism, Trocchi sought to destroy his brain with his prick (his success with this appaled [*sic*] me) you passed from Sade to Kierkega[a]rd via Bataille and political events. Out of all this I found a major artist – Brecht, to whom, if he will have me, I can attach myself.[31]

But they were still serious about themselves.

Collection Merlin was quickly replaced by the Traveller's Companion Series. Olympia produced, among its more meaningful endeavours, work by Samuel Beckett, William Burroughs, J. P. Donleavy, Lawrence Durrell, Jean Genet, Henry Miller,

Vladimir Nabokov and Alexander Trocchi. *Hedyphagetica* aside, there is no doubt about Girodias's role in the history of erotic literature. Four of John Phillips's nine landmarks of modern French eroticism – Guillaume Apollinaire's *Les Onze Mille Verges* (1907), Pierre Louÿs's *Trois Filles de leur mère* (1926), Georges Bataille's *L'Histoire de l'oeil* (1928) and Pauline Réage's *The Story of O* (1954) – were published in English by Girodias's Olympia. The overall project was what Justin Beplate has called 'a heady mix of *avant-garde* literature and pure pornography'.[32]

The first great literary (non-erotic) 'discovery' was Samuel Beckett, lauded by Seaver as 'one of the two or three most important writers of the twentieth century'.[33] The future New York publisher came across *Molloy* and *Malone Dies* – in French – in 1951 or 1952 and was persuaded by Trocchi to write about Beckett in *Merlin*, the first of many Beckett pieces in the magazine. In his later Grove collection of Beckett's writings, Seaver evoked the jolt of this initial encounter with *Molloy*: 'I will not say I understood all I had read, but if there is such a thing as a shock of discovery, I experienced it that day. The simplicity, the beauty, yes, and the terror of the words shook me as little had before or has since.'[34] He told Trocchi that he had never read anyone like Beckett, 'Totally new, totally different. Maybe more important than Joyce.'[35] Seaver also determined that there was an unpublished Beckett novel in English called *Watt*, which had done the round of English publishers without success. *Watt*, with its numerous editorial and printer's typographical errors, was published as an Olympia Press and Collection Merlin book in 1953.[36]

But it was Patrick Bowles who translated Samuel Beckett's *Molloy* from the French, an intensive process taking fifteen months for some 240 pages, and involving, as Bowles recalled, 'meeting with Beckett on a regular basis to revise the draft translation ... slow, painstaking work ... wrung and thrashed and hammered out. Every day we revised a few pages, pen in hand, but debating virtually every word.'[37] The bilingual parrot in the English version of *Molloy* emerged from such negotiations, swearing in both English ('Fuck the son of a bitch, fuck the son of a bitch') and French ('*Putain de merde!*').[38] Beckett chose Bowles for his writing skills as much as his translating abilities: 'Time and again Beckett said that what we were trying to do was to write the book again in another language – that is to say, write a new book.'[39]

The 'Merlin juveniles', as Beckett called them, translated many works of note, making them available in English for the first time.[40] Baird Bryant told Kearney that he took certain liberties with their first translation of *The Story of O* (1954): 'I simply overstated and exaggerated the proposition that such sadistic treatment of "O" was subjected to would "free" or "liberate" her (from her bourgeois conditioning).' He accomplished this, he said, 'by simply translating *livrer* (to deliver) as *liberer* (to liberate)'.[41] Austryn Wainhouse would translate the later editions, correcting Bryant's version to produce *The Wisdom of the Lash* (1957) and *The Story of O* (1959, 1965).[42]

However, Wainhouse's main accomplishment, under the name Pieralessandro Casavini, was the translation of Sade's *Justine* (1953), *The Bedroom Philosophers* (1953), *The 120 Days of Sodom* (1954) and five volumes of *The Story of Juliette* (1958–61) (another translator completed the project).[43] Wainhouse, as Casavini, translated Restif de La Bretonne's *L'Anti-Justine* as *Pleasures and Follies of a Good-Natured Libertine* (1955, 1956, 1961 and 1965).[44] He anonymously translated Jean Cocteau's *The White Paper* (1957).[45] He was also responsible, under the name Audiart, for the English versions of Georges Bataille's *Madame Edwarda* (*The Naked Beast at Heaven's Gate*, 1953) and *L'Histoire de l'oeil* ('The Story of the Eye'), published as *A Tale of Satisfied Desire* (1953), more of which in due course.[46] His correspondence shows that he approached Girodias, sometimes indirectly, pitching possible publications and translations: *Teleny* (which Girodias published); Andre de Nerciat's *Le Diable au corps* ('The Devil in the Flesh', which did not eventuate); and Bataille's *Le Bleu du ciel* ('The Blue of Noon', which Girodias passed on too.)[47]

Wainhouse's contribution was remarkable. He had begun his Sade translations with little expectation of ever publishing them. Sade's 1947 French publisher had been prosecuted for 'crimes against morality', and English publishers were very wary – 'the market was not yet ready for this material'.[48] Nonetheless, Wainhouse started with *The Bedroom Philosophers* and *Justine*, seized, much as Seaver had been with Beckett, by the power and difference of the language. 'Sometimes it happens that reading becomes something else, something excessive and grave', he wrote several years later; 'it sometimes happens that a book reads its reader through'.[49] And so he toiled away. 'I can say that I translated *La Philosophie dans le boudoir* before I ever met Girodias', he later wrote to Seaver, 'and read aloud passages to you, Alex Trocchi, Jane Lougee, and Christopher Logue at 8, rue du Sabot, in your room, long before I showed the texts to Girodias'.[50] Wainhouse knew that he was onto something with Sade: 'On the outermost edge of literature, as good as outside it, beyond its pale, banned, the value Sade represented and the influence he exerted were immense'.[51] Then he met Trocchi and the Merlinois, who wanted to publish his translation of *The Bedroom Philosophers* (Wainhouse was cautious), and Girodias, who actually had the means of delivering.[52] 'George Bataille has spoken to me about you. I understand you have some texts', was the publisher's opening gambit.[53] Wainhouse's diaries record his elation when Girodias's patronage made anything seem possible: 'there seems almost no limit to the quantity of translating that lies ahead'. His head reeled with the promises of work, endless Sade, perhaps Musset and Apollinaire, 'writers like Nerciat might well be done into English. In short, I can translate as long as my strength lasts and estimate that six months work will supply me with nearly a million francs, or enough to live an entire year'.[54]

They were not the earliest translations of Sade into English; those had occurred in the nineteenth century.[55] Olympia was not the first to substantially publish Sade; Jean-Jacques Pauvert was doing this in France from 1947 and being prosecuted for his trouble.[56] The press was not the first to intellectually and artistically appreciate Sade; as Alyce Mahon has shown, that honour goes mainly to the French surrealists of the early twentieth century.[57] Henry Miller first encountered Sade in Hollywood in 1941: 'Man Ray the photographer, whom I see occasionally, is nuts about Sade', he wrote to the bookseller Barnet Ruder, 'and talks to me interminably about the subject. Quite fascinating, I tell you. Probably the last word on sex, or rather, sexual perversions.'[58] Olympia was not even the first to publicise Sade to an English-speaking, intelligent audience; Edmund Wilson did that in the pages of the *New Yorker* in 1952, already feeling confident enough to refer to 'The vogue of the Marquis de Sade'.[59] However, the Girodias/Wainhouse/Olympia translations were the most systematic and wide-ranging. Wainhouse had moved from translating without hope of publication to musing in *Merlin* in 1953 at the heady, impending prospect of tourists purchasing affordable English-language copies of his Sades on the Parisian quays and in the kiosks: 'Sade suddenly become available!' 'Is it really a service this dauntless young publisher is rendering, who with his scorn for censorship, his defiance of confiscation, his intrepidity before the *brigade mondaine* [vice squad] and the magistrates, issues pocket editions of Sade?'[60] Amy S. Wyngaard has described Wainhouse's collaboration with Girodias on the Sade translations as 'perhaps the most daring endeavor' that the publisher ever undertook.[61]

The brief for the Traveller's Companions was simple: 'Let me be candid', Girodias told Christopher Logue and the *Merlin* writers, 'I require simple stories of a wholly pornographic kind. Character drawing, social context are of no importance. Disadvantages even. I want constant, heavy, serious fucking.'[62] 'My publishing technique was simple in the extreme', Girodias wrote, 'when I had completely run out of money I wrote blurbs for imaginary books, invented sonorous titles and funny pen names ... and then printed a list which was sent out to our clientele of book-lovers'. These customers responded with orders and prepayment, 'thanks to which we were again able to eat, drink, write, and print. I could again advance money to my authors, and they hastened to turn in manuscripts which more or less fitted the descriptions'. He recalled those days fondly: 'It was great fun. The Anglo-Saxon world was being attacked, invaded, infiltrated, out-flanked, and conquered by this erotic armada.'[63] Quality literature and dirty book were twinned in this campaign.

Girodias did not publish just any old thing. Logue's proposal for 'The Abominable Circus', about acrobats in a dizzying array of sexual contact, was turned down by his editor: 'Christopher ... this ... will never do. You are not writing pornography to amuse yourself.'[64] Marilyn Meeske was paid to write another dirty book, 'The Porridge Tasters', but instead worked on her envisaged Proustian novel. When she eventually sent the typescript, Girodias was 'horrified': 'not one word, not one reference to sex; not one erotic passage ... *Had I become a devout Catholic?* It was not publishable.'[65] (She tried elsewhere to place the book but was turned down by at least six different publishers.[66]) Alternatively, Iris Owens maintained that Girodias asked her to tone down the book that became *Darling* (1956): 'He explained that every single word I wrote did not have to be sexual! The book was just a little more than what his readers seemed to go for. So I tried hard to rein in my sexual fantasies. But, I was young and passionate and quite crazy, and the book went its merry course.'[67]

Girodias certainly stressed both his 'glorious authors' (Bataille, Beckett, Burroughs, Donleavy, Durrell, Genet, Miller, Nabokov, Sade, Queneau) and 'dirty books' ('dbs'), 'that meat & potatoes part of my production', as he phrased it in a letter to Beckett.[68] That was in retrospect. In earlier times, the distinction between the two genres may have been more imprecise. The young Patrick Kearney worked as a runner for a London dealer in under-the-counter Olympias, and he remembered that the man's customers began to complain about some of their more serious literary products: Beckett, Donleavy and Miller were 'either not dirty enough or else too "arty"', Sade had too much 'philosophizing' and *The Young and Evil* was over-experimental.[69] (What would they have made of *Hedyphagetica*?) When Kearney corresponded with Girodias in the 1970s about Bataille's *The Naked Beast at Heaven's Gate*, the publisher told him of a scheme to publish the book in a limited edition with engravings by the artist Hans Bellmer, but that he had decided against it: 'I felt there was no market for it. Hans Bellmer's engravings were too sophisticated for the U.S. 6th Fleet.'[70] Yet it is unlikely that the fleet would have liked Bataille's work anyway, with its serious preface musing the links between sex and death, pleasure and pain, 'the identity that exists between the utmost in pleasure and the utmost in pain: the identity between being and non-being, between the living and the death-stricken being'.[71]

It was not often clear in which category a prospective publication fell: glorious author or dirty book? Girodias was reputedly unimpressed when he first saw William Burroughs's *The Naked Lunch* in 1957, saying that it was 'formless' and that there was not enough sex; 'his readers wanted clarity, sex on every page, and no ambiguity'.[72] Terry Southern has told the story of the editor's first encounter with the manuscript: '"There is no fucking in the book," he said. "No sex at all in the book." We pointed out something on page seventeen. "Ah, yes!" he said triumphantly. "All the way to page seventeen! And still it's only a blow job!"'[73] As for the title, it was no good: 'What does it mean, this "*Naked Lunch*?"' He was mollified when told it 'was American slang for sex in the afternoon'.[74] Girodias revived his interest in the book after published extracts from it in America prompted prosecution. Burroughs thought that the deal with Girodias was the best that he could get: 'Please understand that Girodias is in a unique position to publish original and valuable work that more orthodox and committed publishers would not touch', he told Allen Ginsberg in 1959; 'His cause is definitely our cause. Who else would have published *Naked Lunch FIRST???*[75]

'You'll have to dirty it up', Girodias told Trocchi before *Young Adam* (1954) was published;[76] 'you know the rule', he wrote to him in a letter reprinted by Andrew Murray Scott, 'one scene per chapter, otherwise my clients will raise hell. They are not much impressed by atmospheres and so on.'[77] Trocchi agreed but was privately disappointed that his novel was 'becoming a mere DB – Dirty book'.[78]

When the African American writer Chester Himes sold Girodias the English-language rights to *Mamie Mason*, published as *Pinktoes* (1961) as No. 87 in the Traveller's Companion Series, he was told that if he 'put in six good sex scenes' he would get a thousand-dollar advance and a contract; 'I put in so many sex scenes I had to take two thirds of them out', Himes claimed later.[79]

J. P. Donleavy was horrified when *The Ginger Man* (1955) appeared as No. 7 in the Traveller's Companion Series, which he saw as little more than a pornography list. *The Ginger Man* is Joycean (the critic and writer Brigid Brophy termed it sub-Joyce) in both its language and its sexual descriptions:

> Chris's willowy fingers dug into his thighs and hers closed over his ears and he stopped hearing the soup sound of her mouth and felt the brief pain of her teeth nipping the drawn foreskin and the throb of his groin pumping the teeming fluid into her throat, stopping her gentle voice and dripping from her chords that sung the music of her lonely heart. Her hair lay athwart in clean strands on his body and for the next silent minute he was the sanest man on earth, bled of his seed, rid of his mind.[80]

With its descriptions of naval fluff and dirt between the toes, the book is too desperate and sad to be titillating. 'The *Ginger Man* must, I think', Brophy wrote, 'owe its fame to a belief that it is a dirty book – which it justifies only inasmuch as the hero, Sebastian, spends some time glorying in not taking a bath.'[81] Onanists must have been hugely disappointed when they purchased it. Nonetheless, its author made over a hundred changes, mainly involving sexual references, when he expurgated the book for publication in 1958 (not with Olympia Press, of course). The revisions included censorship of the passage quoted above, and the excision of a whole chapter where the book's hero takes a train journey with his penis unknowingly exposed.[82]

Donleavy was uncomfortable with being in the same stable as *The Enormous Bed* (No. 1), *The Whip Angels* (No. 9), *The Sexual Life of Robinson Crusoe* (No. 13) and *White Thighs* (No. 14).[83] He was not really mollified by the simultaneous publication by Olympia of

Beckett's *Molloy*, Genet's *The Thief's Journal* and Nabokov's *Lolita* because they had not initially appeared under the imprint of the Traveller's Companion Series.[84]

For his part, Nabokov was oblivious to Olympia's reputation:

> I had not been in Europe since 1940, was not interested in pornographic books, and thus knew nothing about the obscene novelettes which Mr. Girodias was hiring hacks to confect with his assistance, as he relates elsewhere. I have pondered the painful question whether I would have agreed so cheerfully to his publishing *Lolita* had I been aware in May, 1955, of what formed the supple backbone of his production. Alas, I probably would, though less cheerfully.[85]

Before Girodias agreed to publish *Lolita*, the book had been turned down by a series of American publishers. One, according to Nabokov, said that publishing the book would land both the publisher and author in prison. Another suggested that Lolita should be turned into 'a twelve-year-old lad' and Humbert into a farmer.[86] *Lolita* was, Nabokov stressed to its publisher, who had issued it in two volumes, 'a serious book with a serious purpose'.[87] It is a study of restraint:

> Once a perfect little beauty in a tartan frock, with a clatter put her heavily armed foot near me upon the bench to dip her slim bare arms into me and tighten the strap of her roller skate, and I dissolved in the sun, with my book for a fig leaf, as her auburn ringlets fell all over her skinned knee, and the shadow of leaves I shared pulsated and melted on her radiant limb next to my chameleonic cheek.[88]

Miriam Worms, Girodias's editorial assistant at the time, later told the writer John de St. Jorre that Nabokov was never able to 'accept that his best book was published by the Olympia Press, which he regarded as a scandalous outfit'.[89] *Lolita* would become the most famous, and lucrative, of the press's stable, though Olympia readers were, reportedly, initially 'disappointed with the tame turn my story takes in the second volume, and do not buy it', as Nabokov reported to Graham Greene in 1956.[90] A sympathetic reviewer in *Partisan Review* said that the 'pornographic promises' implied by *Lolita*'s 'publication by a Parisian erotica house, seem only ghosts to be dispelled almost in the very first chapter'.[91] *'Damn!! ... It's God-damn Litachure!!'*, a disappointed soldier was said to have exclaimed.[92]

Girodias was not afraid to publish innovative, unconventional literature. After its editor suggested substantial cuts, Olympia Press published Philip O'Connor's *Steiner's Tour* (1960).[93] The eccentric British poet's challenging novel was No. 83 in the Traveller's Companion Series, and, although its author's life story could have formed the subject for a dirty book, *Steiner's Tour* is definitely in the serious category.[94] 'Seized by the epileptic grandeurs which obscurity begets', its opening sentence began, 'to make money and to make me glad, I begin my book.'[95] 'Your face is a minestrone of what you don't mean and what you want me to think you really mean', O'Connor writes later in the book, 'which you must learn to believe *is* utterly dispensable.'[96]

Paul Ableman described approaching the publisher after his 'schizophrenic fantasy', *I Hear Voices*, was rejected by English publishers: 'I happened on Molloy by Samuel Beckett in an Olympia Press edition. I thought such a firm might prove receptive to my own non-mainstream novel.'[97] And so, what Philip Toynbee, writer and critic for the *Observer*, termed '[t]his brilliant and terrible little book' saw the light of day: 'I look and see the familiar sights, the mines with their charge and volley, the cross pitch and the laggings. Cardinals pass, beating for shells, avoiding both asps and swallows and sinking their percipient lines deep in the fiber.'[98]

Girodias's response to *The Young and Evil* was initially negative, even though his father had previously published the avant-garde queer classic. Charles Henri Ford told Parker Tyler that the Olympia editor thought it 'too "tame" for his list – his policy now is to publish only those books which can't be done in America. He said Grove Press would be the best bet for us'.[99] However, Girodias had changed his mind within days: 'He wants to step-up production for the Spring Tourist Season. Says he'll give *Y&E* special treatment – with slick paper "illustrated" jacket as he did for *The Naked Lunch*', and there was talk of a blurb by Tennessee Williams.[100] The contract was signed in April 1960, witnessed by Gregory Corso and Miriam Worms, and published in June as No. 80 in the Traveller's Companion Series.[101] By early 1961, Girodias was reporting a negative review while simultaneously hoping that it 'might prove to be positive publicity': 'D.H. Lawrence's work is positively virginal when compared with *The Young and the* [*sic*] *Evil*, a completely evil, degenerate, and depressing book … A good thrashing is what the authors deserve'.[102]

The poet Gregory Corso's somewhat surrealistic *The American Express* (1961) is No. 85 in the Traveller's Companion Series but is certainly not a dirty book. Corso was rather self-deprecatory about his work, written, he said, in less than a month: 'Syntactically and grammatically it's fucked up.'[103] A French friend claimed 'He didn't want to publish it. He didn't put his soul into it at all. He was on junk most of the time anyway.'[104] One of the main characters in the novel, Mr. D ('He stands for danger! disaster! death!'), was said to be based on his friend Burroughs.[105] Again Girodias played with his genres. He even toyed with the idea of calling the book *Fuck* to taunt the British censors, for the word is never used in its text.[106]

Olympia Press also published Burroughs's experimental novels *The Soft Machine* (1961) and *The Ticket That Exploded* (1962), produced using the cut-up and fold-in methods, developed with the artist Brion Gysin, where a variety of texts are broken up (amid prolific use of the dash and lower case) to form a new word mosaic: 'Tell Laura I love her sucked through pearly genital woman off your big fat shower of sperm – Diamond rings spurt out of you – Should be brought to mind – Ejaculated bodies without a cover – I learned to love you pale adolescents – Someone took you out of the creature charms'.[107]

Girodias was not reluctant to *refuse* serious literature too. He rejected a novel written by Burroughs's collaborator, Gysin: 'Won't do me any good and won't do your career any good.'[108] The Olympia editor passed on J. R. Ackerley's *We Think the World of You*, a homosexual, cross-class love story involving a dog, destined to become a literary classic, because it was 'not nearly dirty enough'.[109] He was not interested in Paul Abelman's second novel, *As Near As I Can Get* (1962), despite his admiration for his first: 'Who could be interested in these pale Soho figures?'[110]

And he was capable of ruthlessness. Richard Thoma had published with Girodias's father at Obelisk Press (as we saw in Chapter 1) and was a friend of Henry Miller. Yet the son was not impressed by the author of *Tragedy in Blue* when he sent him his latest offering: 'It's low-grade sh[i]t. Perfectly stupid drivel', he told his assistant Muffie (Mary) Wainhouse, 'the man is the most asinine old pederast I've ever heard of. What a shock. It's quite clear that Miller recommended him only because the ms contains frequent and ridiculously delirious references to himself [Miller]. Disgusting. I'm going to send the man a letter of refusal which I hope will kill him.'[111]

There is no disputing Girodias's ingenuity. He paid Frank Harris's widow an exorbitant amount for the manuscript of the fifth volume of her husband's *My Lives and Loves* (the other volumes had been published by Obelisk, as we saw in an earlier chapter). When the manuscript turned out to be less complete and less erotic than anticipated, Alexander Trocchi was engaged to rewrite the volume. 'We decided that the fifth volume of Monsieur Frank Harris's world-famous memoirs should be made into a really sumptuous work of art, to make Monsieur Harris's name even more illustrious', Girodias wrote later, 'When the brand new fifth volume was delivered about ten sleepless days and nights later, tingling with sex and fun, I felt that Frank Harris himself would have been proud of it.'[112] Trocchi later bragged that the imposture had not been discovered for several years and that Eberhard and Phyllis Kronhausen, academic experts on pornography, had taken volume five as genuine Harris.[113]

It is possible to detect Trocchi's additions by comparing the original Olympia volume with the Grove edition, which used the fragments of Harris's envisaged fifth volume rather than Trocchi's rewrite.[114] Thus we have supplemental descriptions of sex in India with a sixteen-year-old widow, with 'pink nipples, as big as small thimbles ... set as coral gems in tarnished brass' (not Trocchi's best prose).[115] Trocchi arranges the sex that Harris never had, in a foursome involving naked leap-frog ('Oh, Mr. Harris, you're terrible!'), Sapphic congress and the memorable narrator's aside, mid-orgy, 'There indeed is evidence to prove the weakness of so much of the thought of Karl Marx. It is only the bohemian who can be free, not the proletarian.'[116] Trocchi enjoyed his writing assignment.

Olympia's portfolio was endlessly imaginative. Humphrey Richardson's (Michel Gall's) *The Sexual Life of Robinson Crusoe* (1962, 1967) rewrote the classic. The incorporation of Crusoe's sexual fantasies, purported dream life and animal adventures certainly gave expansive opportunities for pornographic invention, a carnal bestiary of varied congresses with goats, quail, a cat ('Cat, by God, that was what he wanted, a cat, not a goat, he had had enough of goats'), a parrot ('he s[e]t to work violating this tender and noisy creature. Poor Poll'), a dormouse-like, banana-eating creature, a monkey, more goats and, predictably, Friday (the man Friday): 'Robinson, as if drawn by some insuperable power, or by his own weight drawn forward, buried himself deep in good old Fri.'[117]

Ed (Edgar A.) Martin's *Busy Bodies* (1963, 1965) is a ghost story which is not so much a story as a series of incidents involving ghost sex. Ectoplasms, ghosts, cadavers, skeletons engage in lifelike sex. Fetishes are on display: paedophilia, gerontophilia, whatever philia involves a fascination with nipples, the fetish (probably unnamed) of trying to put the testicles as well the penis into the vagina, a fascination with 'milking' balls. Female ghosts are perpetually randy; male ghosts are constantly erect. 'Couldn't you stay solid another second?' Tom asks Helen. 'There's nothing like coming in a bunch of bones.'[118]

Though the sex lives of the Olympia writers are not really relevant to their literary output, it is a question that readers are bound to ask, and the lives of some of the Olympians may not have been too far removed from their fiction. (Recall that Anaïs Nin referred to a 'wind of eroticism' passing through her group of anonymous pornographers in 1940.) Based on conversations with some of those involved, de St. Jorre has information on the many Olympia in-house liaisons, involving Trocchi, Owens, the Bryants, Lougee, Meeske, the Wainhouses, as well as other writers who we will meet in due course, including John Stevenson (better known as Marcus van Heller), Mason Hoffenberg and Norman Rubington. Girodias called Rubington (who was involved with the bookseller Gaït Frogé) 'a sexual predator', and Miriam Worms referred to an encounter with him in 1965 in which he 'promised to put a fat prick into my hand if I went to see him ... Great charm as usual!!!'[119] The British publisher John Calder, who had a salacious preoccupation with such matters, relayed example after example of Girodias's affairs; he also claimed to have witnessed a Stevenson/van Heller rape.[120] Muffie Wainhouse, on hearing in 1956 that Owens was pregnant to Baird Bryant, wrote to Christopher Logue, 'hearing it, I was suddenly depressed and realized I am tired to death of these poor people playing this mad game which is ultimately sad'.[121] The Wainhouses themselves split but continued a long and intimate correspondence, now housed in the Austryn Wainhouse Papers in Syracuse.

In terms of life imitating art, Trocchi seemed preoccupied with the sadomasochistic *L'Histoire d'O*, writing to Lougee in 1954, after she had left him, 'this, I feel is what love – if it is to be taken on the level of passion – must become if it is not to die', and 'I can be your Sir Stephen' (O's master in the novel).[122] Austryn Wainhouse claimed that Trocchi had a hair-brained scheme in 1956 to enact the sadomasochistic doings of *L'Histoire d'O*, and had assembled the personnel: 'everything was ready, he advised me, everything but the trimmings: hygienic, chromium-plated chains, whips of quality, and the château'. Wainhouse calculated that the enterprise would cost up to £30,000, and the project was dropped.[123]

Most of the Olympia writers used pseudonyms. A manifesto published in English in Paris in 1930 had advocated anonymity as a means of sacrificing individual personality for the creative common good: 'All art becomes the joint manifestation of every individual artist. The poet is merged with poetry'.[124] Perhaps Girodias was aware of this (anonymous) work by Michael Fraenkel and Walter Lowenfels and felt inspired by the notion that the anonymous writer/artist wanted 'his' work rather than 'his' name known. However, pseudonymity is not the same as anonymity, for the former still presents a sense of self, even if fabricated, and some of the Olympia writers were to achieve a measure of fame under their false names. The Olympia authors were guided more by a desire to avoid potential prosecution or to preserve their good names or their literary identity.

Bataille was Pierre Angélique for *The Naked Beast at Heaven's Gate*, although, cheekily, he penned its preface under his own name. Nabokov had contemplated using the anagram Vivian Darkbloom when writing *Lolita* but decided to use his real name – 'I toyed with the idea of publishing Lolita anonymously but wished to affirm my authorship in code'.[125] Likewise, Girodias claimed he offered Donleavy the option of publishing under a pseudonym, but the writer was eager to use his true identity.[126] The real author of *The Story of O* (1954), Dominique Aury (born Anne Desclos), a respected French literary figure, employed the pen name Pauline Réage, a secret that was kept for many years.[127] Diane Bataille, who wrote *The Whip Angels* (1955), was known as XXX.[128] Denny Bryant, the wife of the future cinematographer Baird Bryant (another Olympia writer), assumed the name Winifred Drake.[129] John Coleman, a poet and future film critic for the *New Statesman* and *Merlin*'s business manager, wrote *The Enormous Bed* (1955) under the name of Henry Jones and *The Itch* (1956) as Stephen Hammer.[130] He wanted his anonymity preserved when Grove Press published *The Olympia Reader* in 1965.[131] The American poet Philip Oxman, a friend of Logue's, went under the name Thomas Peachum when he wrote *The Watcher and the Watched* (1954, 1959).[132]

Michel Gall (we have noted) became Humphrey Richardson, but he was also Homer & Associates, the author of *A Bedside Odyssey* (1962), a spurious, newly discovered, sexual version of the

Odyssey: 'Odysseus gazed entranced by the sight of so much beauty. The part of him which Athena had blessed jumped up with so much force that the olive-branch he held before him was knocked from his hand and went floating off down the slow river.'[133]

Robert Waltz, who was commended to Girodias by Chester Himes, published his book *Abandon* (1958) as Bernhardt Von Soda: 'It was more a catharsis than a novel. I depicted real Chicago encounters, affairs, early wives and children and my Great Dane dogs as characters in that book. I was surprised that Olympia Press wanted the manuscript.'[134] William Talsman, the pseudonymous author of the Genet-inspired novel *The Gaudy Image* (1958; 'if given the right amount of encouragement, every man is a woman in the ass') was James M. Smith.[135] Kearney thought that Talsman 'may' have been Smith, but the permissions files for *The Olympia Reader* in the Grove Press Archives confirm that Smith, who died in 1964, was indeed the author.[136] Girodias had great hopes for this book, telling Barney Rosset at Grove that he thought that it would be a best-seller.[137]

The poet Logue became Count Palmiro Vicarion; he told Kearney that all he knew about Vicarion's *Lust* (1954) was that he wrote it.[138] He also compiled the witty *Count Palmiro Vicarion's Book of Bawdy Ballads* (1956, 1957, 1959, 1961, 1962; 'Recent extensive researches/ by Darwin, Huxley and Ball/ Have conclusively proved that the hedgehog/ Has never been buggered at all') and *Count Palmiro Vicarion's Book of Limericks* (1955, 1956, 1957, 1959, 1962; 'There was a young maid named Clottery/ Who was having a fuck on the rockery./ She said, "Listen chum/ You've come on my bum!/ This isn't a fuck, it's a mockery."')[139] Both volumes appear to have been big hits if the number of editions is any guide.[140] Legman claimed that the contents of the *Book of Limericks* had been stolen from his own published collection.[141]

We have already noted that Austryn Wainhouse adopted the names Pieralessandro Casavini and Audiart. The Canadian poet John Glassco was Miles Underwood when he wrote *The English Governess* (1961), though he used his own name for his supplemented version of Aubrey Beardsley's unfinished work *Venus and Tannhäuser*, published by Olympia as *Under the Hill* (1959).[142] Willie Baron, author of *Play This Love With Me* (1955), and owner of the words 'my prick felt like it was caught in a hot punching bag full of hardboiled eggs', was really Baird Bryant.[143] Robert Desmond, one of Olympia's most productive writers, had only slightly masked his real identity, which was Robert Desmond Thompson; he worked for a bank in Antwerp.[144] Wu Wu Meng was actually the South African beat poet Sinclair Beiles, who initially tricked Girodias by recycling a reworked, translated version of a Chinese classic, *Psi Men and His Many Wives*, as *Houses of Joy* (1958), a supposedly rare erotic novel that he claimed to have translated himself. Girodias quickly discovered the deceit but considered Beiles's 'gorgeously doctored' version 'worth every yen we had paid him'.[145]

Mason Hoffenberg and Terry Southern (later a famous screenwriter) used the name Maxwell Kenton when they wrote their highly successful *Candy* (1958); Hoffenberg was also Faustino Perez and Hamilton Drake.[146] Their correspondence while writing *Candy* is hilarious: 'I've been looking over the work and strongly agree now that it was a real error to say "pussy" and "nooky"', Hoffenberg wrote to Southern in 1958. 'This comes from the careless smuttiness I'd adapted in my previous work. Delete them at any rate and put "sugar dripper" "jelly scoop" "butter-pouch" "Dixiecup" "spice-box" "lamb-pit" or "stink tank".'[147]

The future British civil servant John Stevenson, another of the Merlin group, became the prolific Marcus van Heller, though that name was also used for some titles that were not by Stevenson.[148]

Stevenson recalled that trying for novelty in his stories was dispiriting – 'You have no idea what it's like writing one scene after another' – but that when it came to motivation he 'just thought about the money'.[149] It still rankled, decades later, that Girodias had objected to his line 'Her fingers were sticky with lubrication from his passion', telling him that he needed to 'see girls more often'.[150]

Norman Rubington, an expressionist artist whose work included paintings of female nudes and chorus girls, employed the pen name Akbar del Piombo to write four dirty books and four collage novels for Olympia during the period 1956–61, two a year in 1956 and 1957.[151] Girodias claimed to have chosen the nom de plume, much to Rubington's discomfort: 'I'm a New York Jew and you've given me an Arab name!'[152] Rubington was an accomplished painter, sculptor and printmaker who won a Prix de Rome shortly before he wrote for Girodias, and Tiffany Foundation and Guggenheim Fellowships while producing his dirty books.[153]

Some men assumed female writing identities. Trocchi was Carmencita de las Lunas and Frances Lengel. *Helen and Desire* (1954) was Trocchi's first work as Frances Lengel; he recalled later that he wrote it in eight days and marvelled over the 'lightness of touch' in both it and its sequel *The Carnal Days of Helen Seferis*, written the same year.[154] Girodias held up the latter as a 'template' for Olympia Press writers.[155] Angela Pearson, who specialised in flagellation literature, was really a 'great Englishman ... with a florid complexion and Cold Stream Guard moustache' who was also known both as Greta X, author of *Whipsdom* (1962; 'I've always wanted to tie men up'), and Ruth Lesse (as in 'ruthless'), author of the appropriately named *Lash* (1962; 'She raised the whip with a cry and laid it down the entire length of his erection'), both Othello Books.[156] The biographer of the Olympia Press discovered who

Pearson was, but did not reveal his identity; Kearney has named him as John Millington-Ward.[157] The man who wrote about a young schoolgirl who enjoyed administering the lash, and described imaginative instruments of sexual pain/pleasure, taught at a private school in Athens and wrote several textbooks on English grammar. His dirty books were certainly grammatically correct.

One or two women wrote as men: Henry Crannach was really Marilyn Meeske. 'We all took glorious pseudonyms', she wrote in an article in *Esquire* magazine in 1965, 'usually gleaned from the lofty worlds of Art and Science. My name, Henry Crannach, was nostalgically inspired by one of my favored painters, Lucas Cranach; also, to have a male name seemed adequately sick enough for the deed at hand'.[158] Meeske, who had come to Paris (like so many others) to write a serious novel, described a scene at the Café Bonaparte in Paris in 1956: 'a gaggle of real life pornographers could be heard and there I was in the thick of it. Conversation flowed as rapidly as the *vin ordinaire*: the finished chapter meant that the rent would be paid'.[159]

Another one of these writers/translators in Paris was a young American, Harriet Sohmers (later Zwerling), who wrote in 1956: 'I'm trying to write an erotic novel for Olympia Press – calling it *The Virgin*. It's hard to get the right tone. I tend to get too dramatic and personal, and that doesn't work.'[160] Though she had no trouble writing in her journal about the numerous sexual encounters she had with both men and women, Sohmers struggled over the erotica: 'I can't seem to get anywhere with the porno I'm trying to write.'[161] She was particularly discouraged after reading the work of Alfred Chester (writing as Malcolm Nesbit), a friend and fellow 'club' member who would become a brilliant but tormented writer and literary critic.[162] 'Especially after reading Alfred's *Chariot of*

Flesh that we smuggled into London, mine seems tame, unimaginative, puritanical. I just don't seem to have the talent for it.'[163] Perhaps that is why *The Virgin* seems never to have been published, although she had translated (under her own name) the Marquis de Sade's *Misfortunes of Virtue* (1953).

Iris Owens, writing as Harriet Daimler, produced five books for Girodias in a mere two years, including (with Meeske) *The Pleasure Thieves* (1956; 'His prick came up urgent to be devoured by the panicky cunt'), and (on her own) *Darling* (1956; 'all the restraints in her body let go, and she felt the pendulum throb in her cunt') and her reprise of Sade, *The New Organization* (1962; 'It's so awful I don't want him to stop. It's so awful, I want to feel it again. It's so awful I can just come and come').[164] Susan Sontag, who had a tortured affair with Sohmers in Paris at that time, and who knew both Chester and Owens, referred to Owens in her notebook: 'from New York, age 28, has written 5 pornos ... Brightest girl of her class at Barnard.'[165] Girodias considered her 'a very gifted novelist' and thought that Owens may never have had the opportunity to publish if it had not been for Olympia.[166]

It is certainly interesting that a significant number of women were involved: Aury, Diane Bataille, Meeske, Owens, Sohmers. Jane Lougee bankrolled *Merlin*.[167] Miriam Worms was an editor and assistant at Olympia Press. She joked with Meeske, 'Maybe we should forestall Nunky [Girodias] and tell the Olympia story hahaha – that would be funny – poor thing: The Olympia sisters or how the Shit was churned out – a great title – very commercial what?'[168] Owens and Meeske were assistant editors at the press's magazine, *Olympia*; they edited the edition that published 'Sicily Enough', Claire Rabe's account of her sexual experiences in Sicily ('I am becoming saturated with sex').[169] According to James Sherwood, Meeske also guided his book *Stradella* (1962) through the Olympia editorial process.[170] Muffie Wainhouse over-saw the publication of *The Ginger Man*, reshaping it with sub-stantial restructuring according to Girodias.[171] Donleavy said that it was 'Mrs. Wainhouse' who initially read the manuscript and recommended it to Girodias.[172] She worked on *The Black Diaries* too. 'I push on through the Casement salad', she wrote to Austryn Wainhouse in 1958. 'It seems there is a bona fide author, a London gâteux [gaga] of 69 years [Peter Singleton-Gates]. It is his curious prose that Maurice rewrites or openly supplements when he feels the muse upon him.'[173] It is a pity that Muffie never wrote a dirty book, for she certainly had a sense of humour, recounting, in a hilarious letter to her ex-husband, an encounter with an American historian who asked her out to dinner after a seminar and whom she made the mistake of asking back for coffee. She refers to 'an oyster like sensation' on the back of her neck, 'a pelvic butt to the buttocks', 'the better half of my face moistened by a sort of wash of a kiss'; 'he was soon bounding about the room, moving chairs, grabbing here and there, planting these washes which, depending on my agility, hit the back of the head, nose, chin, and occasionally, mouth which, under the circumstances registered as much sensa-tion as an elbow being cleaned in a lemon'. He told her that he had 'made love in 5 languages'. The historian left unsatisfied.[174]

Denny Bryant translated *The Story of O* with her husband Baird Bryant and, as Winifred Drake, wrote *Tender Was My Flesh* (1955).[175] Ataullah Mardaan, the pseudonymous author of *Kama Houri* (1956; 'If you live here with us you must learn the joys of complete sub-mission') was, according to Girodias, a Pakistani woman, educated at Columbia University and married to a Dutch photographer. Her (or his?) true identity has never been revealed.[176]

For the Olympia writers, then, this was an opportunity to write, to be published, to have some fun, to rebel and, more often than not, to make money. 'Most of us romantic expatriates went to Paris to be free of the conventional horrors at home', Owens told de St. Jorre. 'Maurice was my ticket to freedom', she elaborated. 'The payment for a book that took a maximum of two months to write, though meager, was sufficient back then for a six-month escape to Sicily or a winter in Hydra, a summer in Saint Tropez, where one was free to struggle with serious literary effort, the kind that didn't get published. We were natural DB writers.'[177]

While Girodias focused on the dirty book and more serious novel, he was not limited to those forms. He published (and co-edited, with Peter Singleton-Gates) the diaries of Roger Casement, the diplomat and Irish patriot who was executed in 1916 for collaboration with Germany.[178] Although *The Black Diaries* (1959) contained details of Casement's wide-ranging reform activity, it was their homoerotic aspects that commandeered attention, with their running total of the number of Casement's sexual contacts, and comments on the attributes of a partner or observed object of lust. Some of the young men were merely admired, others were paid for sex, with costs recorded, as in this Dublin entry for 5 March 1911: 'Enormous 19 about 7″ and 4 thick', '2. 6.' (2 shillings and 6 pence), '12' (twelfth sexual contact).[179] These homosexual diaries (actually cash ledgers) were included in *The Black Diaries*, the first time that they had been published (extracts had been passed around secretly to discredit Casement at the time of his unsuccessful appeal). John Sparrow anonymously reviewed the book in the *Times Literary Supplement* in 1960, pointing out the shortcomings of the editing and blunders in presentation but accepting it nonetheless as 'an important book'.[180]

Then there was the briefly lived but impressive literary magazine *Olympia*, or *The New Olympia*, designed both as a 'house organ' for the press and, as its founder put it, 'to attract and help in the discovery of new talent'.[181] It was banned by the French authorities three days after the first issue came out. Girodias provided a hilarious description of the Attorney General providing a description to the non-English-speaking judges: 'This is simply disgusting, no poetic inspiration, no redeeming qualities. Beatnik stories.'[182] Only four issues of *Olympia* appeared: with prize-winning essay entrants' stories, some of which became books (Stephen Schneck's, Claire Rabe's); poetry (Gregory Corso); photographic essays (one on tattoos, for example); essays by Brion Gysin and Ian Sommerville on the Dream Machine, with cut-outs to enable the reader to construct their own machine on a gramophone turntable; a brief appearance of the fictional Professor Henry Crannach (Marilyn Meeske), with an essay on chastity belts; and, of course, extracts from Olympia's novels (*Stradella, Sexus, The Ticket That Exploded*, among several).[183] Girodias was the named editor, but Owens and Meeske seem to have done most of the editorial work. Owens complained about her role in 1963, 'I am horribly bored with all of it, since the journal has no unity and Maurice less ... But, but, I need money, and he's giving me a day to day stipend.'[184] Meeske came tantalisingly close to landing the iconic comedian Lenny Bruce for an article, but took too long to get back to him: 'Love, you', he wrote to Meeske. 'Sorry I never got a chance to fuck you but I told everybody I did and made up a lot of rank stories about how you like to wrap tvillin [tefillin] around your arm and make believe you're a junkie Rabbi who's taking his blood pressure.'[185]

Finally, there were Olympia Press's precursors to the graphic novel. Rubington's slim collage projects are intriguing, anticipating both the Monty Python visuals and graphic novels with their bizarre imagery, recycled from a stash of old nineteenth- and early twentieth-century pamphlets and books 'picked up in the flea market'.[186] Severed from their original context (penny dreadfuls, scientific and medical magazines, travel prints, government reports, trade magazines), the engravings are provided with new text as a parodic critique of some of the major issues of the post-war world: the paranoia surrounding the drug culture, militarism, the space race and nuclearism.[187] In *Fuzz Against Junk* (1961), for example, the reader is invited to mock the efforts of Sir Edwin Fuzz to combat crime associated with the drug trade, with imagery of the ingestion of opium and heroin through an inventive range of gadgetry (the 'Ear, nose and throat-adapter injection system employed principally in New York circles', the 'osmotic intra-cranium absorption of liquid Heroin (rare)' and the 'pressure-blower system employed by California females'), as well as incongruous pictures of supposedly stoned subjects – including the amusing image of a suited man standing on a similarly garbed figure, suspended horizontally between two chairs, 'New York detective demonstrating [the] complete inflexibility of [a] stoned subject'.[188]

Although, like his father, Girodias's aim had been to use Paris as a base to avoid the literary censorship of the US and Britain, Kearney has shown that Olympia Press fought a constant battle with the French censors. The publisher's practice of retitling books was one of his strategies of evasion: police working from a list of banned items were confused by even the slightest change in title. Thus, *The Woman Thing* became *Woman, Candy* was also *Lollipop*, and *Helen and Desire* was reprinted as *Desire and Helen*.[189] Girodias joked that *Fanny Hill* was banned in 1956, 'was immediately reissued by Olympia under the thinly disguised title of *Memoirs of a Woman of Pleasure*; was banned again as such; was republished as simply *Fanny*; and banned again. The police never found out that they had thus banned the same book three times in succession.'[190] Bataille's *Madame Edwarda* became *The Naked Beast at Heaven's Gate*, Wainhouse told Kearney, to throw the police off any link to the French version of the book.[191] Miles Underwood's (Glassco's) *The English Governess* was reissued as *Under the Birch*, without the author's initial knowledge.[192]

Girodias paid bribes too. Austryn Wainhouse recorded in 1954, presumably from the mouth of the editor himself, that Olympia's editor was paying a million francs a year in bribes but that it was 'not enough to guarantee him against annoyance'.[193]

How successful these strategies were is up for debate. Kearney has calculated that fifty-five Olympia titles were prosecuted either under the Decree of 1939, giving the Minister of the Interior the right to ban publications in foreign languages, or the 1949 statute against providing forbidden material to minors (those under the age of eighteen); twenty-two titles were prosecuted under both laws.[194] Girodias claimed that he had become so familiar with the corridors, courtrooms, offices and cells of the Palais de Justice and the Préfecture de Police that he felt like 'one of the family so to speak; the judges know me, and also the ushers, and even the charwomen'.[195] He wrote gleefully of running circles around the police in their effort to determine the real author of *Story of O*, of Jean-Jacques Pauvert ringing the police:

> Girodias tells me he told you that he knew who I knew was the author of the book but that he was convinced that I was wrong. Well, that's a lot of nonsense. He always refused to tell me who he thought I thought was the author of the book: so how can he assume that I was wrong? That fellow's been reading too much pornography or something; he's simply illogical. No, my position is unchanged: I know who wrote the book, and I won't tell you. And even if you ask me if Girodias wrote it himself, I won't answer.[196]

Olympia Press was harassed overseas too, with the intended green-cover camouflage becoming a target. The future famous US sociologist Daniel Bell had his copy of Genet's *Our Lady of the Flowers* confiscated by New York customs in 1958 after a trip to Europe. The officer 'saw the distinctive green color of the unhidden book and immediately said, "Oh, you have there some of those Parisian books."' He was told by the inspector that 'all Olympia Press books are confiscated on the presumptive basis that they are obscene'.[197] The American Civil Liberties Union, of which Bell was a member, sought clarification from the Secretary of the Treasury, who eventually denied that all Olympia books were banned and returned Bell's book for research purposes – which in itself indicates some kind of alert.[198] We know that Burroughs's *Naked Lunch* was intercepted by the US postal authorities and that both Olympia and Grove Press were alert to such monitoring.[199] Judith Schmidt at Grove, aware that packages from Olympia in Paris were failing to arrive at their intended destinations, joked in 1960: 'By this time the Customs Department must have so many NAKED LUNCH's on hand that they could easily open a bookstore to compete with us when our edition is published.'[200]

Olympia sent their prohibited wares to England too. Sometimes they were disguised under false dust jackets; *Rape* (1955) and *Cruel Lips* (1956), both by van Heller (Stevenson), as well as *The Enormous Bed* and *The Sexual Life of Robinson Crusoe*, the Postal Services Department noted, were wrapped 'in dust jackets which might escape notice'.[201] Sometimes the entire dispatch details were fictionalised. A package of Olympia Press books seized at the London Airport in 1955 had been classified as 'music books' consigned by 'Musique de Folklore de Provence'.[202] The Home Office papers record numerous instances of seizure by the postal authorities and customs. A list of obscene matter seized in 1956 contained photographic material and some familiar Obelisk (by then Hachette) names (Miller's *Tropic* titles, Harris's *My Life and Loves* and Hanley's *Boy*), but most of the items intercepted were Olympia Press books, including *Thief's Journal, Count Palmiro Vicarion's Book of Limericks, Fanny Hill, Black Spring, Quiet Days in Clichy* and various unnamed consignments – '117 Olympia Press Books' were seized on 23 December 1956.[203] There was an assumption that if a publication was under the Olympia imprint, it was obscene.

The British Government repeatedly petitioned the French to stop the flow of Olympia publications into their jurisdiction, providing details of individual titles in an effort to stem the tide. The Home Office had approached the French Ministry of the Interior as early as 1953, informing them 'of a firm within your territory who have been discovered sending through the post, parcels containing books of a grossly obscene nature', and urging them to take action against the firm, Olympia. The titles mentioned in the first letter were *Plexus, Justine, Bedroom Philosophers* and *Amorous Exploits of a Young Rakehell*, but the list expanded in subsequent letters.[204] By October 1956, the Home Office had a list of over sixty Olympia Press titles.[205] The implication of the series of correspondence between London and Paris was that the French had been either rather slow to proceed or ineffective in their actions. The last letter of 1956, arranging a meeting with the French authorities and referring to their earlier agreement to act, impressed on M. le Prefet, Ministere de L'Interieur, that 'The publications of this Press, especially in the Traveller series, continue to give the most serious concern to the Central Authority for the suppression of obscene publications in England.'[206] We have seen that the French did act. Home Office files for the 1950s also refer to periodic searches of Girodias's offices, with material seized, books banned and prosecutions instituted, and to the French Ministry of the Interior's desire to 'liquidate' Olympia Press, but also indicate that the process had been hampered by the need to get the books translated into French before prosecution could occur.[207]

Girodias's Paris career reached both its zenith and nadir in the late 1950s and early 1960s. He dined out on the success of *Lolita*; actually, he bought the whole restaurant, which he had wanted to call Chez Lolita but instead (for legal reasons) called La Grande Séverine. From 1959 to 1964, La Grande Séverine became a multi-level entertainment centre with restaurants, bars, clubs and a theatre.[208] But it absorbed his money as well as his attention. His collaborations with Barney Rosset of the US publisher Grove at this time, discussed in a later chapter, were beset with Girodias's constant demands for advances on future royalties and telegrams begging for loans – Rosset's patience was sorely tried.[209] Girodias notoriously fell out with his writers, apart from the longstanding disagreements with Nabokov and Donleavy (who got *his* revenge by purchasing the bankrupt Paris Olympia Press).[210] The cases are too numerous to list, but Rosset summarised the situation perfectly in 1965, in one of many heated exchanges: 'What you offhandedly dismiss as your carelessness with money is more often than not taken to be something far more serious by your authors, translators, etc.', he wrote to Girodias, 'and finally you alienate them completely by your failure to honor commitments. I could name a dozen instances with a dozen different people, all of whom feel that you betrayed them completely, failed to live up to your contracts if you had any, and more often than not failed to make a contract in the first place.'[211] It was a perfect synopsis of Girodias's lack of professionalism and chaotic business practices.

The regime of censorship and suppression became untenable too. Girodias famously accrued massive fines, long (unserved) prison sentences, publishing bans and continuing indictments – mitigated only by his numerous court appeals.[212] 'Maurice is collapsing', Owens wrote to Meeske in 1965. 'It's sometimes like sitting with a patient who has terminal cancer, and you say, well Christ, when do they finally close those eyes and die.'[213] Miriam Worms said to Meeske that she was 'convinced that he is mostly responsible for the situation he is in today – that infallible way he has of pushing himself into auto-destruction and self-punishment that is stronger than anything else that drives him'.[214] From the perspective of New York, his next venture, Girodias saw his brief career as an entertainment entrepreneur as an extravagant folly: 'I should have fled the ugly police-infested Paris scene, and followed my authors and my books to America. It was so clear, so evident. What awful blindness …'.[215] It would become his regret that he had not left France earlier. And go to America is what he eventually did.

4

Repurposed pornography:
the role of erotic classics

The republication of erotic classics was a feature of the Olympia Press. As we saw in Chapter 3, Olympia published Austryn Wainhouse's impressive renderings of the Marquis de Sade's works and his translation (as Pieralessandro Casavini) of Nicholas-Edme Restif de La Bretonne's *L'Anti-Justine* (1798) as *Pleasures and Follies of a Good-Natured Libertine* (1955, 1956, 1961 and 1965). They issued, under the Ophelia Press imprint, *Histoire de Dom B****, *Portier de Chartreux* (1741) as *The Adventures of Father Silas* (1958), a reprint of an earlier English translation of an eighteenth-century French classic rather than one of the original translations that the press's editor favoured. The attributed author, Beauregard de Fariente, was merely a name fabricated by Girodias.[1] Olympia repeatedly reprinted the pornographic staple that was John Cleland's *Memoirs of Fanny Hill* (originally *Memoirs of a Woman of Pleasure*, 1748–49) in 1954, 1956, 1960 and 1962.[2] Girodias also republished a rare nineteenth-century classic, Alfred Musset's *Gamiani, ou Deux Nuits d'excès* (1833). Appearing as *Passion's Evil* (1953), and translated by Audiart (that is, Wainhouse), the book is notable as an attempt to write erotica without 'the crude old words which besmirch our ancient language'.[3]

We should also include Aubrey Beardsley's unfinished work, *The Story of Venus and Tannhäuser* (1896), added to by its editor John Glassco and published by Olympia as *Under the Hill* (1959) in a stylish, green, silk-covered, hardback, numbered version, with numerous illustrations by the artist.[4] The prose was equally sumptuous. 'The place where he stood waved drowsily with strange flowers, heavy with perfume, dripping with odours', the narrator begins (Beardsley rather than Glassco). 'Huge moths, so richly winged they must have banqueted upon tapestries and royal stuffs, slept on the pillars that flanked either side of the gateway, and the eyes of the moths remained open and were burning and bursting with a mesh of veins.'[5]

Olympia also published *Teleny, or The Reverse of the Medal* (1893) in 1958, narrating the love of Camille Des Grieux for the concert pianist René Teleny, with its powerful, prolonged descriptions of homosexual sex: 'While our lips clung together, his hand slowly, imperceptibly, unbuttoned my trousers, and stealthily slipped within the aperture, turning every obstacle in its way instinctively aside, then it lay hold of my hard, stiff, and aching phallus which was glowing like a burning coal.'[6] *Teleny* contains portrayals of female–female sexual encounters, trans-like characters and male–female trysts, sometimes erotic, often voyeuristic, and Teleny was sexually involved with both men and women (including Des Grieux's mother); the text might be more accurately described as queer or sexually polymorphous rather than homosexual. But the principal purpose of such imagery is to privilege the relationship of Teleny and Des Grieux. The descriptions of what are perceived to be effeminate sexual liaisons likewise valorise the higher sodomy of the two main protagonists: 'I hurried on, sick at heart, disappointed, hating myself and my fellow-creatures, musing whether I was any better than all these worshippers of Priapus who were inured to vice.'[7] Though their love affair is doomed, the focus is on Teleny and Des Grieux: 'He shivered with delight as he felt the crisp locks upon his cheek and neck; then, taking hold of my phallus, he pressed his lips upon it. That seemed to electrify him; and then the tip and afterwards the whole glans disappeared within his mouth.'[8] When, in the book's preface, Girodias attributed *Teleny* to the authorship of Oscar Wilde, he was following an established tradition, though there is no compelling evidence for this linkage.[9] As Colette Colligan has outlined, Wilde certainly knew those involved in the book's production, but that is not to say that he was involved in its composition, even as part of what has been claimed was a multi-authored project.[10]

Then there are the translations of early twentieth-century works. Alexander Trocchi, using the name Oscar Mole, translated Guillaume Apollinaire's *Les Onze Mille Verges* ('The Eleven Thousand Rods', 1907) as *The Debauched Hospodar* (1953, 1959 and 1962).[11] Richard Seaver was puzzled how Trocchi, 'with his limited French', was able to '"translate" Apollinaire' and suspected that he had had help.[12] When working on it, according to George Plimpton, Trocchi would 'stand on a table in the Café Bonaparte and recite parts of the translation he had just completed'.[13] Seaver translated Apollinaire's *Les Exploits d'un Jeune Don Juan* as both *Amorous Exploits of a Young Rakehell* (1953) and *Memoirs of a Young Rakehell* (1959 and 1962).[14] We should also include Pierre Louÿs's *Trois Filles de leur mère* (1926) in this category. Published in 1926 after its author's death but thought to have been written in 1913, it was translated anonymously for Girodias by William Robinson (who would become Professor of English at San Francisco State University). It was published under Olympia's Ophelia Press imprint as *The She-Devils* by Peter Lewys (1958 and 1965).[15]

Translation and repurposing of older texts formed an important part of Olympia's publishing strategy. It is an impressive list of republished erotic classics.

It is strangely fitting that in his quest for literature and pornography, Girodias drew on the philosophical erotica of the eighteenth-century world, when pornography, as Lynn Hunt once put it, was 'most often a vehicle for using the shock of sex to criticize religious and political authorities'.[16] Robert Darnton has called this period 'the golden age of pornography', but strictly speaking it was a time of pornography before pornography when sex and philosophy were inextricably bound (forgive the pun).[17] Sex did not appear purely for titillation. As Darnton has explained, conceptions of a 'pure' pornography treat any disruption of a sexual narrative ('psychological complexity, philosophy, humor, sentiment, or social comment') as deviation from its erotic purpose, but this philosophical porn was full of such interference.[18] 'At supper they debated the following questions, namely what purpose sensitivity served in man, and whether it was conducive to his happiness?' is not a sentence one would normally expect to read in a pornographic novel; yet it, and many like it, can be found in Sade's *120 Days of Sodom*.[19] Even *Memoirs of a Woman of Pleasure* – which some historians have seen as coming close to being limited to sexual arousal, and which, as the story of a sex worker, was literally pornographic (*pornographe*, writing about the activities of prostitutes) – had an Enlightenment message built into the narrative and was interpreted by some commentators as a serious romantic novel.[20] Pornography as an end in itself, sex for sex's sake, came later.

The important point here is that in the premodern world, sex was used to challenge societal norms, so there was a certain logic in Girodias's attraction to such texts. Girodias said he had 'acquired over the years the urge to attack the Universal Establishment with all the means at my disposal … to fight French intolerance or Anglo-American moral conventions really came to the same thing'.[21] Sounding like Sade himself, Girodias argued: 'The imbecile belief that sex is sin, that physical pleasure is unclean, that erotic thoughts are immoral, that abstinence is the proper rule which may be broken at rare intervals, but merely for the sake of procreation – all those sick Judeo-Christian ideas were exposed for what they were … immature delusions.'[22]

The allure of Sade is perfectly explicable. As Alyce Mahon has shown, the French intellectuals and the avant-garde were drawn to what she terms the 'transgressive Sadean imagination'.[23] Robert Desnos captured the current in 1923: 'In essence, all our current aspirations were formulated by Sade, he was the first to posit the integrity of one's sexual being as being indispensable to the life both of the senses and of the intellect.'[24] Girodias would have been sympathetic to such sentiments and he later moved in those circles.

On another level, Girodias's choices seem bizarre. His greenbook readers were unlikely to seek out discussions on the existence of God ('there is no God', says Coeur-de-fer to Thérèse in Sade's *Justine*. 'Nature sufficeth unto herself'[25]). They were probably less shocked than their forbears when God's name was taken in vain: 'one of my largest pleasures is to swear in God's name when I'm stiff', 'Oh double name of God be fucked! Sacred bugger-God! I come!'[26] It is doubtful that the 1950s reader was much concerned about the ills of *Ancien Régime* society or clerical hypocrisy; they may not have appreciated the significance that so many of the protagonists in these texts were figures of authority, the four libertines in *120 Days of Sodom*, for example, being a bishop, a judge, a nobleman and a financier – a financier, moreover, who derived sexual pleasure from exploiting the poor ('Evil acts make me hard'), and a judge who felt 'a sensual tingling' when he sentenced innocent people to death.[27] It is uncertain whether modern readers would want advice about eighteenth-century contraception: 'to cheat propagation of its rights and to contradict what fools call the laws of Nature, is truly most charming. The thighs, the armpits also sometimes provide asylum to the man's member and offer him retreats where his seed may be spilled without risk of pregnancy.'[28] They are unlikely to have sought instruction on how to be an effective male or female libertine: 'I shall employ the better part of the time educating the young lady', Madame de Saint-Ange tells her brother at the beginning of *Philosophy in the Bedroom*. 'Dolmancé and I will put into this pretty little head every principle of the most unbridled libertinage, we will set her ablaze with our own fire, we will feed her upon our philosophy, inspire her with our desires'.[29] And how did modern readers respond to premodern humoral theories of the body and sex? What did they make of female sperm? 'Oh, heavenly fuck! How I love to play the whore when my sperm flows this way!' says the same Madam de Saint-Ange in *Philosophy of the Bedroom*.[30] '"What!" said Susan to the Sister, "was that spunk that you discharged just now?" – "Yes, indeed it was", said she', was just one of many such interactions, this time in *The Adventures of Father Silas*.[31] How did Olympia's readers respond to the obsession with virginity and pretended maidenheads ('my imaginary jewel') in Cleland's *Memoirs of a Woman of Pleasure*?[32]

While philosophy and desire mingle in these texts, their aim was also to titillate. Sade's *Philosophy in the Bedroom* focuses on sex-for-pleasure with its descriptions of extended sessions of tutelage reinforcing that message, amid pauses for philosophical discussion ('Start from one fundamental point, Eugénie: in libertinage, nothing is frightful, because everything libertinage suggests is also a natural inspiration').[33] Arousal was expected in this literature:

'Pleasure is the "primum mobile" of all human actions', *The Adventures of Father Silas* proclaims, but the 'sentiment of pleasure is ... twice as powerful in a woman as in a man'.[34] Darnton refers to works 'so shot through with autoeroticism that it can be sensed on every page'.[35]

The works in Olympia's repurposed pornography varied in their sexual explicitness. The nineteenth-century *Passion's Evil* (*Gamiani*) was supposedly written to avoid crude language but is no less sexually intense in its portrayal of male–female and female–female lust and convent orgies, including sex with a donkey: 'Oh what an extraordinary spending! What an orgasm! I felt it shoot from me like spurts of flame, and then fall drop by drop to the bottom of my womb. Everything in my inmost being was steaming with lust.'[36] Sade's *Justine*, the story of the virtuous sister, is marked by passages of circumlocution. Even anal sex is cloaked in an apian metaphor: 'Nothing can betray a girl from this quarter, however rude or multiple the attacks may be; as soon as the bee has left off sucking the pollen, the rose's calix closes shut again; one would never imagine it had been opened.'[37]

Despite the book's notoriety, the descriptions of Fanny's sexual awakening in *Memoirs of a Woman of Pleasure* rarely employ the usual pornographic terms. Other words and phrases convey the experienced passion: 'licentious courses', 'a lambent fire', 'enflamed', 'her lascivious touches had lighted up a new fire that wanton'd through all my veins', 'tears of pleasure gush'd from my eyes and somewhat assuaged the fire that rag'd all over me'.[38] The vagina (or cunt) is 'the main-spot', 'that dark and delicious deep', 'soft-pleasure-conduit', 'neither [or nether] mouth', 'luscious mouth of nature' or 'soft laboratory of love'.[39] The penis (or cock) is 'that capital part of man', 'this weapon of pleasure', 'the engine of love-assaults', 'that delicious stretcher', 'master member of the revels' and much else; indeed, Peter Sabor has counted 'over fifty metaphorical variations for the penis' in the novel.[40] Scott Juengel has referred to *Memoirs of a Woman of Pleasure* as functioning 'like a tropological machine, producing a spectacular array of metaphors and equivalences for the sexual parts'.[41] Yet desire is no less powerful for the absence of sexual explicitness, as in Fanny's early encounter with Charles:

> I began to enter into the true unallay'd relish of that pleasure of pleasures, when the warm gush darts through all the ravish'd inwards; what floods of bliss! what melting transports! what agonies of delight! too fierce, too mighty for nature to sustain: well has she therefore, no doubt, provided the relief of a delicious momentary dissolution, the approaches of which are intimated by a dear delirium, a sweet thrill, on the point of emitting those liquid sweets in which enjoyment itself is drown'd, when one gives the languishing stretch-out, and dies at the discharge.[42]

Cleland was aware of the 'extreme difficulty' of picking a path 'between the revoltingness of gross, rank and vulgar expressions, and the ridicule of mincing metaphors and affected circumlocutions'.[43] His long descriptions of mutual ecstasy are unlike anything in erotic literature. In the book's publisher's trials for obscenity in New York in the 1960s, a witness for the prosecution was extremely puzzled by its sexual descriptions: 'I was expecting to find a quite different work.'[44] *Memoirs of a Woman of Pleasure* is erotic without much of the language of pornography.

In contrast to *Justine*, Sade's *Juliette*, the narrative of the sister given over to vice, is explicit in its sexual descriptions. 'Charlotte waxed drunk on my sperm', Juliette recounts of an encounter with the Queen of Naples. 'We entwine ourselves, each buries her face between the other's legs; tongue to clitoris, libertine finger in asshole and cunt, we sot ourselves upon each other's fuck'.[45] Or there is Juliette's interaction with Olympia and her servants: 'We cunt-sucked those who had just been cunt-sucking us, and those who had just been cunt-sucked by us in turn sucked our cunts; and the music played on.'[46] 'Sade's heroines are ferocious in their pursuit of pleasure', writes Kathryn Norberg, 'and they are not particular about the gender of those with whom they have sex.'[47] The cultural critic Angela Carter has observed that whereas women are normally fucked in pornography, women fuck in Sade: 'Whatever else he says or does not say, Sade declares himself unequivocally for the right of women to fuck ... he urges women to fuck as actively as they are able, so that powered by their enormous and hitherto untapped sexual energy they will then be able to fuck their way into history and, in doing so, change it.'[48]

Peter Lewys's *The She-Devils* (1958 and 1965; Pierre Louÿs's *Trois Filles de leur mère*) is shockingly graphic, all the more since it involves incestuous, sodomitical relationships between a family of sex workers – a mother and her three daughters, the youngest of whom, Lili, is ten.[49] 'Mother and her sisters were all acrobats and double-jointed to boot', explains the mother, Teresa, in a narrative within a narrative, 'and each one of them could suck her own pussy if she wanted. But what they did most often was to bend themselves double and suck the balls of a man who was cornholing them.'[50] Teresa boasts that she is not a normal whore who submits to the sexual whims and vices of men: 'I give them mine. I teach them new ones, give them the tastes I have.'[51] John Phillips has termed Louÿs's fiction 'the most obscene writing of his day'.[52]

Olympia's portfolio of repurposed pornography is a veritable erotic encyclopaedia. Voyeurism is key: what Jean Marie Goulemot has called 'The Reader as Voyeur'.[53] Roger, the young protagonist in *Memoirs of a Young Rakehell*, hides and listens to his aunt's confession: how she had taken her nephew's 'member in her mouth' while he was sleeping and how she had seen her maid using a candle to pleasure herself; 'this performance had made such an impression on me that from then on, my Father, I couldn't help trying the same thing ... Yes, I've fallen low, Father.'[54] Characters become stimulated watching other characters engaging in sex or talking about their sexual histories, and presumably the book's readers become sexually excited too. 'One moment', exclaims one of Sade's libertines, who had been listening to pornographic stories, 'I cannot hear these things with a cool head – they have a hold on me that is difficult to convey. I've been holding back my come since midway through the tale – be so good as to let me spill it now.'[55] *Passion's Evil*, which begins with the narrator spying on a tribade (lesbian), is awash with voyeurs overcome with desire at what they have just witnessed or heard: 'What hellish lubricity! I had not the strength to move from my post of observation. My mind was wandering, my eyes were fascinated. These furious transports, these brutal fits of lascivity made me giddy. My blood was boiling with voluptuousness, debauchery, and I was raging with lust like a beast.'[56]

Steven Marcus has described *The 120 Days of Sodom* as reaching 'one kind of perfection' in pornotopia.[57] Six hundred 'passions' are related and acted in that book's narrative, stories within stories of fictive memories and actions – layer upon layer of voyeurism.[58] 'The time has come, friendly reader, for you to prepare your heart and mind for the most impure tale ever written since the world began', the narrator states, 'for no such book may be found among either the ancients or the moderns.'[59]

The passions vary. Throughout *Justine*, every act of Thérèse's trust or kindness (her virtue) is met by treachery, deceit and violence. She is coerced on every page, raped, beaten and tortured for the pleasure of others – never her own: 'Never in my life have I suffered so much'; 'Séverino was in an ecstasy ... he was in a delirium at least the equal of my agony'.[60] Angela Carter has remarked of Justine that in her suffering she achieves a 'kind of ... masochistic mastery over herself'.[61] On the other hand, Madame de Saint-Ange and Eugénie are more open to the pleasures of perversion in *Philosophy in the Bedroom*. 'May atrocities, horrors, may the most odious crimes astonish you no more, my Eugénie', the older female libertine tells her young pupil, 'what is of the filthiest, the most infamous, the most forbidden, 'tis that which best rouses the intellect ... 'tis that which always causes us most deliciously to discharge.'[62]

There is masturbation in the Olympia books: 'Eugénie, *frigging herself* – Oh Christ! You drive me wild! See what your frigging speeches do!'[63] The Hospodar in *The Debauched Hospodar* 'had only to think of a Parisian woman, à la Parisienne, to get an erection and to be compelled to toss himself off, slowly, into beatitude'.[64] Charlotte, the eldest daughter in *The She-Devils*, tells the male protagonist: 'I don't like fucking. I don't like people to eat me either because it tires me out'; What does she do for pleasure? '"I do the same as any other young girl. I finger myself", said Charlotte with a sad smile.'[65] 'I don't ever try to hide anything', she expands. 'I don't care who I'm in front of, I finger myself whenever I feel like it.'[66]

There is much licking and sucking in this literature: of breasts, penises, clitorises, vaginas, mouths, tongues, anuses, even noses. There are numerous orgies in *120 Days of Sodom* 'where many little abominations were carried out: many mouths and arses were sucked'.[67] 'I licked her furiously', says the hero of *Pleasures and Follies of a Good-Natured Libertine*, 'keeping a sharp eye open for the gushing descent of her virginal liquor, awaiting that instant to hurl myself upon her and encunt her: she came with the sixth thrust of my tongue, but came with well nigh unbelievable abundance'.[68]

Then there are the whippings, such as in *Justine*: '"Ah my friends!" says the exalted monk, "how are we to avoid flogging a schoolgirl who exhibits an ass of such splendor!" The air immediately resounds to the whistle of lashes and the thud of stripes sinking into lovely flesh.'[69] The title of *Les Onze Mille Verges*, noted at the start of this chapter, refers both to rods and the penis, and the book does not disappoint in the lashing area. In the intense flagellation and torture in this literature, the bodies of the victims always appear to recover miraculously for further abuse – except for the hero of *The Debauched Hospodar*, who dies by two thousand blows and whose body becomes 'a sort of pork mincemeat'.[70]

There are vivid descriptions of the pleasures of sodomy: 'No, no, in the wide world there is no pleasure to rival this one'; 'it is a titillation so lively, it is of so piquant a voluptuousness ... one becomes giddy, one ceases to reason, stammers; a thousand kisses one more tender than the next do not inflame us with an ardor in any way approaching the drunkenness into which the agent plunges us'.[71] Predictably, the four main libertines in *120 Days of Sodom* 'idolized arses'.[72] The hero of Apollinaire's *The Debauched Hospodar*, Prince Mony Vibescu, fucks and is fucked: 'bugger me while I furbish this delightful girl', being one of many such scenarios.[73] His name, Vibescu, Frans Amelinckx has explained, when broken down into syllables, is *vit-baise-cul*, referring both to 'fuck' and 'arse'. One of his female partners in crime is Culculine d'Ancône, the repetition in the name of the word *cul* (arse) again invoking sodomy.[74] Apollinaire, a poet and bibliographic expert on erotica, had a sense of humour when it came to the subject, writing of the Prince:

He rang to send for the masseur, who massaged him and buggered him properly. The performance brought new life to him. He took a bath and felt clean and fit when he sent for the hairdresser, who dressed his hair and buggered him artistically. The manicurist came up next. He attended to his nails and buggered him vigorously. Then the prince felt completely at ease.[75]

The prince then proceeded to a sex marathon with two women.

The anal sex in these Olympia texts very much includes women. Madame de Saint-Ange tells Eugénie that once the pain threshold has been passed, 'nothing can equal the joy one tastes upon the entrance of this member into our ass; it is a pleasure incontestably superior to any sensation procured by this same introduction in front'.[76] The mother and daughters in *The She-Devils* are specialists in sodomy. The daughters do a calculation, based on daily averages, allowing for special occasions and including dildos, that their mother has been 'cornholed [buttfucked]' 'well over thirty thousand' times.[77] But she says that she has not had vaginal sex 'more than thirty times in my whole life'.[78] There are at least 147 references in the book to 'cornhole [buttfuck]' or its derivatives.[79]

There is even a reference to fisting in this classic erotica, belying the claim in the sexual historiography that fisting is a modern sexual invention. 'Madame, look to my ass; it's ready for you', Dolmancé encourages Madame de Saint-Ange in *Philosophy in the Bedroom*, 'Do you see how it yawns? Do you not see how it calls your fingers? By God's fuck! my ecstasy is complete ... drive them in further, to the wrist!'[80] In a fanciful variant on the practice, the youngest sister in *The She-Devils* puts her hand into her mother's vagina and clasps and manipulates her mother's sexual partner's penis while he is anally penetrating on the other side of the membrane.[81]

There is much discussion of the clitoris in this literature. As James Steintrager has expressed it, the libertines 'knew a good deal about the clitoris before sexologists such as [Shere] Hite came along'.[82] Thus *Philosophy in the Bedroom* refers to 'a little tongue-shaped thing – that is the clitoris, and there lies all a woman's power of sensation', and provides advice to 'insist your clitoris be frigged while you are being buggered: no two things harmonize so sweetly as do these two pleasures'.[83] Madame Champville, one of the sexually experienced storytellers in *120 Days of Sodom*, 'a faithful follower of Sappho', has a clitoris 'that jutted out more than 3 inches when aroused'.[84] There are around twenty-five references to the clitoris in *120 Days of Sodom*, though some relate to torture rather than pleasure. Unsurprisingly, given that it was a book about a tribade, the clitoris is mentioned in *Passion's Evil* and in connection with extreme pleasure: 'two strong lips took my clitoris, pinched it and sucked it till it drove me mad. No, Fanny, it is quite impossible to feel such sensation and to spend as I spent then more than once in a lifetime.'[85] The clitoris is very much visible in Apollinaire's novels as a means of arousal ('They felt one another, he pinching her clitoris, and she pressing her thumb on the hole of his prick'), and once as a faux penis when a woman with a 'clitoris as long as a little finger' fucks a teenage girl ('"It's funny", said Wanda, "how I've upped you with my clitoris and yet I'm still a virgin"').[86]

Incest is crucial to this literature – fathers and daughters, fathers and sons, brothers and sisters, nephews with aunts, women with their brothers, mothers and daughters. We have already noted the incestuous family in *The She-Devils*. 'He has four legitimate daughters, now married; he wants to fuck all four of them', notes Sade in his uncompleted section of *120 Days of Sodom*, 'he gets all four pregnant so that one day he can have the pleasure of deflowering the children he has had with each of them and whom the husbands believe to be their own.'[87] The protagonist in *The Adventures of Father Silas*, while still a boy, leaves sex with his purported sister to fuck the woman who is supposedly his mother, 'Thus at the first stroke, I made a cuckold of my imputed father'.[88] Roger, the central character in *Memoirs of a Young Rakehell*, has sex with his younger and older sisters, and with his aunt, impregnating a sister and the aunt – 'all children to the same father, though they will never know it'.[89] Similarly, *Pleasures and Follies of a Good-Natured Libertine* (*L'Anti-Justine*) is a virtual cornucopia of incest: 'No pleasure in the world can be compared to that of plunging your hard cock in the depths of the satiny cunt of a cherished daughter.'[90] In the book's opening pages, the young libertine has sex with his sisters and his mother ('And thus it was in the maternal womb I began effectively to sow my wild oats').[91] 'I had begun my career by making a cuckold of my father', he summarised. 'I had cornified my brother-in-law, fucking and causing his wife to discharge and impregnating her into the bargain'.[92]

Underage sex is key to many of these narratives. One of the daughters in *The She-Devils* is ten years old and another is in her teens, but the reminiscences in the book relate explicit sexual activity going back to early childhood. The female protagonists in Sade's novels are twelve- and fifteen-year-old virgins when their stories begin. A school in *Justine* in which the students of both sexes are routinely whipped and raped by their teacher limits its intake to those aged over twelve and under sixteen. And the boys and girls that the 'agents of sodomy' acquired for the orgies in *120 Days of Sodom* were of ages also 'set between 12 and 15'.[93]

The Olympia portfolio employs all the exaggerations that became the staples of pornographic imagery. *Memoirs of a Woman of Pleasure* has a penis glans the size and colour of a 'common sheep's heart'; as an academic witness explained somewhat condescendingly in defence of the book in one of its twentieth-century US trials, the amplification in the descriptions of male organs in the book was called hyperbole, 'the literary term for exaggeration'.[94] A gardener in *Philosophy in the Bedroom* has a penis 'fourteen inches in length'.[95] The procured fuckers in *120 Days of Sodom* boast members 'nothing less than 10 or 12 inches long by 7 and a half around', and one of them, Brise-cul (Break-arse), had a 'prick' with a head that 'resembled an ox heart'.[96] The hero of *The Debauched Hospodar* has balls 'like the Bells of Notre Dame' and a member 'like a Norwegian fir', while the lover of a chambermaid has 'a prick and balls which must have weighed at least three and a half kilos' (that is, heavier than a house brick).[97]

Ejaculations – male and female – are of flood-like intensity: 'God, what abundance of sperm! … with what power it springs forth! … Behold the traces of the initial jet: it shot ten feet, nay, more! By God's fuck! The room's awash'.[98] Charlotte in *The She-Devils* produces a 'foaming stream': 'It overflowed her vulva and passed through the forest of hairs … I got out of the way just in time.'[99] Sexual combatants come over and over again. The Duc de Blangis in *120 Days of Sodom* has 'the ability to spill his sperm as often as he wished in a day', and in his youth 'had come as many as 18 times in a single day without ever seeming any more exhausted after the final spurt than he had after the first'.[100] The Debauched Hospodar's valet 'buggered him eight times in succession without dis-arsing. They called these daily affairs their penetrating pleasures.'[101] And when he fucked Culculine, he 'didn't come out of her cunt until he had discharged three times and Culculine ten'.[102]

The heroes and heroines of erotic texts, Goulemot has observed, are not bound by the usual rules of society and physiology. They have 'a quite remarkable aptitude for pleasure … creatures of desire, always ready'.[103] The Duc de Blangis engaged in both active and passive sodomy, and had once 'withstood 55 assaults in the same day'.[104] 'You can play in my pussy if you want', Charlotte offers the male narrator in *The She-Devils*, 'in my ass, in my mouth, between my breasts, under my arms, in my hair, on my face, in my nose if that will amuse you. I can't do any better than that, can I?'[105]

Then there are the orgies of perplexing combinations – 'I am in the second fucker's arms, stretched out on top of him, tis I [Juliette] who do the fucking while he lies quietly still; I handle, I maltreat a cunt with my right hand, my left is socratizing an ass, my tongue is licking a clitoris.'[106] Iris Owens (as Harriet Daimler) had immense fun with this in her book for the Traveller's Companion Series, *The New Organization* (1962), when a group reenact Sade: 'If you're in her ass, she's got to be with her back to you, and to me, so how can she go down on me?'; 'No, I couldn't bear another description of anybody being frigged, not by mouth, hand, toe, or frog's legs.'[107] This regulation for the proceedings framed by the storytelling in *120 Days of Sodom* is but a fragment of the orgiastic nature of that book: 'everyone shall be naked there – storytellers, wives, young girls, young boys, old women, fuckers, friends – everyone pell-mell, everyone sprawled over cushions on the floor, and like animals everyone shall change places, switch roles, incestify, adulterate, sodomize, and … surrender themselves to all the excesses and debauchery that may best fire the imagination'.[108] Apollinaire's *The Debauched Hospodar* is similarly just one long orgy.

Individuals engage in a bewildering range of acts. 'I've done everything with men and women and boys, and little girls', Charlotte declares in *The She-Devils*, 'I've drunk the come of donkeys and horses; I've done everything … I've lived my whole life in come and shit.'[109] The reader will have gathered that sexual identity in the modern sense has little purchase in these texts. Their protagonists, to quote Goulemot, are 'always polymorphous' in their sexuality.[110]

Juliette terminates with what some might be tempted to interpret as the logical conclusion to the violent core of pornography, with truly depraved scenes of rape, buggery, torture, mutilation, incest, filicide, cannibalism and mass murder – 'Crime holds no terrors for anyone when in the act of fucking; and one must always ponder its attractions when swimming in tides of sperm.'[111] Apollinaire's *The Debauched Hospodar* out-Sades Sade with its extravagant violence. A penis is bitten off, buttocks are stabbed, part of an ear is severed and swallowed, an arse is roasted and then buggered and eaten, a mistress strangles her maid with her thighs during oral sex, there is necrophilia, children are molested, a man is skewered on an iron stake, his girlfriend impaled on his dying erection and then shot, a boy is sodomised and decapitated to increase the sodomite's sexual pleasure, a baby is raped, a nurse is fucked while (in a sexual frenzy) she fondles the open wounds of her soldier patients, and numerous people are whipped into a bloody mess. Critics have argued that Apollinaire's motive and approach was parodic, *The Debauched Hospodar* 'almost a comedy of black humor'.[112] For Peter Michelson, the book is a parody of Sade – sans the philosophising.[113] Yet, parody or not, the horror remains horrific. The comicality of its violence may be lost on modern readers.

Finally, there are fetishes that must only appeal to particular tastes. The coprophilia of *The She-Devils* stretches credibility: 'Give your mother a child with your ass', a customer tells Charlotte. 'Shit my come into her cunt.'[114] And that was how her little sister was conceived. 'Shit in my mouth', Charlotte tells the narrator. 'Your cock sets me on fire. I want your shit as well as your come.' The narrator professes incredulity: 'Even today, I can't understand how I managed to keep myself from leaping up from the bed at those words.'[115] The endless shit-eating and wallowing (and wanking) in *120 Days of Sodom*, which put the American critic Edmund Wilson off his breakfast in the 1960s, surely has limited erotic appeal.[116]

The Olympia classics employ all the pornographic literary techniques discussed by the academic experts on the genre to achieve what Lucienne Frappier-Mazur has termed 'the pornographic effect'.[117] *Pleasures and Follies of a Good-Natured Libertine* (*L'Anti-Justine*) is structured according to fucks: everyday fucks, preliminary fucks and major fucks.[118] The obscene word, effective in itself in the right context (and we have seen many such examples), holds more power when uttered by an aristocrat rather than a peasant or when it comes from the lips of a woman. Narrative (however weak) is more engaging, especially in the first person, and, for many readers, more sexually powerful if that narrator is female. As Frappier-Mazur has noted, stories within stories enable shifts in the gender focus of the narrative (in both narrator and narratee), thereby increasing erotic intensity and variety.[119] Verbal (and non-verbal) communication is essential too, with breathless exclamations, ellipses, where speech (or lack of speech) indicates approaching sexual climax.[120] Apollinaire was a master of this, but there are similar passages in every one of the Olympia texts:

> Go quicker … rub your tongue hard against the little button … do you feel it growing, my clitoris? … listen, make scissors of me … that's right … force your tongue right in my cunt and your index finger in my arse … that's right … aah! It's good, it's good … oh! … you hear my belly growling with pleasure? that's right … your hand on my tits … crush the strawberries … I'm coming! ooh! feel my arse curves, feel my bottom jump! ooh, you bastard, that's good! … come fuck me honey … your big prick quick! I'll suck it … make it hard … 69 … you and me …[121]

Voyeurism, we have seen, is fundamental. 'Everything turns on the gaze', writes Goulemot, 'the reader must be made to see, for the book can give rise to the desire for *jouissance*, for pleasure, only by describing those bodies offered up to stimulate desire or by depicting the gestures and postures of the moment of climax itself.'[122] These are books, Goulemot insists, that are supposed to have a physiological impact on their readers.[123] Restif de La Bretonne notoriously becomes inflamed while reading *Histoire de Dom B**** and embarks on a sexual rampage that in itself becomes a piece of pornography.[124] The introduction to *Pleasures and Follies of a Good-Natured Libertine* (*L'Anti-Justine*) stresses the arousing effects of erotic literature. Sade's *Justine*, he writes, provoked him to 'excesses'; 'Pick up my book, gentle reader, leaf through it, and ... you'll see whether it has not a similar effect upon you.'[125] The narrator in Sade's *120 Days of Sodom* admits that not everyone will be pleased by all the 'various excesses' described, but that there will be some that will 'inflame you to the point of spilling your come, and that is all we require'.[126]

The perceptive reader will have noticed mention of humour and parody in this repurposed pornography. We have already noted Apollinaire's wit: '"And I", said she, "am Culculine d'Ancône, I am nineteen, I have already emptied the balls of ten exceptional men in sex-play, and the purses of fifteen millionaires."'[127] *The Debauched Hospodar* has a character whose mother thinks that she is a chamber pot: 'She became dangerous and cried out for the lavatory attendant to come and empty her.'[128]

There is humour in Sade too. How else would the reader react to the anatomical details of the giant Minski in *Juliette*, in a state of permanent tumescence, with 'a pike eighteen inches long by sixteen in circumference, surmounted by a crimson knob the size of a military helmet'?[129] 'Oh, golly, sweetheart! Keep your cunt to yourself, I beg you', a client tells a sex worker in *120 Days of Sodom*, when she instinctively raises her skirts. 'Thanks to you I might not be able to come all evening ... not until I've got that fucking cunt out of my head.' He then turns her over, worships her posterior and masturbates: 'Oh, good God! What a fine arse!'[130] The examples in *120 Days of Sodom* are endless. There is the case of a man 'who fucked the three children he had by his mother, including a daughter whom he married to his son, so that by fucking this girl he was fucking his sister, his daughter and his daughter-in-law, while forcing his son to fuck his own sister and mother-in-law'.[131] Or consider the man who had gold pins pushed into his 'bottom' until it began to 'resemble a saucepan rather than an arse'; 'he would sit down, the better to feel the pinpricks'.[132] There is delicious self-mockery too. 'Everyone knows the story of the Marquis de ..., who, as soon as he learned he'd been sentenced to burn in effigy', Sade has one of the libertines say, with clear reference to himself, 'pulled his prick from his breeches and cried out, "Holy fuck! Here I am just where I wanted to be, here I am covered in opprobrium and infamy – leave me be, leave me be, I need to come!"'[133] When confronted by the sheer bizarreness of many of the six hundred 'passions' described in *120 Days of Sodom* – vomiting in the mouth, for example, or farting in the mouth, with 'farteurs' and 'farteuses' against 'swallowers' – the reader's reaction must oscillate from incredulity to appalled mirth.[134]

Some commentators have claimed that humour and pornography are incompatible. As John Phillips said of Apollinaire's *Les Onze Mille Verges*, 'The novel's images function above all to vitiate the pornographic elements, not merely because they are amusing (most are, some are simply bizarre) but because they interfere with the arousal of erotic and/or sadistic responses in the reader.'[135] Phillips goes as far as to claim that the humour and parody in

Louÿs's *Trois Filles de leur mère* disqualifies it from being considered pornographic: 'Louÿs's erotic fiction may be the most obscene writing of his day', Phillips writes, 'but its irrepressible humour also makes it curiously *un*erotic, which is why it might be argued that he was not a pornographer'.[136] The logic seems to be that if one is laughing, they are not masturbating, or at least the focus on arousal is somewhat disrupted. As Goulemot has put it, 'the erotic novel, by its very nature, excluded all forms of humour, as if irony, by the very act of creating a distance between reader and text, could interfere with the novel's effect'.[137]

The problem with this argument is that all pornography is parody, all pornography consists of sexual exaggeration, so are these critics referring to a parody of parody? Moreover, parody, as Frappier-Mazur has explained, can be flattering, censorious or transgressive; its effects are complex.[138] Surely parodied pornography, as Susan Sontag once observed, is still pornographic.[139] As we will see again in the next chapter, the most proficient erotic writers employed both humour and parody.

There is no denying Girodias's pornographic perspicacity. Darnton has termed *The Adventures of Father Silas* (*Histoire de Dom B****) a 'pornographic masterpiece'.[140] Not legally published in the US until the 1960s and in England until 1970, its case making its way to the US Supreme Court, Cleland's *Memoirs of a Woman of Pleasure* has become a classic; according to Hunt, it is possibly 'the single most read pornographic novel of all time'.[141] Apollinaire had moments of brilliance: 'She had two superb titties, hard as marble, ringed with blue, and topped by a delicate strawberry pink; the right one was prettily blemished by a beauty spot, stuck there like a fly, a butchered fly ... Her thighs were hot and her buttocks were cold, which is a sign of good health.'[142] John Phillips included Apollinaire's *Les*

Onze Mille Verges (*The Debauched Hospodar*) and Louÿs's *Trois Filles de leur mère* (*The She-Devils*) among his 'landmarks of modern French eroticism'.[143]

Sade is in a league of his own – Annie Le Brun refers to 'the inconceivable outrage' of his writings.[144] Can we ever erase the image of Clairwil killing a child, plucking out his heart and fucking herself with it while she chews the boy's tongue? Juliette promptly follows suit: 'The fiendish creature was right, for dildo this is without peer; for warmth, for elasticity where will you find its match. And the moral parts, my friends! How they are fired by these horrors.'[145] This is pornography at the absolute limits. To quote Alyce Mahon, 'Sade locates the reader at the very syntax of the sexual imagination'.[146] The sexual violence of his work – its sadism, which, after all, is named after Sade – is unique. The misogyny is shocking: 'the best thing that can happen to a woman is to die young', it is observed in *120 Days of Sodom*, before the book deteriorates into a series of notes on sadistic, despicable and murderous actions against women – nearly always women. For the libertines in that book, 'the life of one woman – did I say one woman? Of all the women inhabiting the earth's surface – is as insignificant as the swatting of a fly.'[147] The modern reader cannot but be repelled, too, by Sade's literary paedophilia; the child victims of Father Laurent in *120 Days of Sodom* are between the ages of four and seven.[148] One modern critic has called Sade's work 'polluting to our moral and intellectual environment', and has accused commentators (perhaps our account is also guilty) of 'bowdlerizing' Sade's atrocity and inhumanity.[149] Even so, Angela Carter sensed the possibility of a new kind of pornography in his very subversiveness, where obscenity might serve to forge 'the acceptance of the logic of a world of absolute sexual licence for all the genders' and project 'a model of the way such a world might work'.[150] Pornography, Michelson reminds us, was central to Sade's purpose: to provoke revulsion or arousal; 'and it was the one kind of rhetoric able to elicit both revulsion and desire, the precise passions upon which Sade's tragic ethos turns'.[151]

To many 1950s and 1960s readers, Sade's oeuvre must have been a jarring juxtaposition of philosophy, atheism, violence and polymorphous sexuality, at a time when sex for sex's sake was coming into its own. Yet it appealed to Girodias, his translators and a wider audience pondering the roles of sex in society and constructions of the self. Grove's *Justine, Philosophy in the Bedroom and Other Writings* would go on to sell 350,000 copies.[152] Although it is doubtful that Sade's belated fame was based on any deep engagement with his work – Steintrager has referred to the serious Sade drifting into something far less earnest, the 'celebration of new sexual freedom in the guise of a frolicsome "kinkiness" and fun-loving deviance'[153] – he did become something of a 1960s icon.

5

Dirty books

Although some, like Gershon Legman and Henry Miller, argued that the enterprise of writing pornography made them creatively (or sexually) impotent, for others (Anaïs Nin and Iris Owens, for example) the works produced during this time hold a special place in their repertoire. Though feeling compromised initially, Nin later saw hers as an experiment in women writing erotica, 'the beginning efforts of a woman in a world that had been the domain of men'.[1] Alexander Trocchi eventually put his own name on his erotic novels when they were reissued by Brandon House some fifteen years after his work for Maurice Girodias; 'Writers should be proud to take on the honored name of pornographer.'[2] He recalled a feeling of freedom, 'innocence' even, in the early years of Olympia: 'M. Girodias' strictures had not yet become, as they certainly did later, a tiresome limitation.'[3] Girodias said, many years later, that he thought that Trocchi and Owens had done their best work under the dirty book structure and 'the freedom to experiment that comes with writing under a pseudonym'.[4]

We have seen that Olympia Press and Girodias produced ready-made (though translated) erotic writing. But they also made their own. The New York syndicate only wrote their own, including their fake Millers. When considering the work of the two syndicates together – Paris and New York – it seems that some writers took their project seriously, others not so much. Peter O'Neil's pulp-like detective novel, *The Corpse Wore Grey* (1962), has a namesake narrator who refers to his penis as 'he', as if it has a separate identity, and who has sex with women with breasts like 'balls of cream' and buttocks like 'alabaster globes'.[5] Let us examine the pornographic writing of the dirty books in more detail.

'Her tongue, with that final swiping lick, was making the glans vibrate and pulse as if it were a beacon flashing out a code into the darkness', writes Marcus van Heller (John Stevenson) in *Adam and Eve* (1961).[6] Another character, this time in van Heller's *Kidnap* (1961), 'encouraged him [Nick] into her as if her pelvic regions were a specially strong vacuum cleaner'; bodies 'lay cooling like steaks removed from the grill'.[7]

According to John de St. Jorre, 'In the netherworld of erotica, the name "Marcus van Heller" approaches the stature of legend.'[8] Stevenson wrote twelve novels for the Paris Olympia Press as Marcus van Heller, but such was the popularity of his dirty books and thus the cachet of the name, the pseudonym went on to be used by the New York Olympia Press, without Stevenson, as a 'house pseudonym' for eighteen further titles.[9] 'Keen collectors of erotica, however, are not easily duped', said de St. Jorre, 'they can tell a "real" Marcus van Heller from a fake one as quickly as a jeweler can distinguish a true diamond from one made of paste.'[10] Although his works were based on a variety of locations and plotlines, he was known for his historical fiction. This included *The Loins of Amon* (1955), *Roman* Orgy (1956) and the two volumes of *The House of Borgia* (1957–58), about the incestuous and murderous Borgia family headed by Cardinal Roderigo (Pope Alexander VI) in the

Renaissance period.[11] This self-claimed 'best-selling author of erotica' for Olympia wrote *Roman Orgy* in 'a fortnight flat'.[12] Stevenson said he would do some research for these works, 'but I soon realized that the less you knew about them [the people, the social history] the better the book would be'.[13] That did not mean that readers ignored historical 'accuracy'. One wrote to 'Marcus van Heller' to say 'I admire your books more than any of the others [in the Traveller's Companion Series] but I don't think you are always quite accurate. There was that bit in *The Loins of Amon* about the donkey and I remember when I was in Egypt I saw this exhibition and, you know, it wasn't like that.'[14] De St. Jorre does not mention whether the reader took similar issue with the ritualized rape of virgins by 'sacred baboons' in the scenes of 'bestial rape en masse' that bookend the same novel.[15]

Christopher Logue's erotic offerings seem inexplicable, unless he was aiming for parody. In *Lust* (1954), which he wrote using the pseudonym Count Palmiro Vicarion, the protagonist says of one encounter, 'I sank into her like a dagger into a perfumed sheath.'[16] He describes another: 'I opened the coverings on my manbody and laid her petal-like hand over its heat.'[17] What woman, even in the 1930s (the setting for the story), would say 'Ram yourself into the very depths of my womanly center'?[18] In *Lust* world, the penis is a 'lusty treasure' and the female genitals 'luscious folds of sex flesh'.[19] A woman has a 'cunt', but she also has a 'liquid orifice', a 'mellow sweet nest of delight' and 'female places'.[20]

Iniquity (1958) by Robert Desmond (Robert Desmond Thompson) begins promisingly with a female pornographer writing a book about boxing and sex: 'I've got the hot parts all worked out, but I know as much about boxing as the average girl'.[21] Its conceit of pornography within the pornography (we are treated to the paid-for smut while the writer herself undergoes constant sexual harassment) might have worked, but the text within the text, which may justifiably be bad in the name of parody, is no worse than the text itself: 'A luscious little temptress such as you – lovely little nipples as firm as hazel-nuts! – must have chaps sleeping with her who could give her all the dope she needs about the boxing fraternity, and for no other payment than the right to sink their teeth into those delicious out-size titties.'[22] 'His penis tossed its flaming head in pride, and nosed the perfumed collar of her womanhood', is literally a random example of the book's lack of quality.[23] Thompson's *Without Violence* (1962), the narrative of a young, middle-class, Belgian woman's casual sex with an older working-class man, has lines like 'He packed himself deeper than deep into the depths of her passion-deep depth, and he depthed her.'[24]

Thompson's *An Adult's Story* (1954) continually has women delighting in their forced degradation: 'The more ruthlessly he thrashed her, rubbed her in the muck, urinated upon her and forced her to eat his excrement, the wilder was her joy in him: everything he devised to hurt her thrilled her.'[25] Willing rape features too in Desmond's *Iniquity* (1958): 'He took her so strongly and expertly that she suffered the added humiliation of getting so excited that she ceased to struggle. Taken against her will, she eventually gave herself with incredible abandon'.[26]

Willie Baron (Baird Bryant) was another of the early Girodias dirty book authors. His *Play This Love With Me* (1955) is awkward pornography at its clumsiest. Thus we have nipples with 'long tips squared off at the ends ... rooted in bulbs the size of golf balls', a penis which stands 'like a pointer sniffing game' and a 'corrugated cunt' which sucks inwards and outwards, 'bump by bump'.[27] When Willy, the narrator, comes, 'each time it seemed like the muscles of my legs were being pulled up and shot in big globs through the burning end of my prick'.[28] The unfortunate reader is entrusted with Willy's thought processes: 'Willy man! When are you ever again going to have the chance to fuck two women all wrapped up in snake?'[29] The snake, regrettably, was not metaphorical. We are treated to his description of what it is like to fuck a woman using a dildo fitted over one's nose, 'the view you'd get if you had eyes in your balls': 'I was fucking her and sucking her at the same time.'[30] These examples convey what Steven Marcus must have meant when he said that 'language for pornography is a prison from which it is continually trying to escape', a 'bothersome necessity'.[31]

Stevenson's van Heller novels are solid examples of the more stereotypically pornographic end of the Olympia dirty book range. They were for the reader who did not want philosophy, literature or existential crisis – meaning too many pages without sex. Some of the language attempted to transcend the raw sex: 'The music beat into their sweating bodies like the sun at its zenith', he wrote. 'It got into their minds, into their blood, seeped through the pores of their skin. She was a dazzling performer – an abstraction of cubes writhing together like a painting by Picasso, a painting with movement, swirling like a Catherine wheel and finally exploding into a feast of spitting sparks before its embers died away, glowing brightly to the very last.'[32]

But these dirty books always returned to Marcus's prison house of language. Women are as sexually voracious as the men in van Heller's novels: 'She wanted the pounding of his cock to obliterate her and she clung with her knees to his shoulders and moaned in the agony of her desire.'[33] 'Get inside me,' breathes Eve in *Adam and Eve*. 'Fuck me; fuck me to death.'[34] For the most part, the terminology of the sex act itself is more literal than figurative in van Heller's work: 'his cock throbbed and thundered against the walls of her moist, tight cunt'.[35] Typical of the wider genre, are the descriptions of the all-powerful erection and male ejaculation:

'His cock was enormous', says Eve of Adam. 'She'd never realized they were so big.'[36] In *Kidnap*, Nick's 'prick felt like lead, a great hard weight of lead, hot lead and sweetly bursting and moist and sticky'. 'The throbbing of his cock as it absorbed her explosion reached a point of unbearable agony', continues the prose, 'before his white-hot relief raced through him so forcefully that he cried out and stabbed into her, wanting to pierce through to her very throat. He gave a great roar like an enraged elephant and the liquid exploded from his prick, the power of his orgasm seeming to splinter his rigid flesh into a thousand tender pieces.'[37] This is Nick's third in as many pages.

So many of these erotic texts contain the staple fare of pornotopia, where, as Marcus has put it, a man is an 'enormous erect penis, to which there happens to be attached a human figure', and all women 'fecundate with lust and flow inexhaustibly with sap or juice or both'.[38] In *The Beaten and the Hungry* (1962), Colette ('My name is Colette Fuck') gushes: 'Then it came – she had it! – a raging torrent of pent up goo, now released, gushing out as a sluice sloshes in spring, a rich candescent flow of hell, its soft oil feel overflowing down her thighs and his cheeks in smooth quiet flood, seeking its own path to oblivion.'[39]

Some of the dirty books escaped the prison. John Glassco was an adept pornographic writer, as is clear in his contribution to Aubrey Beardsley's *Under the Hill*, discussed in a later chapter (though we argue that he is not as skilled as Beardsley). His book *The English Governess* was a rewritten version (at Girodias's urging) of a previous work, *A Firm Hand* or *The Dominant One*, rejected by another publisher but which would later resurface (in 1967) as *Harriet Marwood, Governess*.[40] As Glassco's biographer Brian Busby has shown, *A Firm Hand* had drawn very heavily on a French work of pseudonymous pornography, published in 1938, Aimé van Rod's *La Governante*. Busby describes the relationship between the French and English works as reinterpretation rather than plagiarism, and Glassco further modified the story anyway when he reworked it for Olympia Press.[41] Nonetheless, *The English Governess* was not an entirely original work.

There is explicit sex in *The English Governess*, but not on every page, even though the whole book is dedicated to sexual arousal. Slowly but surely, the narrative increases the sexual tension as the reader waits for – expects – the final pay-off. A wealthy father, Arthur Lovel, hires a disciplining governess, Harriet Marwood, to deal with his onanistic fourteen-year-old son Richard; masturbation is a leitmotif of the book, in true pornographic fashion. The governess tantalises him, disciplines him, building up to her own heightened arousal, knowing that the tactic of punishment, suppression and temptation will culminate in even better orgasms for him (and her – and the reader?). Glassco draws on classical pornography. The father's country house, to which the governess eventually takes her young charge, is the sequestered space where, Sade-like, no one hears the screams. The book features flagellation, so beloved by many pornographers; the whole story is premised on the pleasure and pain of the whip. There is sodomy (recall the repurposed pornography): 'Mr. Lovel, like many Englishmen of his station at that period, greatly preferred to sodomise his women'.[42] There is also the voyeurism that we have seen is crucial to the erotic text; the reader is treated to the narrator's lingering, longing description of the boy's penis, 'an instrument of extraordinary beauty … almost Gothic in its rigid springing line', and are told what happens to it 'under the accustomed ministrations of his fingers'.[43] Again, Richard's body is described, but through the eyes of Harriet as she supervises his bath: 'for all her air of outward calm she was deeply stirred by the beauty of this adolescent body'.[44] At one point, the boy's father and his mistress experience heightened arousal while listening to the sounds of the boy's punishment, as the governess administering the lash feels her own mounting excitement, and the boy later beats off to the memory of the incident: 'Upstairs, Arthur Lovel was still panting in the utter exhaustion induced by the most violent and pleasurable orgasm he had ever known; while in the darkness of his room his son was already rubbing his wildly erected member in a veritable ecstasy of pain, humiliation and rapture.'[45]

The reader, of course, looks on, while the writer sadomasochistically toys with the literary spectator by constantly deferring the denouement. It is at the end of Chapter 4 that we are told, although we have already guessed, that behind the governess's 'cold and placid demeanour she was inwardly maddened by the desire to begin whipping' her charge.[46] It is not until Chapter 5 that she first beats him and kindles new desire in her student: 'He was as if stupefied; an intense heat was devouring his beaten flesh, seeming to penetrate from his smarting palms to his very shoulders; he felt an overpowering disturbance of his nerves; but the impression of shame and sensuality dominated every sensation.'[47] By page 56 of the book, the governess is bringing the boy to the point of orgasm, but preventing it at the last moment: '"You see, Richard", she said softly, "you are in my power … With this, and with the whip, I will teach you the habit of self-control."'[48] It is not until page 119, after the passage of four years, and after they have married, that Richard sees Harriet's vagina, yet not until page 127, after cunnilingus and fellatio – and a vasectomy! – that the story's 'climax' occurs in the book's epilogue:

> The only omission we are obliged to make is one that is enforced on us by the sheer limitations of our ability, for the ecstasy in which Richard literally swam when he at last plunged his fine nervous member in Harriet's vulva is something that our poor pen cannot

describe, and we must be content to indicate the excess of his sensations by saying that his first orgasm in the womb of his beloved was so violent that he fainted quite away.[49]

The author masterfully withholds from the reader.

Only as the book is about to end, is the perseverer treated to a full description of congress, spurred on by a punishing lashing ('"Ah! Yes, yes!" He cried. "Again – Again!"'). 'She took him from above like a goddess or a savage queen, her back arched, her breasts with erected nipples thrust out, the splendid hips crissating [rippling] with an urgent, imperious motion; her vulva gripping him like the oiled fist of a wrestler'.[50] The narrative is of a woman in complete control: 'Harriet had made of him a finished libertine, a connoisseur of every kind of delight to be enjoyed with a woman.'[51] Glassco gives quite a pornographic performance. He thought so too. He would later recommend the book to a student of Margaret Atwood as one of the rare 'intelligent' works on flagellation, without mentioning that he was its real author.[52]

Thomas Peachum's *The Watcher and the Watched* (1967) was really written by a poet called Philip Oxman (encountered in an earlier chapter). *Watcher* is about a teacher, a part-time photographer, Masefield Hopkins (a rather obviously poetic name), who persuades Jill and Toni, two sixteen-year-old schoolgirls, into posing for him and to stage sex with two boys so that he can watch ('I don't want those boys to know that I'm there watching you').[53] The voyeurism is unrelenting. It includes the pleasures, or rather the compulsions, of watching: 'It was all to come to an end, a climax where he would not be present but outside, pressed in the chilly night against the metal fringe of the screen. He would watch, longing, until it was all over. But for him it never would be over.'[54] The voyeurism also entails the appeals of being watched (hence the title). There is a knowingness in the observees: 'They watched him, watched him watching them ... Toni felt herself doubly naked, once for Jill, once for him.'[55] Jill performs in a school tableau, naked under her costume: 'She knew they could all see her, all of them. When she heard the sounds of the cadets straining forward in their chairs, she felt she could taste their excitement.'[56] Even the back-stories and sub-plots involve looking – a doorman watching a couple make love in a hotel, for example. Oxman provides accounts of anal sex and rape, yet the sex is never really explicit – 'she held what she had not known in her hands'; 'His freedom nodded its response, assenting up and down.'[57] The described acts of congress are few. Most of the book involves anticipation and preparation, prolonged desiring. There are layers of gazing. Hopkins leaves an album of nude photographs that he has taken of Jill and Toni so that they and the boys look at the images while he watches them (as the reader of the book watches on too). While the plot goes off the rails at the end of the book with rather unlikely gerontic sex, and the protagonist dies, *The Watcher and the Watched* was certainly a superior dirty book.

The quality of the dirty books varied, then. The content of all this commissioned written pornography both confirms and challenges the tropes of Marcus's pornotopia, with literature sacrificed on the altar of sex and where everyone 'is always ready for anything'.[58] Most of the books discussed so far were male-authored erotica. But, as we have seen, women wrote pornography too. Diane Bataille's *The Whip Angels* (1955), one of Girodias's dirty books, employs the fictive device of the discovery of an old diary containing a fourteen-year-old girl's account of forced sex, which, as one might expect of the genre, she comes to enjoy: 'those blinding sensations, those sensations which had hurled me beyond the edge of any conceivable morality into a world of indescribable damning

delight'.[59] The very writing of the diary, the record of her humiliation, becomes part of that forced sex.

> 'Write', he said ... 'Put everything down, everything. We are going
> to provide you with all the material you need.' I have been writing.
> Kenneth has his prick under my left armpit, and is watching me tell
> of all these horrors, horrors, horrors. My journal is defiled forever,
> defiled, defiled, defiled, and every time the dreadful thought stops
> my writing, he pinches the skin of my back between two fingernails
> and the pain is excruciating. I am so tired.[60]

Whip Angels contains underage sex, BDSM, incest, bestiality
(involving a kitten and a snake), oral and anal sex, threesomes, and
humiliation – all female-narrated and written by a woman.

Olympia Press's female writers included established authors as
well as promising beginners. Edith Templeton's *Gordon* was first
published in 1966 by Olympia under the New English Library
imprint, with Templeton using the pseudonym Louise Walbrook.
It was banned, although New York Olympia Press reissued it in
1968 as *The Demon's Feast*, still under the pseudonym. Here was an
established author – Templeton had published four books in the
1950s and had short stories in the *New Yorker* – writing a novel with
explicitly sexual content, and with Girodias the only publisher willing to issue it. Templeton later revealed her authorship, and *Gordon*
is now a Penguin book.

Gordon is no normal dirty book. Faust and Goethe are quoted
in the German. There are references to Mann, Huysmans, Pascal
and Mallarmé. Templeton writes beautifully. The sexual scenarios are graphic in conception but never pornographic in terms of
actual detail. There is no lingering; the descriptions are effectively
economical.

The story, set in London in 1949 and, as she later revealed,
based on her own life, is about the female narrator's (Louisa's)

sadomasochistic relationship with a Scottish psychiatrist, Gordon (his surname). He is forty-eight years old; she is twenty-eight. The mood is established early in the narrative when the man forces her onto a stone bench (the narrator is very particular that it is not a push or a throw) and penetrates her: 'He laid me down; a hard edge cut into the backs of my knees while my feet were still on the ground, and as soon as I was extended, he was inside me.' It was not a rape, she insists: 'I was neither willing nor unwilling. I was nothing at all.'[61] She was aroused by his actions but felt ashamed too: 'the thought that this man whose name I did not even know had managed, without any additional effort on his part, to give me this pleasure by his short, indifferent, careless act, filled me with embarrassment'.[62] The relationship continued. He probes her psychologically and sexually. He takes her when he feels like it, more or less at whim, always cold and aloof. He rapes her in public places – on rubble in city courtyards. There are descriptions of 'dissolution, of loss of my being', of anger, pain and shame, but also of wanting to be brought 'to the brink of darkness', of a 'yearning for him to shatter me and to break me down', of wanting to feel 'helplessly dominated'.[63] It is Gordon's detachment that is so chilling. As Louisa narrates, 'He always plunged into me, without fondling or caressing me, whether I was willing or unwilling'.[64] Elsewhere, she describes it as 'his invasion ... relentless, ever returning, like the sea beating against the shore'.[65] It was the possession that was important to him, cold, calculated, as he would grind, grimly, relentlessly on. Any other contact, Louisa observes, would have been 'weakness on his part, a superfluous gesture of unnecessary contact'.[66] She never really touched or saw his genitals. Their only kiss was once in her dream.

Yet Louisa experiences pleasure in this humiliation and obeisance, what she terms 'that exquisite feeling of helplessness': 'I was pervaded by a marvellous sweetness which streamed through me, and its spreading flow would have made me willing, as Faust was, to let such a fleeting moment of fulfilment be his last'.[67] Templeton, the real Louisa, later describes it as 'the fundamental event' of her life.[68] The fictional Louisa is aware that she has never before received such satisfaction but thinks that 'the longing to be violated, body and soul, must always have been inside me'.[69] Gordon penetrates her anally, and although she hates the physical experience (indeed cries for an hour afterwards), she responds psychologically. He watches her when she goes to the toilet. He refuses to let her wash between her legs when she stays overnight with him. He takes pleasure from her obvious discomfort while undergoing analysis. He humiliates her by smoking a cigarette while they have sex. He tells her, 'I'll hold you for ever. Because I shall always find new ways of torturing you.'[70] Years later, when in her eighties, Templeton described the relationship as psychological rather than physical 'enslavement'.[71]

Domination was only one trope in female-written pornography. Women could be, and often were, sexually autonomous in Olympia novels, some more inventively than others. In *The Pleasure Thieves* by Harriet Daimler (Iris Owens) and Henry Crannach (Marilyn Meeske), Carol is so sexually aroused by her new merkin (pubic hairpiece) that she wants 'to push the Empire State Building in there tonight'. But 'what was she to use', she pondered, 'her fingers were not enough, not now … She stretched behind her and pulled off [a plaster mannequin's] arm, smashing it at the elbow, and rammed the forearm up into her.'[72]

The work of Anaïs Nin is in a different style of female-authored pornography altogether. Nin thought that her erotica 'wasn't literary enough'.[73] But from first reading, John Ferrone, Nin's editor at Harcourt Brace Jovanovich, never doubted the literary quality of the stories in *Delta of Venus* – originally written to order, we have seen, for a collector of pornography. We have to allow for the reshaping of the original text. Ferrone was a ferocious editor and Nin gave him carte blanche in the making of *Delta of Venus*. He explained later that stories 'had to be carved out of long, episodic narratives that contained tales within tales. They needed beginnings and endings, and often titles'.[74] Seven titles in Nin's original manuscripts became fifteen in the published book.[75] The story 'Elena', for example, yielded 'The Basque and Bijou', 'Pierre' and 'Elena' itself.[76] Nevertheless, the literary merits of Nin's writings are still evident.

Although a single story could encompass many of the tropes or themes of the larger cohort of money-per-page pornography – 'Life in Provincetown' includes voyeurism, urination, slashing, asphyxiation and a sex toy, a 'heavy rubber tongue with rubber spikes all over it' – Nin's writing style was unique.[77] The similes and metaphors, the rhythm of the poetic prose, represented the sex less explicitly but no less powerfully. For much of the beginning of 'Life in Provincetown', the 'Portuguese' listens night after night to his neighbour having sex through the walls: 'The walls were so thin he could feel it all in his body. Ah … ahh'.[78] The reader listens on with the auditor. 'The Portuguese's body was burning, tortured with desire. Each cry of the woman raised his penis in the dark. And how it burned.'[79]

Smaro Kamboureli has claimed that 'Nin never uses words like "cunt", "cock", and "fuck"' in her erotica.[80] In *Delta of Venus*, Kamboureli notes, Mathilde's sex is 'like the gum plant leaf with its secret milk that the pressure of the finger could bring out'.[81] Any realism in sexual action is rendered figuratively, a merging of 'erotics and poetics'.[82] 'I have dipped into obscenity, dirt, and his world of "shit, cunt, prick, bastard, crotch, bitch" and am on the way up again', Nin said of the work of her lover Miller. 'Again and again I have traversed the regions of realism and found them arid. And again I return to poetry.'[83] More than one cultural commentator has noted the difference between Nin's 'brocade' (Miller's term) and Miller's 'four-letter words'.[84] Nin herself said that she was aware of 'a great disparity between Henry Miller's explicitness and my ambiguities – between his humorous, Rabelaisian view of sex and my poetic descriptions of sexual relationships in the unpublished portions of the diary'.[85]

This said, a directness does creep into Nin's diary writing, which, we noted earlier, was sometimes provided to her pornographic broker. *Henry and June* has 'deft, acute core-reaching fucking'.[86] 'Henry and I are tasting each other's flesh', she writes of Miller. 'We fall together into our savage world. He bites me. He makes my bones crack. He makes me lie with legs wide open and digs into me. Our cravings grow wild. Our bodies are convulsed. "Oh, Anaïs", he says, "I don't know how you learned it, but you can fuck, you can fuck."'[87] Her diaries contain some of the most convincing of her erotic prose. When she reread and revised her diaries 32 to 38, presumably with a view to selling extracts to the collector, she described herself as 'overwhelmed': 'such consuming pages, what ecstasies, what fever, expansion, dilation. Such joy and drunkenness ... At moments I feel it is the first time that a woman has opened herself. This is more revelatory than Proust – more than Gide'.[88] *Fire*, the published extracts from her diaries for 1934–37, record an encounter with a businessman, George Turner: 'We stood up by the window. "Can I slip my finger there, can I?" By the window he lifted my dress and I felt the honey flowing. And the dizziness, the sense of falling, melting, yearning for mouth and sex.' They have sex in the elevator – 'I had his penis in my hand, it was so hard, so big and a little wet already, and he took me right there in the little elevator' – and thereafter, in her mind, she relived the experience every time she entered a lift.[89] She has an 'orgy' with the publisher Donald Freide and another woman: 'For a long while the three of us lay entangled, caressing, sucking, biting, kissing, with fingers and tongues.'[90] The prose is compelling in its honesty, especially when it works against pornographic expectations. Nin says that she did not like the taste and smell of the woman's vagina ('a strong seashell dish'), that neither she nor the woman (Arline) had orgasms ('She was not even wet').[91] She philosophises about casual sex: 'If someone asked me, Do you know Donald, do you know Arline? Well, I would answer, I have slept with them, I know every part of their bodies intimately, their smells, their tastes, their textures of skin, but for the rest, please introduce me.'[92] She advocates not talking to male partners during brief encounters because it will undermine the moment. 'To hell with knowingness. Fuck. Fuck. Fuck.'[93]

Still, Nin preferred poetry: 'The quietness and hardness of his penis filling her completely, so that when the womb began to breathe, as it were, inhaling and exhaling there in the dark, to envelop him, encompass him and then open like a mouth and close again, she felt a quiet, long, drawn-out pleasure, which made her silent.'[94] Matilde's 'sex' 'curl[ed] like a leaf at each caress'; she had nipples that 'would harden like a fruit pip in his mouth', a 'womb' that 'burned from his plowing'.[95] But it did not require a lover for arousal, as in 'Life in Provincetown' when Pietro watches a woman sunbathing:

> The sun had caressed her all over, even to the secret places between the legs. It had warmed her mouth and her nipples, and the heavy, thick lips of her sex too. In answer to its caresses somehow, her own hand moved slowly to the place between her legs where the sun seemed warmest. As if seeking its rays, as if it were another hand, she searched for its incisive caress to meet it … and found the lips it had touched into sensibility.[96]

Nin even rendered necrophilia poetic. As a youth, Pierre had sex with a recently drowned woman: 'Her body had the taste of dew, of wet flowers, of wet leaves, of early morning grass. Her skin was like satin under his fingers. He loved her passivity and silence.' When he penetrated her 'water flowed from between her legs, as if he were making love to a naiad'.[97]

Commentators have interpreted Nin's erotic stories very differently. For Angela M. Carter they are subtle feminist texts, where even the most unpromising scenarios – female submission and male dominance – are explorations of restraints on female sexuality and 'a valid depiction of women's struggle and search for sexual freedom'.[98] Anna Powell has hailed them as experimental, stylish, transgressive, modernist texts.[99] Edmund Miller, on the other hand, considers Nin's erotica a narrative and sensual failure – though his condemnation tells us more about his male sexual preferences than it does about Nin's work.[100] In any case, plot may be irrelevant for both modernist status and pornographic effect. Edmund Miller aside, there is little argument over the literary quality of the erotic stories. As Smaro Kamboureli has expressed it, Nin's is a 'new kind of pornography', one infused with her 'poetic sensibility'.[101]

Then there is Pauline Réage's *Story of O*, which was published almost simultaneously in French and English in 1954; the respective publishers, Jean-Jacques Pauvert (publisher of Sade) and Maurice Girodias, shared an office.[102] The 1957, 1959 and 1965 editions of the book were No. 44 in the Traveller's Companion Series. It was, it was later revealed, a love letter from one French literary figure to another when the two were engaged in an affair, though the writer employed a nom de plume at the time. Given the nature of the novel, there was speculation about both the identity and gender of the author. Some American feminists thought it was inconceivable that anyone other than a man could have written such a clear case of male sexual wish fulfilment. Indeed, much of the early conjecture focused on male writers. The assessor for Grove Press in the US said that he took it 'for granted that the author, or at least part-author, is a man'; it was 'a tour de force of literary transvestism'.[103] But, as we have seen, the author was female: Dominique Aury (born Anne Desclos), writing her night-fantasies for her lover Jean Paulhan, an influential writer, literary critic and publisher, who then urged the book's publication. 'Why did I write it?' Aury explained to Régine Deforges in the 1970s, 'Let's say that it was a way of expressing a certain number of childhood and adolescent fantasies that persisted into my later life, that not only refused to go away but came back time and again.'[104] Aury told John de St. Jorre: 'I couldn't paint. I couldn't write poetry. What could I do to make him sit up?'[105] She knew of Paulhan's admiration for Sade but drew on her own fantasies, claiming that she had not actually read Sade until after she had finished her own book.

When de St. Jorre asked her about the male-fantasy criticism of her work, she replied: 'I've always been reproached for that. All I know is that they were honest fantasies – whether they were male or female, I couldn't say. There is no reality here. Nobody could stand being treated like that. It's entirely fantastic.'[106] So these were what she called 'dream castles':

> one could without fear build and furnish clandestine castles, on the condition that you people them with girls in love, prostituted by love, and triumphant in their chains. So it was with Sade's castles, discovered long after I had silently built my own, never surprised me ... But Sade made me understand that we are all jailers, and all in prison, in

that there is always someone within us whom we enchain, whom we imprison, whom we silence. By a curious kind of reverse shock, it can happen that prison itself can open the gates to freedom … free this unknown creature whom we have kept locked up.[107]

Odile Hellier, the owner of the Village Voice Bookshop in Paris, who read *Story of O* in the 1960s, said that she was impressed by the fact that O was not a simple victim: 'O was the initiator, the one who controlled the imagination, enacting her *own* fantasies. She was daring and took responsibility for her perversity.'[108]

O is the story of a woman's willing enslavement, shocking for many readers, it should be stated from the outset; Alyce Mahon has observed that its provocation lies more in 'O's willingness to be a victim' than in the details of her slavery.[109] Paulhan, being typically presumptuous as to the gender of the readership, wrote that 'the *Story of O* is one of those books which mark the reader – which do not leave him entirely, or at all, such as he was before'.[110] The book does describe pornographic situations: 'she watched every time O was tied to the wooden bedstead', the narrator relates of a young woman obsessed with the fashion photographer O, 'watched her writhe under the riding crop, watched the kneeling O receive the thick, uprisen sex of Sir Stephen in her mouth, watched the prostrate O spread her own buttocks with her own hands to open the passage into her behind'.[111] Yet *Story of O* does not employ the languages of hard-core erotica (recall Nin). There is no fucking or frigging in O's world, no references to cunt, cock, prick, arse, or even penis, vagina or clitoris. The actions are described without the vulgarity of sexual usage. Cunt is womb, her sex, or belly, as in 'the stranger who chewed her womb', 'Her sex gaped', 'dug his other hand so roughly into her belly that she thought she might faint'.[112] The penis is also the sex, as in 'all the sexes that had been sunk into her'.[113] The clitoris is 'the already burning morsel of flesh'.[114] The anus is mentioned, but never the arse or ass, merely the buttocks and behind, as in 'the two well-opened cracks of her womb and her behind'.[115]

It is a psychological study of a woman's desires – it was this that made it, in John Phillips's terms, 'literature as well as pornography'.[116] O's lover, René, takes her to a chateau, Roissy. There she is prepared as a sex slave: 'Your hands are not your own, neither are your breasts, nor, above all, is any one of the orifices of your body, which we are at liberty to explore and into which we may, whenever we so please, introduce ourselves.'[117] There are the usual accoutrements of BDSM, a riding crop, whips, chains, restraints, wrist bracelets, a leather collar, gags, uniforms. She is fitted with a series of ebonite rods to distend her anus for anal sex. She must obey a series of Sadean rules. (Mahon calls *Story of O* a 'modern Sadean novel'.[118]) She has to be naked under her skirt, even when she leaves Roissy, and wears an iron ring so that she can be identified. Later, when she is handed over to an older man, Sir Stephen, her labia are pierced and a chain and token attached, she is branded with her master's initials on her buttocks, and she wears a corset ('it hurts terribly') to narrow her waist.[119] After her sojourn at Roissy, she is treated as sexually available by all those who desire her and is at the constant beck and call of Sir Stephen once René has effectively relinquished his custody. She is whipped regularly. Her pubic mound is depilated at the whim of a master. She is raped orally, vaginally and anally.

The justification – her justification – for such subservience, as hinted by Aury in the quote about dream castles, was love, 'prostitution for love'.[120] The third-person narrator explains the motivations of the lovers, though the initiative is René's:

> For a long time he [René] had desired to prostitute her, and it was gladly he now discovered that the pleasure he reaped from it was greater than he had even dared hope, and increased his

attachment to her as it did hers to him, and that attachment would be the greater, the more her prostitution would humiliate and soil and ruin her. Since she loved him, she had no choice but to love the treatment she got from him. O listened and trembled from happiness; since he loved her, she trembled, consentingly.[121]

Love of René leads O into slavery, but then slavery leads her into love with Sir Stephen. 'O told herself', explains the narrator, adopting her perspective, 'that she had only loved René as a means for learning of love and for finding out how to give herself better, as a slave, as an ecstatic slave, to Sir Stephen.'[122]

O's longings are complex and conflicted. The book's author once said that what was daring about O was that she was fulfilling the dream of many women: 'To be able to sleep with anyone they wanted, without the slightest twinge of guilt.'[123] O desires women (Aury was involved with the writer Édith Thomas before and after her affair with Paulhan), but only when she takes the initiative and as a means of experiencing what Sir Stephen must feel when he dominates her.[124] ('I love you the way a man loves a woman', the feminist Aury told the feminist Thomas, according to the latter's diary.[125]) Sir Stephen asks O to have sex with the model Jacqueline so that he can secretly watch – she 'fetched cry after cry from Jacqueline until she broke like a pane of glass, and relaxed, soaked from joy' – but she was already attracted to the young woman.[126] When their relationship ceases, 'What O missed wasn't Jacqueline, strictly speaking but the use of a girl's body, a body with which she could do as she liked.'[127]

What if, O (via the narrator) muses at one point, 'her abasement, her abjection were sweet to her?'[128] And it seems that they were. There is reference to O 'lost in a delirious absence from herself', to 'this state of being dispossessed of her own self'.[129] Susan Sontag

observes that O 'progresses simultaneously toward her own extinction as a human being and her fulfillment as a sexual being', attain-
ing the annihilation of the self 'required of a Jesuit novice or Zen
pupil'.[130] Aury herself reflected on submission being 'a formidable
weapon', that in fact O uses her male dominators rather than they
her: 'Doesn't she bend them to her will? And the fact is, she does
get what she wants in the end' – even if it is her own extinction.[131]
Phillips has mused the significance of O's name: the O of a pout,
the O of female orifices, the O of jouissance, of submission, of
disapproval and, finally – with homage to Sontag – the O of nul-
lity, zero.[132] Gregory Stephenson has posited that O might signify
emptiness but it could also 'symbolize a having come full circle,
the achievement of completion, fulfillment'.[133] The writer herself
imparted no such significances. O was merely 'that faceless, ageless,
nameless (even first-nameless) girl'.[134] A nameless woman had written about a nameless woman.

We have seen that some dirty books were irredeemably pornographic and that others had more literary merit. Were *Gordon*,
Story of O and Nin's erotica even dirty books? But there were also
dirty books of superior quality, though dirty books nonetheless. *The
Chariot of Flesh* (1955), the book which discouraged Harriet Sohmers
from writing pornography, was breathlessly extravagant. Malcolm
Nesbit (Alfred Chester) provided the sexual act on every page that
Girodias had reportedly requested. There are indeed monstrous
pricks in *Chariot*. 'Nothing existed but this wild painful lunge', a
female protagonist recalled of sex with her husband, while she and
the book's male narrator engage in preliminary mutual masturbation; 'that tremendous instrument. It beat like drums and affected
every part of my body ... past my belly, into my chest, beside my
heart. My heart throbbed with its throbbing.'[135] There are copious

amounts of ejaculate: 'Boris's juice was pouring out of him, spilling into me like a fountain into the sky.'[136] Women are always wet: 'He seemed to be drinking the slime of my loins, drowning in it, while his tongue sloughed through my meat.'[137] They ache for sex, literally: 'I'm all aching ... I'm all one piece of aching cunt.'[138] The writer uses the tried technique of the sexually aroused voyeur or listener: 'I couldn't help – I overheard the story and it excited me. Will you fuck me, Mr. Cunningham?'[139]

But *Chariot* is different to the normal run of porn. Chester insinuated homoeroticism into his prose scenarios in a way that was unusual for the heterosexually leaning Olympia dirty books. He was skilled in his construction of layers of voyeurism, multiple narratives that allowed for the switching of genders in the pornographic descriptions. His plot stretched credulity, but at least he provided a narrative – and even a twist at the book's end – that held the story together in a manner incommensurate with the normal inconclusiveness of pornographic writing.[140] Chester was endlessly inventive, with upside-down fucking, nipple-to-anus stimulation, chicken sex, a daisy chain of anal contact that had not been broken for three years, and the inerasable image of a bath, half-filled with warmed sperm.[141]

For Chester and the more skilled writers, playing with the tropes of pornography ran the risk of stretching them to a comedic breaking point; indeed, some seemed to embrace that course. There was a sense of fun about some of these books. The famous *Candy*, which in heavily pirated form was to sell millions of copies, was 'a satire on pornography' that 'might be mistaken for pornography', as one of the endorsers of its US publication wrote.[142] Terry Southern would later say that in agreeing to publish it, Girodias himself had mistaken 'Quality Lit erotic-humor-allegory for porn trash'.[143] (Though he also credited Girodias's skills in enticing 'impressionable young

American expatriates ... to churn out this muck by convincing us we were writing *Quality Lit!*'[144]) *Newsweek* would call *Candy* 'the first genuinely comic pornographic novel'.[145] 'If you'd read my book, you'd understand how I feel about these things', the authors make the psychiatrist character say to a colleague. 'In the fifth chapter of *Masturbation Now?* I state expressly that heterosexual love-making is the root of all neuroses, a shabby illusion which misleads the ego, that we must endeavor to keep it in its true place – as an aid, and adjunct to masturbation, which is the only sex-mode that permits complete fulfilment and mental health.'[146]

Akbar del Piombo's (Norman Rubington's) numerous green books are generally considered to be 'outrageously funny'.[147] The Olympia author Marilyn Meeske, who would have known, singled out del Piombo for particular notice in 1965: 'he writes the best contemporary pornography. His trilogy, *The Fetish Crowd*, is genuinely hilarious, ribald, and the writing is excellent. It would not be considered prurient – it is too absurd.'[148] (She did not disclose Rubington's true identity, except to say that he was an expatriate American painter in Paris.) The erotica experts Eberhard and Phyllis Kronhausen cited *Candy* and del Piombo in a discussion of the role of erotic wit and humour in what was for them (writing in 1964) the pornography of the future.[149] 'Gently I stroked her abundant mop, coaxing out the bare lips of her organ', the narrator wrote in *Who Pushed Paula?* (1955), the first book of del Piombo's trilogy *The Fetish Crowd* (1965). 'The vulva rolled and rippled between my fingers, became drizzling wet, then a murmuring, gurgling swamp, under the relentless advance to the tributary source.'[150] In this Rabelaisian romp, we have anal and vaginal play with nuns, sodomy, bestiality with a (jealous) Great Dane, a Sapphic servant orgy, horse sex (by means of pulleys and ropes) and double penetration – all in the first three chapters. The book then proceeds to a mass orgy, prompted by a sex education lecture: 'I screwed, blind-drunk, grabbing at buttocks, squeezing on thighs, biting on titties, smelling on cunts. Nothing was spared in our lavish abuse, not an inch of flesh which didn't offer itself in the sacrificial heap, not a hole which went unscathed by a finger, a tongue or even a foot.'[151] On it goes, with brutal BDSM encounters, grotesque sex of truly fantastical proportions, all amid the hero Henry Pike's never-ending sexual encounters – 'I never saw a man who ran around so much without his pants!'[152]

Rubington's *The Traveller's Companion* (1957; the same name as the series in which it appeared as No. 43), in which Henry Pike makes a comeback, so to speak, is a veritable relay race of fornication in an aristocratic chateau; the only contact is sexual contact, every entry to a room becomes carnal entry, with (exceeding Girodias's ideal) at least one sex act on every page as the story builds to the 'Grand Orgy'. In one descriptive scene, the narrator takes the reader to window after window, with a sexual tableau in every room.[153] The frequent descriptions of masturbation (male and female) mirror what presumably the book's one-handed readers would be doing. This male author certainly provides portrayals of female pleasure, as in this description of the Duchess and the Baroness: 'The Duchess, who was atop her friend, swung round and bared the Baroness' bush to her tongue', the narrator tells the reader, 'Her own, smooth pussy was enjoying the thick juicy surface of the Baroness' organ. Soon they were nothing but a whirling rainbow of colors, panting and moaning in a rising tempest of flooding vaginas which only ceased when the gurgling current of orgasm exhausted the last of their strength.'[154] And there is humour: '"If you mean the position you are in now", answered the Baroness, "I can think of none more suited to matrimony. You have your prick in your wife-to-be and your tongue in your boss' cunt. It is an enviable position."'[155] In true pornotopian style, and with some narrative ease, all reality is sexualised in *Who Pushed Paula?* and *The Traveller's Companion*; as Marcus has remarked of the genre, there is more interest in organs and sexual positions than there is in emotions and people.[156] In *The Traveller's Companion*, nipples are mentioned 36 times, the clitoris 37 times, ass 45 times, fuck, fucked or fucking 50 times, orgasm 55 times, buttocks 67 times, breast or breasts 104 times, cunt 147 times and the cock 294 times.[157]

Some of Olympia's product was experimental, even surrealistic. Take, for instance, James Webster Sherwood's *Stradella* (1962), No. 101 in the Traveller's Companion Series. 'She was standing so close I swallowed her lips by accident', the narrator says of his first encounter with Stradella, his love interest. 'Offering to shake her hands, I stroked her buttocks with my free hand'. Sherwood's prose is genuinely innovative: 'She plucked me like a dandelion. I sank my toe in her apple', the narrator continued in his creator's inimitable style. 'I threw her against a wall. She stuffed me in a drawer. She sighed and swung from a lamp. I crawled up the Venetian blinds.'[158] The book's genesis was as surrealistic as its contents: lost, rewritten from memory, found again, restructured without the author's consent and, according to Sherwood, falsely claimed by Girodias as his own work ('my writing *Stradella* was easy').[159]

Some readers may be surprised that humour has been mentioned, given that, as we saw in the last chapter, some literary experts have claimed that humour and parody are inimical to the pornographic effect. Perhaps this is what Girodias had in mind when he told Samuel Beckett that the dirty books were 'a parody of pornography, rather than the real thing'.[160] This was a claim that he had anticipated in a letter to the *Times Literary Supplement*, accusing a critic (ironically) of a lack of a sense of humour in failing to recognise that the dirty books were anything other than 'pure parody'. They were, Girodias claimed, 'intended to make fun, at the same time, of genuine pornography, and of the hare-brained censors who want us to believe, in the middle of the twentieth century, that it constitutes a monstrous social evil'.[161]

Yet humour is clearly present in the work of some of the most adept erotic writers. We have noted in this chapter the hilarity of Norman Rubington, the authors of *Candy*, Iris Owens and Alfred Chester, and in previous chapters that of Gershon Legman, Robert Sewall, the fake Millers, Apollinaire and Louÿs. Anaïs Nin could be humorous, too, as a reviewer in the *Times Literary Supplement* noted of the vignette in *Delta of Venus* where a rubber woman gives syphilis to its sailor-users.[162] 'We have comical conversations', Nin said of her coterie of writers. 'We tell a story and the rest of us have to decide whether it is true or false. Or plausible.'[163] One such story was 'Manuel', told to Nin by her lover Gonzalo Moré and mentioned in her diary. 'His favorite theater of denudation was the Bibliothèque Nationale', where he would linger waiting for a young female reader to raise her head from her researches, and there would stand Manuel, 'exhibiting his prize possession in his hand. The shock, the flush, the reaction delighted him.'[164] Manuel goes to extreme lengths to expose himself and 'exhibit his rather formidable member. The more people there were, the better ... Women tended to run away from him. He had to beg them to stay'.[165] He only needed a glance, 'then he would fall into a trance, his face would become ecstatic, and soon he would be rolling on the floor in a crisis of orgasm'.[166] He did not have much luck, but eventually reached an agreement with the wife of a literary agent 'who was dying of starvation and overwork'. He would do her housework for her in exchange for her watching him strip and then commenting on his penis. 'She had to look at his penis as she would look at food she liked … It's a beautiful penis you have there, the biggest I have seen in Montparnasse. It's so smooth and hard. It's beautiful.'[167] This admiration would turn into 'undulation' as, 'still holding his penis and shaking it under her face', he would collapse to the floor and 'roll himself into a ball as he came, sometimes all over his own face'.[168]

We know that it was the humour in Henry Miller's *Tropic of Cancer* which was one of its attractions for the publisher Jack Kahane (as we saw in Chapter 1). Alfred Perlès, a friend of Miller, both confirmed and denied the proposition about laughter and pornography. 'A sense of humour does not go with sex', he wrote in 1955, just as Olympia was beginning. 'Sex is a dead serious matter … Sex and laughter don't mix – at least not until a man like Henry Miller comes along!' He elaborated: 'The crudest, the most obscene passages in Miller's books are pervaded with a sense of humour that takes the unwholesomeness out of eroticism.'[169] As for Vladimir Nabokov, a writer for *Partisan Review* deemed *Lolita* 'just about the funniest book I remember having read'.[170]

Girodias might have claimed that his dirty books were parodies of the 'real thing', whatever that was, but he wanted them to sell – 'done convincingly enough to satisfy the sex-obsessed whose sense of humor is notoriously blunted', as he also told Beckett.[171] If the description 'funny pornography' is so oxymoronic, why was comicality favoured by some of the better writers? Presumably they did not need lecturing about the pornographic effect. We may have to reconsider the role of laughter in erotic writing.

A few of the Olympia authors moved beyond a mere focus on sex. Trocchi's pornography could be more philosophical: 'Once again I have experienced the terrible joy of annihilation', writes the female narrator in *Helen and Desire* (1954), 'the deliverance of my whole being to the mystery of sensual union, and this time with a male whom I would not recognise in daylight. There is perfection in that. I want nothing more of him.'[172] It is difficult to know whether the intellectual impulse behind her characterisation was existentialism, or a renewed interest in Enlightenment erotica, where bodily experience leads to freedom of the mind; but something was happening other than sex for the sake of sex. Hers was a 'new and purer existence'; 'Mine is the true culture, all that is deep, all that is not surfaces'.[173] While it is debatable whether liberation can be achieved by lying on one's back in the desert, in captivity, being serviced by a procession of nomadic partners, the Helen of *Helen and Desire* was defiant of the norm. 'What a fool he was!', she said of an early sexual contact:

> The thought of marriage had never crossed my mind. To be a house slave as my mother had been, to lose my freedom and adapt myself to his absurd male requirements! That was my first experience of this kind of idiot male presumption – why do they assume that because we have need of their bodies we will be willing to submit ourselves to the drab pattern of their everyday existence?[174]

The Scots publisher John Calder has observed that Trocchi wrote top-quality pornography: 'He wrote with style, he created real people, he created backgrounds.'[175] This does not mean that his pornography was unproblematic. *Thongs* (1956), which Trocchi wrote under the name Carmencita de las Lunas, is an unrelenting tale of sadomasochistic sex, culminating in the willing crucifixion of the female narrator (the fiction being that her notebooks were found by her editor). The book begins with the crucifixion so that the reader is aware from the start that there will be no happy ending.[176] There are shades of the *Story of O* (with a labial piercing), but the violence is on another plane, starting with the marking of a woman's thighs by the removal of a triangle of flesh with a razor, and progressing to complete degradation (and revelling in that debasement) by forced group sex. It is the most misogynist of Trocchi's dirty books, a lingering on women's bodies like a 'lecherous mortician', as one critic has described it, almost a bodily revulsion, and, in the words of another, 'authorial pleasure in the violent use of women that is deeply unsettling'.[177] When Trocchi met Sally Child in the 1970s, he gave her *Thongs* to read; 'I was completely horrified', she recounted, 'because I'd been making love to this man who'd written this book and I can remember saying to him, you know, my God, Alex, where did this stuff come from and he said oh, just off the top of my head. I kept thinking my God, if that's at the top, what's at the bottom'.[178] However, there is no denying Trocchi's talent.

Harriet Daimler (Iris Owens) operated at another level too. *Woman* or *The Woman Thing* (1958, 1965), No. 61 in the Traveller's Companion Series, has the required sex scenes: 'He fucked her until she was a hot river, until he could feel her not knowing or caring who or what the thing inside her was, just plunging it up and down inside of her with lavish fascism.'[179] But Owens, as Girodias intimated, was a real writer. Although the critic George Steiner was generally critical of the Olympia project, he did see Owens's novel as one of its more exciting products: '*The Woman Thing* uses all the four-letter words and anatomical exactitudes with real force; it exhibits a fine ear for the way in which sexual heat compresses and erodes our uses of language.'[180] In the achingly claustrophobic *Woman*, much of the action occurs in an apartment – indeed, in a bed: 'When Martha was in the room she was in the bed, that being a genuine syllogism, because when she was in the bed, there being no other area in the room, she was in the room.'[181] *Woman* is about being down-and-out in Paris, sexual politics, co-dependency (though the term is not used), class and male privilege (the male character Macdonald is reputedly based on Trocchi).[182] The dialogue is bracing: '"Oh Macdonald", Martha implored, "don't hit me again. Why don't we fuck instead? It's practically the same thing." "None of your Freudianisms", Macdonald warned.'[183] The work is full of social observation:

> Impoverished men, she upbraided destiny, why always poor men? They are certainly not more intelligent, they're not amusing. And so plentiful. They multiply, they destroy, they're like white cells in my blood stream. My parasites of poverty. And they have no style, so dedicated about having nothing. Treating everything like wives – men, women, children, animals, birds, reptiles, fungus, concierges, their misery marries them to everything.[184]

It is witty:

> 'James is a painter', Conrad began, 'all the while he was organizing his wills, trusts, investments, inheritances, property, lands, houses, peons, stocks, bonds, accounts, coupons, oilwells, tennis courts, orange groves, rubber plantations, steel mills, atomic plants, stables, kennels, and aviary, he was thinking of being a painter. Am I correct so far, James my boy.'
> 'For ten years I've thought of little else', James confessed.[185]

Far from being porn masquerading as literature, *Woman* is literature disguised as porn. Gerald Howard has called works such as those of Owens and Trocchi 'quality-lit pornography': 'The reading experience they offer is a curious one, suspended somewhere between the purely pornographic and the Euro-literary … Art-house porn'.[186]

Marilyn Meeske saw erotic writing as an opportunity to experiment: 'The chance to use language in a free, shocking way could lead to a great unleashing of creative inhibition and also serve as an exercise in the understanding of the powers of the written word.'[187] But she also said that one of her books, *Flesh and Bone* (1957), 'was a wordy sex-hash off the top of the head. I knew it wasn't literature;

I understood the formula; I needed money.'[188] Although parody was certainly produced (as we have seen), the situation was far more complex than that. Olympia's editor had both an eye for literary talent and a sense of what might sell as masturbatory material, while recognising potential tensions between the two.

Perhaps Mason Hoffenberg, as Hamilton Drake, was right in *Sin for Breakfast* (1957) when Margot says: 'Let's face it – the thing that's unique about these particular books is that, for once, the writers have the liberty to deal with sex as frankly as they wish.' 'If they do it well', continues the character, who was reputedly based on Owens, 'they accomplish something that's really significant: they throw light on a very, very important subject that's always been a forbidden one for authors. If they don't do it well then their books may be what a lot of people claim them to be – pornography.'[189] Was the distinction between literature and porn the outcome of a kind of erotic natural selection? It is an issue to which we will return in a later chapter.

6

Sexual revolution: Olympia, New York

Maurice Girodias founded an Olympia Press in New York that ran from 1967 to 1974, repeating his Paris formula: young, pseudonymous and named writers, women authors, a mixture of avant-garde literature and experimental pornography. He also reprinted older Olympia titles – nearly thirty at our count – utilising the tried and true.[1] Girodias tapped into Ed Martin's fantastical world again, reprinting his ghost-sex dirty book, *Busy Bodies* (1968, 1970), as well as newly written titles, including *Frankenstein '69* (1969) with its mechanical sex dolls and never-to-be-forgotten mermaid sex scenes: 'There were tits rubbing and slapping at his back. A man with tits? Or a woman with a cock? He was suddenly aware of the tits in front of him. They were working together. He was being massaged by four tits, and the cock and cunt were working together too.'[2] Norman Rubington, as Akbar del Piombo, continued with his preposterous orgies. In the narrative preliminaries to *Into the Harem* (1970) the hero's permanently erect (and predictably massive) penis breaks out of his trousers at a genteel tea party and erotic chaos ensues: 'Round and round I went, faster and faster, shoving in and out, fucking the entire company one by one.'[3] Akbar liked to see himself as 'the Groucho Marx of erotica'.[4]

Girodias viewed the New York Olympia Press as a venture of the sexual revolution, which made clear the role of his earlier work in the heritage of that revolution. As he wrote in 1970 in the midst of his brief New York undertaking, 'Our primary object then [in Paris in the 1950s and early 1960s] was to dismantle censorship; today [in New York in the 1960s], with the sexual revolution well on its way, our aim is to normalize the situation, and help integrate the erotic side of life in creative writing, as being one of its most natural and essential components'.[5]

Girodias attempted to negotiate with Barney Rosset, the editor of Grove Press and the US publisher of Henry Miller. Girodias and Rosset had cooperated in the past. Girodias petitioned Miller and gave Rosset inside publishing information in his successful bid for the rights to *Tropic of Cancer*: 'I gave you all these details because you have to be acquainted with the whole situation if you want to avoid wasting time and making blunders.'[6] The two publishers lobbied prominent authors over the French prosecution of Jean Genet's *Our Lady of the Flowers* in 1959.[7] They collaborated in the same year over the publication of the politically sensitive Roger Casement *Black Diaries*, issued by Olympia in Paris and by Grove in New York.[8] Again in 1959, they reached agreement over the publication in the US of William Burroughs's *Naked Lunch*, another original Olympia book.[9] Grove published *The Olympia Reader*, a showcase of Girodias's authors. Olympia Press also distributed Grove Press in France in the late 1950s, including the *Evergreen Review*.[10] Rosset advised Girodias on his lucrative US deal for *Lolita*, including offering to broker the money, paying him in instalments (presumably for tax purposes).[11] Girodias even persuaded Judith Schmidt at Grove to scour New York bookshops for old images to be used in the collages in Rubington's *Fuzz* series.[12] There had been mutual cooperation.

However, behind the scenes, most of these projects were beset with dispute. Their partnership on *The Black Diaries* was nightmarish ('One thing which you do not seem to understand Maurice, is that your way of dividing the book into mathematical units means absolutely nothing to us').[13] Girodias, under self-inflicted financial pressure because of his ill-fated restaurant project, harassed Rosset for royalty advances, and even loans: 'I hope you will now be able to arrange the $20,000 loan without delay in order to avoid my untimely collapse.'[14] Future yields on the *Reader* and *Naked Lunch* were levied by court order to cover debts to the Diner's Club, of all institutions (the restaurant again).[15] And Girodias's desperation led him to pressure Rosset to publish *Naked Lunch* when the Grove publisher had a careful strategy to see Miller's *Tropic of Cancer* through the courts first. He agitated Grove to publish other Miller works when the danger was that the market would have been flooded. 'If you think you can sell NAKED LUNCH to anybody else', Rosset wrote to Girodias in late 1961, during an acrimonious exchange about the delay in the US publication of the Burroughs book, 'you are sadly mistaken. We are not defending over fifty people, arrested on criminal charges, on the TROPIC case, just to be pushed around by you. Believe me, not only will it not work but it will destroy any hope of future dealings with you.'[16] The two publishers also fought in the late 1960s over the rights to *The Story of O*, originally published by Girodias but which proved to be a lucrative acquisition for Rosset.[17]

Based presumably on their shared past, Girodias stressed their common interests, when in truth they were competitors and Rosset seems to have outwitted his French counterpart.[18] In fact, when Grove published their collected works of Sade, translated by Richard Seaver (now an editor at Grove) and Austryn Wainhouse, they drew heavily on Wainhouse's earlier work for Olympia, so much so that Girodias claimed the rights to this work and expected royalties.[19] Simply put, Girodias claimed that Wainhouse was a writer for hire and the copyright for the translations belonged to his employer ('commissioned, published and paid for by me'), while Wainhouse argued that he was an independent writer, had translated *The Bedroom Philosophers* before he even met the French publisher, and that, in any case, the Grove editions were significantly different, 'bettered versions of the work I did thirteen years ago'.[20] This aside, we know that Seaver and Wainhouse *were* duplicitous in their dealings with Olympia. The latter was offering his Olympia translations *Madame Edwarda* and *L'Histoire de l'oeil* to Grove as early as 1964.[21] At one point, Wainhouse was in possession of the galleys for both the Olympia and Grove versions of Sade's *Juliette*, and, at Seaver's bidding, held back on the Olympia corrections so that Grove could publish first.[22] Girodias was oblivious to Grove's strategy. 'The poor devil is going to go mad the day he discovers the little farce that has been played upon him', Wainhouse wrote to Seaver in 1968. 'Indeed, with every passing day I feel worse about this sabotage, and am eager to hear that Grove has started printing and has moved into the lead: this will enable me to return Girodias' proofs to him with an I'm-awfully-sorry letter which will bring an end to this really very ignoble business.'[23] As a result, the New York Olympia version of *Juliette* never appeared – though Brandon House and Lancer pirated the Paris Olympia Press edition.

The relationship between Girodias and Rosset was tortured and complex. Both men were aware of its quirks yet seemed compelled to continue. 'Maurice is a strange, difficult and unpredictable man', Rosset counselled Ian Ballantine of Ballantine Books (who was printing the paperback of the *Reader* that Girodias and Grove were doing together), 'and through long experience I have learned that the best way to deal with him is to ignore him. Anything he says today you may be sure he will contradict tomorrow.'[24] 'It's funny, don't you think', the unpredictable Girodias wrote at a time when funny would have been the last word on Rosset's lips, 'the kind of relationship that's been developing through the years between us. It is an ambiguous thing indeed, part (genuine) friendship, part business competition – although it is competition of a very one-sided nature as I have never tried to compete with you, whereas the reverse seems to be all too true.'[25]

At one point in 1966, the presses even drew up a contract, with Grove participating to produce Traveller's Companion books in the US and Canada, but the negotiations collapsed over publishing terms and editorial control.[26] The collaboration never happened. Olympia Press set up in the US without any Grove partnership, apart from a short-lived distribution agreement ('we do seem to be about to distribute some books for Maurice', Rosset wrote to a German publisher in 1968, 'because we are crazy and greedy').[27]

Girodias also approached Brandon House, according to one of its editors, 'asking us if we'd like to go 50–50 on his books, in a partnership operation. We refused of course. Why pay for something that's free.'[28]

At first the American undertaking seemed to go well. Girodias became an entity. He was interviewed by Peter Collier in a perceptive piece for the New Left publication *Ramparts* magazine in 1968: 'The pilgrimage of Maurice Girodias, most celebrated of pornographers, to his true spiritual home in America seems to be a momentous event in our erotic history.'[29] The celebrated pornographer ensconced himself in the famous Chelsea Hotel, where he met Valerie Solanas, more of whom later. He held Chelsea Hotel soirees of the type that Hunter S. Thompson's copy editor Margaret

Harrell was invited to in 1968: 'Monsieur Girodias wishes to meet some beautiful, intelligent women'.[30]

Gerald Williams, a young African American who had worked with the publisher as an editor and translator in Paris, met up with him in New York in 1967, and Girodias seemed full of life and schemes: 'His enthusiasm was contagious.' Someone was writing a porno *Alice in Wonderland* for his dirty books. There was to be a film about his life, 'with Peter Sellers playing Maurice and Maurice playing a gendarme'.[31] In 1968 Girodias was interviewed about another film featuring him, the 'first big-budget Dirty Movie', provisionally called *The Olympia Reader*. Melvin Fishman, an LSD aficionado who was to be the film's producer, said that it would be a mixture of biography ('loosely' biographical) and fantasy, 'And frank, all so frank, no nonsense – The public is ready for Real Blue Movies, of a studio excellence, isn't it?'[32] The film was never made. Fishman went on to produce *Steppenwolf* (1974) and then died.[33] But the point is that Girodias had arrived. He wrote an upbeat letter to William Burroughs in 1969, saying that he should have moved to New York ten years earlier: 'I am going through a completely unexpected renaissance. Weird, eh?'[34] He floated the idea of a new literary magazine called *O*, 'as in Oscar, or Olympia' (or, he should have said, *Story of O*), to be edited by Girodias, with Rubington as art editor and Sam Abrams in charge of poetry; 'it is meant to serve as a medium for what is probably the most diversified group of young writers in America today'.[35] Girodias flirted with counter culture, appearing as a judge at the first American Erotic Film Festival in the Presidio Theatre in San Francisco in 1970.[36] He negotiated to distribute the Amsterdam-based sex magazine *Suck* in America, which would have been an interesting development had the scheme not faltered. He tried to take over *Suck*'s Wet Dream sex film festival as the Olympia Festival ('isn't Wet dream synonymous to Olympia Press, etc.'), but the *Suck* editors knew their history: 'Maurice was trying to swallow *Suck*. Just the way he had conjured the Merlin group in Paris during the Fifties.'[37]

It should be stated from the outset that Girodias was no slouch when it came to publication numbers. According to Patrick Kearney's catalogue of New York Olympia Press titles, nearly four hundred appeared between 1967 and 1974 (compared to under two hundred Paris Olympia titles during the first phase of Girodias's activity).[38] He had a *New Olympia Reader* only two years into his enterprise in the US, nearly nine hundred pages of work by over forty authors.[39] His books sold in respectable numbers too, as we know from the records of Grove Press, which distributed Olympia Press before the arrangement broke down in late 1969. Forty-five thousand copies each of books by Frank Newman (Sam Abrams) and Benjamin Grimm (Spencer Lambert), for example, were distributed in the first months of their publication.[40] Twenty-two Olympia titles sold a total of 196,000 copies in 1969 (taking into account book sellers' returns); Grove had distributed 700,000 copies of Olympia New York titles by early 1970.[41]

Girodias established his well-worn publishing modus operandi, what Harvey Hornwood has referred to as locating 'writers with an abundant sexual imagination and acute shortage of money'.[42] The *Ramparts* interviewer noted that the publisher was attempting to locate the equivalent of his Merlin group: 'He hasn't yet found such a centralized source in America, although he is beginning to tap the legion of marginal writers in this country who always have trouble getting into print.'[43]

We know that Girodias employed Marilyn Meeske, a former Olympia Paris author and editor, to help out with his US venture. He asked for inspiration with titles for his books, offering $25 for each title used. She came up with 'Flying Upside

Down', 'Mouths of Babes' and 'Bunny Fur', for example, while Girodias suggested 'Honey Finger', 'The Moan' and 'Who's Coming Next?' 'Keep trying', he urged her. 'We need some more raunchy ones also, for the Ophelia series, which is more aggressively sexy and truck-driverish.'[44] Meeske clearly had an editorial role. They discussed what would become Lyn Raskin's *Diary of a Transsexual* (1971), which Meeske was editing, an early, very explicit trans autobiography, an important work in the history of both transgender medicine and trans sexuality: 'Make the story more grotesque, more extreme – and also more sexy: well, sexy – I mean, pertaining to sex, not necessarily seductive; one would like a little more about those masturbation scenes, and the endless fantasies that must haunt the author, to the extent that his-her whole life is dominated by that problem of sexual definition.'[45] Girodias's advice was not exactly trans-friendly, but it does show that he was engaged in his publishing. Meeske's archives contain undated memos from 1969–70, with a stream of requests and suggestions from Girodias: give priority to Pekinpah, Moline and Peter Rabbit (see later); see if di Prima is writing a sequel (see later); does she agree that 'In Bed with [the] President' is slapstick, and that the sex scenes in Louis Atcheson's typescript become perfunctory; should they set up a newsletter, 'a sort of literary Rolling Stone'?[46] She wrote publishing blurbs for Olympia Press books.[47] '[I]t's really good to know that you are part of this bizarre renaissance', Girodias told Meeske, 'and your participation in this is for me a lucky omen'.[48]

Ghost writers were another possible source for prospective Olympia authors. Collier located one in San Francisco, Norman Singer, who, under his own name, would go on to write nine Olympia titles, seven in 1968 and 1969 alone, including *The Cannibals Next Door* (1969) and *The Man Who Raped San*

Francisco (1969).[49] While ghost writing, Singer had written *Curtain of Flesh*. 'I think that it's a good study of nymphomania and marital cannibalism', he told Collier. It had been rejected many times: 'Then my agent happened to send it to Mr. Maurice Girodias. Mr. Girodias liked my book. He asked me to put in some more, really outspoken sex scenes. I did, he bought it, and it was just recently published.'[50] Singer was perplexed by his good fortune in landing full-time employment. He had promised Girodias a book every two months: 'You know, it's kind of strange, all of a sudden writing scenes of gang bangs, group congress, and all sorts of weird sex stuff. But I get $2000 a book'.[51]

A sardonic piece in a local newspaper in 1971 said that when Girodias had first arrived in New York, the publisher had placed advertisements in the *Village Voice* calling for manuscripts, 'and received responses naturally, from every stock clerk with dementia praecox who had been working on the Great American Novel for some time, and had stacks of it in his closet'.[52] The call for more sex certainly recommenced. 'Gobs of words would go off to New York whenever the rent was due', Diane di Prima wrote in her afterword to *Memoirs of a Beatnik* (1969), one of Girodias's commissions. They would 'come back with "MORE SEX" scrawled across the top page in Maurice's inimitable hand, and I would dream up odd angles of bodies or weird combinations of humans and cram them in and send it off again.' The 'prurient interest had to be added, like oregano to tomato sauce'.[53] And Girodias certainly got his oregano. 'My right hand slid down, one finger sunk deep into his asshole, the others stroking the skin behind his balls', di Prima wrote in one of the book's many such passages. 'I could feel his cock grow still larger against the soft flesh of my stomach. My cunt convulsed in a spasm that left me moist and aching with desire.'[54]

The standard dirty books were reprised, then. Girodias did a mail-out to New York literary agents, and the future leading sports journalist George Kimball answered the call. He was paid $1,000 in advance for *Only Skin Deep* (1968), a *Candy*-like pornographic parody, published when the author was twenty-four years old. Kimball becomes Susie, a fifteen-year-old schoolgirl, with the action beginning, predictably, in the showers in the girls' changing room: 'My young nipples hardened as Judy time and again smoothly slid the bar of Lye soap across my chest; then, as she tucked it through and between my legs, I was startled to feel the searing pain as she inserted a corner of the bar into my twinging rectum.'[55] The journalist Hunter S. Thompson, tongue-in-cheek, called *Only Skin Deep* 'the foulest, most rotten thing I've ever laid eyes on. It goes far beyond pornography as to approach a new form of some kind'.[56]

Girodias approached already working pornographers, or they contacted him. He got in touch with Victor Banis's agent who told Banis, 'Girodias said he thinks of you as being a star of the Greenleaf stable. He asked which other Greenleaf writers I represent and if I could get them to write for him.'[57] Girodias was setting up a homosexual series called 'The Other Traveller' and wanted Banis to write for him. He did, as Victor Jay, and *The Gay Haunt* was published in 1970 and 1972. According to Banis, the business relationship did not go well. He got a $1,500 'advance' (which arrived after publication) and was cheated out of royalties.[58] Greenleaf's Earl Kemp claimed that Olympia got the idea of catering for the gay market from them and that Girodias stole their writers, including Larry Townsend and Richard Love (aka Richard Amory), as well as Banis.[59]

The veteran pulp writer Robert Turner contributed a couple of Olympia texts, under his own name and as K. K. Klein, though he had many pseudonyms to choose from.[60] *Pretty Thing* (1968) is a comedic pornographic romp featuring a young, naive, Candy-like female southern governor, and some questionable racial stereo-types, including a man who is able to 'have an instant erection' at will, rendered in exclamatory prose: 'Oh, Big Daddy, *look* at you! Oh. I'm *dying* for it even though it'd probably *kill* me! Oh, a flag-pole! Oh, a redwood *log*! Oh, the nose of a *jet* plane!'[61] Despite its title, Klein's *The Sex of Angels* (1968) is a puerile, comic-book-like story about a faux preacher with a penchant for underage girls (who turn out to be older than they are pornographically imagined) and an obsession with breasts, rendered in truly awful prose imagery: 'The great, white, hard-nippled breasts rolled and shimmered like molds of blancmange', is but one such description.[62]

The previously mentioned Norman Singer was certainly adept at writing crudely efficient, nasty pornography: 'Her body heaved and throbbed with each inner blow of his prick, the pain and dreadful shame shooting throughout her flesh and mind, her senses whirling in endless waves of shock leaving her dazed with the dim threat of gruesome pleasure that was slowly building up against her will.'[63] Singer could have produced a thesaurus of sexual descriptions, and the flow of words is unending in his hyphenated descriptions: 'oh flushing and swim-popping the wet-splattered velvet-tipped cock in this tongue-trapping mouth-watering cunt and heaving lung-bursting death in the tangled oceans'.[64]

Inspired perhaps by Burroughs's *Naked Lunch* (1959), Olympia was responsible for several key texts in what Jay Gertzman has termed 'Porno Noir'.[65] Charles Platt, a science fiction writer and future computer programmer, wrote *The Gas* for Olympia's rivals Essex House, but the book was rejected as 'disgusting, abhorrent, repulsive, and unpublishable'; not so for Girodias who published it in 1970 under his Ophelia imprint.[66] 'A letter was waiting for me from Maurice Girodias, telling me that he would buy *The Gas*',

Platt recalled many years later. 'He thought it would be perfect for his Ophelia imprint, which was the less-literary subsidiary of Olympia Press. Yes, my book was disgusting, abhorrent and repulsive, but he seemed to like that kind of thing, and offered to buy it for $1,500.'[67] Platt then went on to publish two more Olympia dirty books, one a regurgitated novel that he had already written, the other, *The Power and the Pain* (1971), he claims to have written in a 'couple of days' – 'It certainly reads that way when I look at it now.'[68]

Then there was the contribution of Spencer Lambert, who, as Benjamin Grimm, was responsible for *Sir Cyril Black* (1969), Girodias's act of revenge against the British politician of the same name, the man responsible for the prosecution of Hubert Selby's *Last Exit to Brooklyn* in the UK several years earlier.[69] Sir Cyril appears at the end of this rather nasty story as the evil, incestuous manipulator who has been responsible for staging the plot of multiple dominations and submissions: '"I have a treat for you, you know", said Sir Cyril, parting the boy's buttocks and probing his asshole with [his] pinky finger. "I have a girl for you ... I'm going to let you use the whip on her ..."'.[70] Girodias clearly found it amusing to name both the book and its pornographic villain after this self-appointed guardian of British morality. Even when his ploy came back to haunt him with Black's successful prosecution of Girodias's libel in the American courts, the former Olympia editor (Olympia had by this time gone into liquidation) attempted to prolong the joke by enlisting the Monty Python crew to testify on his behalf – 'such an occasion could be turned into a rather wild occasion for both publicity and fun, rolled into one'.[71] Michael Palin seems to have been momentarily tempted.

Lambert was an effective pornographic writer. His (Grimm's) *Nightland Spell* (1969), a second person narrative – 'Aurelia continues her assault upon your face by stretching wide the lips of her cunt and rubbing them back and forth against your cheeks and chin and eyelids' – is darkly compelling, like a never-ending, spiralling dream, where repressed and shunned impulses (incest, paedophilia, rape, sexual slavery) are acted upon and delivery from this carnal labyrinth seems impossible as one perverse scenario leads to another more intractable situation and the nightmare goes on and on.[72] It is polymorphously perverse. The dreamer, whom it transpires is the reader, is fucked while cunnilingus is forced upon him – 'You feel yourself melting at both ends, drowning in the orgasms of your greedy lovers' – and then compelled into vaginal sex while being fucked in the mouth – 'Again, the rhythm of the pain feeds your fire, making the upsweep of your heat all the more exquisite, its down-sweep all the more desperate.'[73] Then, as his captors sleep and he remains unfulfilled, he is fellated by a mysterious fifteen-year-old girl: 'But who *is* this girl, reader? Who is this girl who comes to you in your moment of greatest need, and with her body and eyes – with her very aura brings you reassurance?'[74] At the end of the story, after disturbing imagery of incestuous sex, a bizarre court scene disintegrates into a dystopian orgy worthy of Sade, involving all the characters encountered in the novel: 'Everywhere, cocks and cunts and assholes glisten with foam and sweat and saliva. Everywhere, asses grind and pussies quiver. Everywhere, women are bent into strange st[r]aining pos-tures, fucked beneath the armpit and behind the knee, explored by the hands and mouths and pricks of a dozen men at a time.'[75] Lambert, at twenty-two, had written five Olympia dirty books. *The New Olympia Reader* quipped that his pseudonym was 'not so much a pen name as an actual facet of the author's personality', that Lambert was waiting for Grimm to depart and that they both lived in New York.[76]

Most dirty books had a hook of some kind. *Love on a Trampoline* (1968) by Sybah Darrich (an anagram of the name of the true author, Richard Ashby), features a man who has pornographic fantasies about women while interacting normally with them – the book opens with imagined sex in the supermarket. Until prompted ('I awoke to the sound of my own snickering'), the reader is never clear which is fictional reality and which is illusion.[77]

Girodias's editor Uta West used the name Rene Auden for her book *The Party* (1971). Like Ashby's *Love on a Trampoline* and (as we will see) Barry Malzberg's *Screen* (1968, 1970), it is about fantasy, though in this case a woman's fantasised sex with idolised pop artists (Malzberg's is about film fantasies). 'She licks and sucks with complete abandon now', she fantasises of Jim Morrison of the Doors.[78] The scenario of rock fandom, of course, lends itself to pornographic typecasting. Morrison does not disappoint: 'Out it pops, in all its splendour. She has difficulty suppressing a gasp ... It is beautifully shaped ... It's the most beautiful cock she has ever seen, but she pretends she's not all that impressed.'[79]

West's other book, *High Thrust* (1971), has another gimmick – robot sex. The narrator, Alma, falls in love with her android, the Elser, 'a figure, somewhat smaller than a man, more like an adolescent boy, with narrow shoulders, and limbs a little too long and thin', as she portrays it at first meeting.[80] She then discovers, by accident, that the robot is in tune with her mind, her thought patterns, and the relationship develops from there. The narrator has sex with humans, even group sex: 'Fingers crawled into my cunt, my ears and nose and mouth, into every orifice of my body, and I loved it, I opened myself wide to the exploring fingers.'[81] But, once initiated, her primary sexual contact (as the sex researcher Alfred Kinsey would have expressed it) was android: 'My skin itched and prickled where he had left red marks upon it, and my nipples were so hard they ached. My entire body was one huge erogenous zone, and my feverish vulva kept twitching as it engorged'.[82] It is not just a sexual relationship – Alma and the Elser discuss Nietzsche's concept of the superman and the Elser writes poems and composes music; however, West never loses sight that *High Thrust* is a dirty book. Alma's boyfriend, Mason, watches her and the android fucking, and then the Elser fucks Mason: 'Mason gave a piercing scream, of joy and terror; I put my hand around his cock, he placed his hand over mine and together we flailed up and down on his cock, while Elser fucked his ass with gentle, masterful strokes.'[83]

Just as he had in his Paris Olympia days, Girodias accumulated a portfolio of talented female writers. Indeed, some of the best Olympia pornography was written by women. There were new-comers, the new discoveries. One was nineteen-year-old Sharon Rudahl, a future famous American cartoonist and one of the founders of *Wimmen's Comix*, but then an art student in New York City's East Village. She (as Mary Sativa) gave Girodias *Acid Temple Ball* (1969), marketed as 'the first authentic account of the hippie trip, told from the inside', the 1960s equivalent to Jack Kerouac's *On the Road*.[84] Based on her own experiences, combined with observations of the scene and pure invention – 'the sex is better and the drugs are better' in the book, she told us – *Acid Temple Ball* is similar to Diane di Prima's *Memoirs of a Beatnik*, though the latter could not have been an influence because the books were published in the same year.[85] 'I used to work on *Acid Temple Ball* after a full day at Cooper Union art college and my part-time file clerk job', Rudahl recalls, 'turning out a disciplined daily quota of words. Thus a template for my future life as a woman artist, never with enough time to waste. It was something less than six months from start to finish'. She had never written erotica before but she knew of Girodias by reputation (a 'freedom fighter' against censorship), looked at some of the Olympia dirty books, and then sent Girodias a proposal and writing sample: 'Girodias was quite charming and urbane and dazzled me with predictions that I would become the next Henry Miller or Nabokov. To my credit, at age 19, I didn't take any of this seriously. I was just delighted with an advance check for a few thousand dollars and being able to quit my part-time file clerk job.' *Acid Temple Ball* was not its original name; Rudahl preferred 'A Season in Paradise', after Arthur Rimbaud's *A Season in Hell*, but Girodias insisted on *Acid Temple Ball*, and the book clearly sold well, with further editions in 1972, 1973.[86] Rudahl also wanted to be known simply as Sativa (referring to a variety of cannabis), but her editor added the Mary, she thinks to make it evident that the author was a woman. (Mary Jane might have been a better choice!)

Drugs and sex certainly feature in *Acid Temple Ball*, which is set mainly in New York and the Bay Area, and mostly narrated in the first person as a young woman's hippie autobiography (she shifts to the third person when describing some sexual encounters not involving her): pot, opium, Methedrine, THC, heroin, acid, kif, Dexedrine, Benzedrine, hash, cocaine, mescaline; couples, threesomes and foursomes in varied combinations (gay, straight, bisexual), and occasional orgies – 'don't just want to be fucked, but actively to fuck' – 'Lying on top of Davy with Eric's finger thrust deep in my ass, rocking back and forth against intensities of pleasure. Eating Jo while Eric and Davy take turns fucking me.'[87] She wants sexual freedom. She is never afraid to act on her longing: 'Making love to Jesse was more like drugs than sex, nothing was static or confined to one role. Under my hands he was a girl, a newborn child, a flowering plant, a sculpture that I was carving inch by inch, the perfection of all my desires.'[88] She has sex with two men: 'His weight grinds me against Nathan's body, he slams into me as though he wanted to ball forever, stretch and iron out every wrinkle in my cunt'.[89] She is active in her pleasure-seeking and never reluctant to express that gratification: 'I was lost in a fog of pleasure deeper than sexual hunger'; 'I felt totally stuffed with cock, couldn't tell which part of me was which, just pressure and stabs of joy and pain'.[90] *Acid Temple Ball* really is an ode to free love. Michael Perkins, who wrote pornography as well as writing about it, considered it one of the best of the dirty books dealing with the hippie subculture.[91]

The advances for Rudahl's second Olympia book, the impressive historical plague novel *The Lovers Crusade* (1971), supported her transition from art school student to freelance illustrator and women's comic book pioneer. Although she admits a fascination with plague as a metaphor for the shadow of nuclear destruction (told to us appropriately during the COVID-19 pandemic), Rudahl remains rather self-deprecating about what we consider one of the best of the New York dirty books – 'I don't think *Lovers Crusade* is a good book', she says – and characterises it as 'Ingmar Bergman's *The Seventh Seal* with naughty parts' (admittedly, there are certain similarities). She claims too, jokingly, that it was the end of her career in pornography: 'Writing it convinced me I had come to the end of writing erotica. I discovered the source of some of the sadism in pornography – we pennies-per-word authors get so fed up with our characters, we are eager to kill them off as painfully as possible. I was also running out of adjectives.'[92]

The Lovers Crusade is an atmospheric story about a band of travellers during the Crusades. Their group expands and then contracts (Rudahl does indeed kill off some of her characters). It starts powerfully with a by now familiar trope:

A line of men waited, watching, laughing, and cursing lustfully, pulling down their trousers and waving their hard, jutting pricks at her, pressing forward to rub them against her body. One had worked his hand into her cunt, jabbing it deep into her belly and swirling his fingers around. One rubbed his sex against her cheeks and open mouth. Her lips began to quiver and roll. She arched her back and groaned, pressing against the mouths and hands and cocks, ravaged with desire.[93]

In this case, forced sex leads to mortality; the young woman is literally fucked to death. But elsewhere there are more tender moments, as the blind, fair-haired, girl-like lute-player, Forest, works his way through the female entourage: 'She felt his heart beating like a trapped bird under the tight skin of his chest, wings beating faster and harder under her hand.'[94] Margaret, the nun, has sex with him. 'He bucked against her', Rudahl writes, 'rolling his hard jutting prick back and forth under the thin chamois trousers like a young deer pounding the hard, hot buds of its antlers against a tree, trying to rip back the bark of his clothing, aching to be stripped and burst free.'[95] There is a scene where a female character watches a man and a boy having sex, and the narrator describes the encounter in detail as the woman becomes more and more aroused: 'Though disgusted, Eleanor was panting and squeezing her damp thighs together as she watched the dark heavy man moving over the naked boy.'[96] After the man leaves, she too has sex with the boy. The book is about sex at a time of plague. It is compellingly evocative, with incense burning, bells tolling, prayers and grim recklessness: 'Whether in fear of Hell or fear of the end of pleasure, men danced their lives out hopelessly, drank and fucked with abandon in the taverns. Convinced that intoxication could save them from the scourge, they hid against the cold miasma of the plague in the thick, hot mist of wine and sweat.'[97]

Rudahl is adamant that she wrote dirty books to survive: 'Well, I'm neither ashamed nor particularly proud of having supported myself as a pornographer while an art student. As in all my work, I expressed myself candidly. Of course, I wrote above all for the easy money. "Better to write about sex than have to do it for a living" was one of my principles.' However, she is also clear that she was writing erotica differently as a woman. When we asked her whether she was merely catering for a male audience, writing to order, or was aiming to achieve something different with her novels, she replied that she 'definitely and specifically wrote erotica I expected women to enjoy', and that (with *Acid Temple Ball*) she wanted to 'convey some of the joy and friendship that really did prevail at the peace and love crest of the hippie epoch'. She also sought to avoid the 'nastiness' and humourlessness of some of the hard-core pornography: 'I did think a porn book was needed that would be as enjoyable and encouraging as a good cookbook about French pastry – not suddenly adding cut off fingers to the crepe, just when the reader was getting into a receptive mood.'[98]

Girodias also published *Ceremonies of Love* (1970) by Deneen Peckinpah, an actress and niece of the famous 1960s filmmaker Sam Peckinpah. *Ceremonies of Love* is surrealistic: 'a beautiful boy stands against the heavy sky. Flowering out of him, where his genitals would ordinarily be, a branch of tiny periwinkle pollen blossoms. I gasp, as, from out of the frame, an enormous lobster claw descends, snaps the brittle but green-growing branch'.[99] It is sometimes horrifyingly Sadean, as in one scene where a poet who looks like Cocteau slices a woman like an orange: 'what looks at first to be the tatters of her clothing, is, in reality, skin and flesh in tatters. Her clothes lie at her feet ... a pathetic heap of gray.'[100] Pekinpah's story has a multi-vaginal woman ('he slips it slowly in and out of the cunt just behind my left knee'), a penis-legged man ('he has to

171

keep a continual erection in order to walk'), a giant female spider (her feelers 'Creeping into my womanplace, and moving over the labia, exploring the clitoris'), and a two-year-old with a head the size of that of a man and whose limb is used for pleasuring.[101] It is a strangely and darkly inventive story of a woman's journey through her own erotic consciousness. Perkins, who knew a thing or two about writing, thought *Ceremonies of Love* 'perhaps the most experimental erotic novel to appear since the work of the French surrealists'.[102]

Marlene Moline (writing as Leila Seftali) had a short but powerful and genuinely subversive career as an Olympia writer (she died in 1972).[103] In *Ride a Cock-Horse* (1970), her only book, she, the narrator, actively pursues sexual pleasure with a parade of characters: a random man glimpsed in a tenement window, a Black rapist watching her from her fire escape (the occasion for some race-inflected sexual descriptions), a cross-dresser ('I crave his trans-sexuality'), an elderly Italian man ('the gaps in his mouth where the teeth are missing set up a wonderful vacuum'), her pet monkey ('I have taught him lots of little tricks, how to twirl the end of an umbrella into my cunt'), a 'suburban-type grandfather' on a train, Puerto Rican youths in a car ('thirty fingers caressing my body'), a young blind beggar on Eighth Street ('his tongue becomes his eyes'), corpulent diners she meets in a restaurant ('They become, lying horizontally on the bed, large sponge cakes, with me as the filling'), a biker ('I am having a public fornication, and I want to shout it'), a 'bull dike', a father and son combination, and a contortionist at the gym.[104]

She is a predator, governed by her longings. 'When my cunt begins to groan', she explains at the end of the book, 'when my fire starts and my thighs are like scissors against my cunt, I know it is time to go on the prowl. It is time to drink someone's breath away.'[105] She is pornographically conscious, describing her body in depth: 'My pubic hair is thick and reddish. It becomes curlier when soaked with semen.'[106] She is at ease as a figure of fantasy: 'I am fantasy. I am masturbation. I am a receptacle for all the male orgasms of the world ... Men would like to masturbate on me, defile me, denigrate me, or put me on a pedestal ... I am a groaning smorgasbord for everyone, a banquet table. It is difficult to reconcile myself to who I am.'[107] She takes drugs: 'I rise and take an amber perfume atomizer from the vanity. It contains LSD in pure liquid form.'[108] She masturbates to vividly recounted fantasies: 'she twists the dildo in my anus, meanders in my ass, causing me to squirm and writhe'.[109] She ventures forth for sexual adventure: 'I put on a red slim dress of fine crepe. No underwear. I step quickly into the street. I desire this elusive male.'[110]

Seftali is a female Sade: 'I think of exploding penises, electrodes placed on the balls, cunts filled with plaster of Paris and sulphur'.[111] She is an advocate of sodomy: 'My body becomes "ani-sexual"', she writes. 'It feels so good to get it in the ass. If more people got hip to the pleasure of sodomy, we would become extinct.'[112] She is a female Henry Miller, with a paean to her cunt – 'I adore my cunt as if it had a brain ... mine is perfect, a treasure. Pale pink and sweet, it can suck the gism out of a man like a child sucking the juice out of a navel orange' – and indeed of all cunts, cunts with surprises, those 'out of character to their possessors', moody cunts, dry ones, deep ones, tranquil cunts and so on.[113] The word 'cunt' is used 110 times.

Seftali likes to shock. 'I want to fuck his head, sever it from his body', she writes of one encounter, 'martyr him, tie it to one of the brass posts of the bed and let the lolling cold tongue caress my clitoris'.[114] There is a long account of menstruating sex: 'I am fucked in the cunt until my blood flows like burgundy wine, until bloody bubbles rise in the air.'[115] And there is sex with an ebony crucifix: 'My nerves have become electric, and my skin white hot. I can delay my passions no longer. My cunt feels like an elastic band ... I spread my legs, plunge the Christ in head first.'[116] *Ride a Cock-Horse* has been justly hailed as the 'most remarkable' of the New York Olympia Press novels.[117]

Finally, there was Valerie Solanas. Girodias first hired her to write 'an autobiographical novel' for Olympia but then published her *SCUM Manifesto* (1968) after she shot the even more famous Andy Warhol in June 1968.[118] Girodias wrote that he had been taken by Solanas's sense of humour and was persuaded by her critique of masculinity: 'the utter uselessness and banality of the male', as the manifesto expressed it.[119] SCUM also advocated an early asexuality, based on sexual experience but perhaps slightly incongruous for a hired pornographer: 'SCUM gets around [...] they've covered the whole waterfront, been under every dock and pier – the peter pier, the pussy pier ... you've got to go through a lot of sex to get to anti-sex, and SCUM's been through it all'.[120] Editor and writer fell out. The rumour was that Solanas had intended to kill Girodias but that he was out of town at the time; however, it has also been suggested that Girodias invented the story to boost sales of the *Manifesto*.[121]

Girodias did not discover writers quite of the quality of his most famous Olympia authors. However, he still maintained the ability to detect literature when he saw it. Hornwood, who worked briefly as an editor at Olympia New York, singled out Barry Malzberg, di Prima, Marco Vassi and Sharon Rudahl as special talents and William S. Burroughs Jr's book *Speed* (1970) as a missed marketing opportunity. But there were others.

Marco Vassi started writing pornography with Girodias's New York Olympia Press and became one of the better-known erotic novelists of the later twentieth century. Vassi wrote four novels for New York Olympia: *Mind Blower* (1970), *The Gentle Degenerates* (1970), *The Saline Solution* (1971) and *Contours of Darkness* (1972). He was assigned to add some sex scenes to Girodias's last published book, *President Kissinger* (1974; a blend of 'current events, science fiction, and pornography'), so may well have ghost-written other material for Girodias.[122] 'I was starving in the East Village in 1970', Vassi recalled, 'when I saw an ad in the *Village Voice*, "Wanted! Writers for adult novels." I wrote a chapter and sent it out and they wrote a note back saying, "It's too literary for the fuck market and it's got too much fucking in it for the literary market."' An agent friend told him to finish the book and he would see what he could do with it: 'he brought it to Olympia Press. They liked it, published it, I suddenly had a market, and I started writing novels.'[123] Girodias told him that he was 'the best since Henry Miller'.[124] In an interview in 1977, Vassi said: 'When I wrote my first novel, *Mind Blower*, my building was next to the St. Mark's Baths. So I spent about eight hours a day in there, partying and orgying, steaming and swimming and running around ripped out of my mind. Then I'd go back to my apartment, where I'd write for twelve hours on speed. So all that sexual energy went into creation.'[125]

Vassi's Olympia novels introduced his notion of metasexuality – sex and sexuality outside the reproductive matrix: 'the nuclear family has been an anachronism for almost as long as it has existed', says Tocco in *Mind Blower*. 'It seems to offer nothing but limitations of freedom, dampening of consciousness, false notions of responsibility, and a general deadening of life forces. It is boring, maddening, inefficient, and perhaps the basic cause of all that is wrong with our civilization.'[126] 'Ultimately', Vassi hoped, 'we may rid ourselves of false notions of perversion.'[127] Michael Perkins gave Vassi, as 'The Metasexual Novelist', a chapter to himself in *The Secret Record*. 'Vassi is the only erotic writer since Georges Bataille to express his perceptions about eroticism along philosophical lines', claimed Perkins, and he had the 'ability to reveal the erotic subtleties of male–female relationships as few writers since D. H. Lawrence have done'.[128]

As Perkins has also noted, Vassi was short on plot and characterisation, and long on sexual description and didacticism.[129] His novels are focused on the questioning of monogamy, conventional relationships and sexual categories, and on immediate and visceral descriptions of sex. In one scene from *The Gentle Degenerates*: 'Her cunt rose up like a fish leaping from the water and swallowed my cock whole. My bowels fell out, my eyes rolled back, and, like an epileptic in full fit, I felt my spine go into great rolling convulsions as I shot a thick volley into her begging crack.'[130] In *The Saline Solution*: 'I exploded into her inner cunt, and felt my energy penetrating up as far as the third chakra. I fucked her in the spine. I lost all self-consciousness at the orgasm. It just scraped the balls of heaven clean … the cunt is the secret smile of God.'[131]

Women are as sexually voracious as men. 'I like to get fucked', Susan tells Michael in *Mind Blower*:

> I like it all the time. In the cunt, in the ass, in the mouth. I like lying luxuriously on a bed with my legs spread wide, feeling a great big cock sliding in and out of me. I also like to go down on my knees in back alleys to suck off perfect strangers. I even enjoy rolling around a bathroom floor while half a dozen guys piss on me. I like to be whipped, I like to be humiliated, I like to have my cunt eaten out, I like to lick cunt. Anything that's got to do with the sexual sensation, I like. I'm a bitch in heat, all the time.[132]

'The world was filled with intelligent sensitive women', the main character in *The Gentle Degenerates* thinks to himself, 'women who enjoyed fucking and who wouldn't involve me in any nonsense concerning promises.'[133]

The same-sex encounters in Vassi's novels are not supplementary to the staple pornographic fare of straight sex but crucial to the characters' sexual experience and to Vassi's questioning of contemporary categories and attitudes. When Cynthia has sex with a lesbian couple in *Contours of Darkness*, she loses 'all concerns over gender; the experience was so thorough, so complete, so implacably right, that she was totally absorbed by it, and her everyday standards of judgement took a timid seat in the back row of her mind'.[134] 'This division into homosexual and heterosexual and bisexual is really very tedious,' Clare later tells Cynthia.[135] '[E]veryone is *at least* a homosexual!' Tocco informs Michael in *Mind Blower*.[136] Vassi writes of anonymous sex between men at bath houses, of the 'meat rack' in the woods on Fire Island, organised orgies with groups of men, all amid the constant supply of amyl nitrate.[137] 'I got something from making it with men that just didn't happen with women', says Vassi's narrator in *The Gentle Degenerates*. 'And there was no one in all of creation who could tell me it was a perversion or a sickness … the simple act of homosexual fucking was as right as anything a man and women did together.'[138] 'When I lived alone', writes Vassi in *The Saline Solution*, 'I could be completely polymorphous perverse.'[139] Norman Mailer has said that, 'Even for the late fifties and sixties, Vassi carried it pretty far … in short, he did everything'.[140]

Girodias also published Roland Tavel's *Street of Stairs* (1969), a fragmented narrative which one critic has compared to the experimental prose of Joyce and Burroughs, with the subject matter favoured by the latter – a Moroccan love story involving drugs, boys and crime, with more than a touch of sexual Orientalism: 'five to eight times a night is not unusual, night after night into week after week'.[141] Girodias had high hopes for Andy Warhol's screenwriter's long book, planning the published condensed version as a prelude to the complete volume. *Street of Stairs* enjoyed critical attention, with extracts and commentary in the *Chicago Review*, but did not sell sufficiently (Tavel blamed its publisher's reputation) and the unabridged version was shelved by Olympia.[142]

Peter Rabbit's *Drop City* (1971) was another significant Olympia Press discovery. The title came from the Colorado commune joined by Rabbit, whose real name was Peter Douthit. Olympia considered the forthcoming book of such importance that they published a sample in *The New Olympia Reader*: 'Little girls who kiss with their eyes open/ hardbrown summer legs/ nights rocking gently on the berth with her thighs clapping out all sound/ my lips full of clit'.[143]

Barry Malzberg, who published eleven books with Olympia and anonymously edited *The New Olympia Reader* under his publisher's name, wrote his commissioned book *Screen* in two weeks after Girodias had suggested the plot. The protagonist, Martin Miller, a case unit supervisor for the Department of Welfare, in elaborate fantasies becomes the stars when watching the screen: 'Everything was possible in that first darkness of the theatre.'[144] He is Marcello Mastroianni with Sophia Loren: 'Why don't you come here and make love to me now?' Sophia says. Marcello replies: 'Because we would have to take our clothes off completely and it would ruin everything. You know how long it takes me to dress.'[145] He then goes to a party and leaves with Elizabeth Taylor: 'I am sick of Sophia.'[146] Malzberg has described his editor's response:

'You son of a bitch', he pointed out, 'you made me crazy, do you know that? I ask you this time for pornography, a simple work of pornography, give you a plot and everything and ask you to keep it simple and low-class ... and what do you do? You give me 40 pages which are beautiful, just beautiful, you even know the color of that one's *bush* how you tell that? And *then* what do you give me? You give me horse-racing, you give me existentialism, you give me despair! You give me terrible anxiety and depression! You give me pain and thwarted desire! This book will sell 400 copies, I have to publish it hardcover too because in paperback everyone will throw it away; I have to publish it because it is a masterpiece, but you *destroy* me, do you understand?'[147]

Malzberg had come to Girodias's attention earlier the same year, 1968, when he penned the opening pages of *Oracle of the Thousand Hands*, 'trying to figure out what might impress Nabokov's publisher's first reader', as he recounted many years later, 'and came up with a crazed pastiche of *Pale Fire* and *Despair*, the memoirs of a compulsive masturbator narrated in the alternating first and third person with quarts of semen spewed over electric fences, cattle mooing nostalgically in the background at the instant of self-defloration and ultimately a powerful shock from that electrified fence at the moment of final consummation.' Malzberg continued, 'Girodias or someone there noticed what was going on, he summoned me to Gramercy Park (the Press and four employees worked out of his apartment, skirting the mattress on the floor as they sidled from room to room) and offered me a $2,000 contract.'[148]

William S. Burroughs Jr's *Speed* was one of Olympia New York's better publications; 'everyone here was very much taken by the book, by its direct style and obvious authenticity', Girodias wrote to its author when accepting the book for publication, pretty much unchanged, and with a $6,000 advance. He suggested that the author use the name William Burroughs Jr rather than William

Burroughs III.[149] (Interestingly, Grove had passed on it as 'ultimately unimportant', 'what kind of name is William Burroughs III????'[150]) *Speed* was reminiscent of Burroughs's father's pseudonymous *Junkie* (1953) rather than *Naked Lunch*, economical, matter-of-fact prose, almost documentary in tone, drug-taking for a newer generation ('Mothers milk was mixed with speed' was the subtitle of Junior's article about life with his father).[151] Burroughs Senior suggested *Speed Kills* as a better title for his son's book.[152] *Speed* is harrowing, bleak, explicit, achingly sad, yet strangely humorous. At the end of the book, after a drug-fuelled expedition to New York, marked by time in prison and interventions by his father's proxy Allen Ginsberg, whom Burroughs Jr did not really know, he returns to his grandparents' house in Florida:

> I stood thinking how strange that I lived there in that house, me, depraved speed freak me, with my crater-pocked arms. I tried to sink it in that I really lived in this nice neighbourhood, me, me whispering to phantoms, I lived in this manicured block with my ragged hair and long fingernails ... But I was not so very strange and was only a freak by the standards I rejected so I quit my signifying. Then I took a deep breath, smelling the jasmine, and I went inside.[153]

Girodias also published the 'Black *Tropic of Cancer*' by the young poet and writer Clarence Major, hailed as a genius by Henry Miller's friend the poet Walter Lowenfels.[154] *All Night Visitors* (1970) has the energy, vibrancy and male sexual bravado of Miller's work – including the misogyny so at variance with present day sensibilities:

> I want to fuck her, like she's a *thing*. The overpowering rapture of just grinding gently with her, without compassion, because I know that there is no future for us, no real reason why we should protect each other's feelings. I don't want to see her eyes when I screw her, because

sometimes they are *too* sad. I feel I can almost see a pig looking at me from her eyes, at times. I touch her pussy now, the dry hair. My sperm dry on it. Little streaks of dry *cum*.[155]

Girodias did not ask Major to add more sex to his novel (his normal editorial intervention) but rather to remove some of the more contextual descriptions. Major complied because he wanted to get his book published, and he told later interviewers that he rather than Girodias made the editorial decisions.[156] Because Major republished the book in the 1990s (as a famous rather than unknown author) it is possible to compare the two versions. The Olympia rendering is much tighter and shorter than the somewhat sprawling preferred edition. The Olympia publication *is* about sex – the Black poet Ishmael Reed's endorsement in red on the minimalistic black-on-white cover describes it as 'The black man at home with his body … healthy hedonism … the new millennium for black art'.[157] But the book concerns more than sex. There is a description of a slaughterhouse juxtaposed against eating a steak meal. It contains a horrific description of violence in Vietnam ('We Is Grunts'). Above all, it is an angry book about race, including the sex: 'My black ramrod *is* me, any man's rod is himself.'[158] Larry McCaffery, who interviewed Major in 1994 as a postmodern innovator, observed that 'the cuts probably made it look more radically experimental than it would have if the full version had been published'.[159] We definitely prefer the shorter Olympia edition.

All Night Visitors is Miller-like. 'I feel a healthy henry miller kind of vitality toward it all', the protagonist observes at the beginning of one of many protracted sexual bouts.[160] But the sex in Major quantitatively outweighs that in Miller. The sexual passages in *Tropic of Cancer* have been exaggerated; most of Miller's prose is about other things. *All Night Visitors*, on the other hand, is pornographically unrelenting. His story 'Anita' contains a twelve-page description of a blow job. Major's metonymy of the penis is reminiscent of what we have previously described as the male camaraderie of porn, though inventive nonetheless: 'black ramrod', 'supernatural enravisher', 'Mr. Ill-Bred', 'blue jacket', 'scudding hammer', 'reclining soldier', 'gun', 'Growing John', 'Mr. Perpendicular', 'the black castle', 'Mr. Rooster', 'vagina-greaser', 'my narcotized sledgehammer-looking pistol', 'my expressive Bridger of Gaps', 'forceful Reconstructor', 'ramrod of existence', 'my huge desperate valve', 'my faucet', 'the ample Chief', 'my *upanga*', 'fruit picker', 'bonanza detector', 'seed-giver', 'Mr. Prick', 'Mr. Hammer', 'my serpent', 'this Bridegroom', 'pendulous totem pole', 'Mr. Tail', 'Him', 'my meat god', 'Life-Giver', 'my screwdriver', 'my silky black dictator', 'my totem pole' and 'my idealistic weapon'.[161]

When influential *New York Times* critic Eliot Fremont-Smith reviewed Major's book in 1969, alongside another talented Olympia author, Barry Malzberg, he asked whether the books were, as the publisher claimed, 'quality fiction ... do they contain sufficient literary merit to justify their endless erotic passages?' His answer was clearly 'no'.[162] But other critics have differed. The precise point about *All Night Visitors* (leaving aside Malzberg for now) is the power and richness of the writing. As Jerome Klinkowitz has observed of Major's novel: 'Scenes of physical excess, whether of sex or of violence, are in fact an excuse for *tour de force* writing, just the opposite of what usually happens in conventional literature.'[163] He placed Major in the company of Olympia's original authors (Miller, Beckett, Genet, Donleavy, Durrell, Burroughs and Himes), where the 'innovative nature of their fiction far outweighed the possible pornography'.[164] Major has been hailed as 'one of the most significant contemporary black avant-garde novelists'.[165] Major's biographer claims that his subject considered writing pseudonymous pornography for Girodias, receiving an advance of $500.

However, the sample provided was considered 'too literary'.[166] It seems that the New York Girodias still maintained a distinction between his dirty books and literary works.

Girodias did not accept just anything that came his way. In the final days of Olympia New York in 1973, Girodias rejected Samuel Delany's truly shocking novel *Hogg*, about an eleven-year-old, nameless rapist. '*Hogg* is the only novel in my career that I have declined to publish *solely* because of its sexual content', he later wrote to Delany. 'Should the book someday appear, please feel free to use this as a blurb, if you think it will help promote sales.'[167] *Hogg* was not published until 1995 (and not by Olympia), after the death of Girodias.

Behind the scenes, things were not going so well. Girodias experienced labour trouble, unsurprising given the history of the publisher's relationships with his writers. In 1971 the Dirty Writers of America protested conditions writing under Girodias: his flat fee payments with lack of royalties, even when, as with Frank Newman's (Sam Abrams's) *Barbara* (1968, 1970, 1971, 1973), the book sold seventy thousand copies in a year. The union held a discussion panel in a back room of the nightclub Max's Kansas City, attended by Abrams, George Kimball (author of *Only Skin Deep*, 1968), Abrams's wife, Barbara, herself an Olympia author, and, inexplicably, the Warhol icon Jackie Curtis (perhaps they were there from clubbing the night before). A journalist from the *East Village Other* tried to broaden the discussion to unionising against all pornography publishers, but the Dirty Writers of America seemed focused on Girodias, who, according to the reporter, was not the worst of the smut publishers. The *East Village Other* has a photograph of the panel with placards saying 'Give us Our Dirty Money', 'Pornographers' Kids Need Clothes Too', 'Olympia Press

Sucks the Blood of [illegible]' and 'We Gave a Hardon – Now We're Hardup'.[168]

Girodias's Paris list was already being plundered when he arrived in America, first by Grove (in Girodias's telling) and then by a host of US pirates: 'Grove having given the example, dozens of mafia-type entrepreneurs set up publishing businesses whose only activity was to pilfer my backlist; and by mid-1967 about one hundred Olympia Press titles, good or bad, had already been pirated.'[169] A managing editor at Greenleaf Classics was quite open about the intellectual theft: 'Mainly we're interested in the "classic", the "long-suppressed item", the book with that intense, building, pressure cooker feeling that the best of Girodias' stuff at Olympia had', he told Peter Collier for his *Ramparts* piece. 'It's pretty hard to come by, so we've relied a good deal on his books.'[170] Earl Kemp, who was the editorial director at Greenleaf, called Olympia Press an 'extensive public domain library'.[171] Kemp said that Girodias was doomed from the start in the US. He had no real idea about the American business and was treated as a marginal entity by his so-called competitors: 'Maurice and Olympia Press NY were at best a minnow floundering and adrift in a rolling sea of high-production, high-activity, month-after-month production sharks.'[172] Greenleaf were publishing fifty titles a month to Olympia's eight.[173] Collier was aware of the competition in what was the initial stage of Girodias's American experience; in Southern California alone, pornographers were producing up to eighty titles a month at around two million copies in total.[174]

Pirating does not quite describe what was happening, though pirating there was. Of the 164 titles in Kearney's Paris Olympia bibliography, we have located 119 reprinted/pirated versions.[175] Greenleaf (who published almost half of these), Collector's Publications, Brandon House and Grove were the bigger players, but other publishers were involved too. Olympia's approach was emulated by its competitors. Perkins has noted that once Essex House instituted its 'line of serious erotic novels' in early 1968, it 'became the West Coast equivalent of The Olympia Press'.[176] Essex House, Samuel Delany explained, followed Olympia's model, approaching 'young poets and aspiring literary writers who were just not making a living, men and women for whom a seven-hundred-fifty or a thousand-dollar advance was a major bulwark against eviction or starvation'.[177] Brandon House either mopped up the disgruntled Paris Olympia writers, getting them to write 'post-scripts' to their reissued novels (as with Alexander Trocchi in *Helen and Desire* and *White Thighs*), or they simply capitalised on fragile copyrights. An editor at Brandon House said of Girodias in 1968: 'Sure he's getting screwed on his books ... but don't forget he made a living screwing people for several years – his own writers and everyone else.'[178] The British publisher John Calder has esti-mated that up to 400,000 copies of Trocchi's Olympia books were printed by other presses in the US without the author gaining any royalties.[179] However, it is likely that the numbers were much more, as many as 300,000 per title just with Brandon House, according to the research of Andrew Murray Scott (with Trocchi never receiv-ing payment for his 'postscripts').[180] Lancer distributed more than 500,000 replicates of Olympia's translated versions of *Justine* and *Juliette*.[181] Richard Seaver, an old associate of Girodias but then a leading editor at Grove, with inside knowledge, said in 1967 that Lancer had sold 2,500,000 of their copied version of *Candy*.[182]

Girodias was not blameless in all this, deceiving his writers and initially doing deals with the pirates while pretending inno-cence to his writers, according to Scott.[183] However, the point is that Girodias was no longer the *primum mobile* of pornographic literature. He told Gerald Williams that not only had Barney

Rosset and Grove stolen authors from him but that '– worse yet –
Barney had stolen his "image"'.[184] There was a new Prince of Porn.
Even Solanas, would-be assassin of Girodias and actual shooter of
Warhol, moved on to Rosset, threatening in 1973 to kill the Grove
publisher.[185]

Literature or pornography?

In 1969 Simon and Schuster published the blockbuster author Irving Wallace's *The Seven Minutes*. Drawing on the recent US censorship battles, the novel was about the fictional publication of a sexually explicit text, *The Seven Minutes*, written by a supposedly dead, invented author, J J Jadway (the lack of punctuation signalling their avant-garde credentials), who had, the fiction went, originally written the book in Paris in the 1930s. It was an 'underground classic', billed both as the 'most obscene piece of pornography written since Guttenberg invented movable type' and one of the 'most honest, sensitive, and distinguished works of art created in modern Western literature'.[1] The story involves an obscenity trial, the intrigue around the prosecution of a Los Angeles bookseller for selling the book, and the contest between an ambitious young defence lawyer and the politically aspiring district attorney heading the case. Was the fictional publication pornography or was it art? *Lady Chatterley's Lover* had 'only thirty pages of sexual matter, and 270 pages of other matter', yet, the defence lawyer reflected ruefully, 'here was Jadway's *The Seven Minutes*, a book in which not merely one page in ten, but rather, every single page, 171 out of 171 printed pages, was given over to sexual intercourse'.[2] There is a twist in the story: it transpires that Jadway is a pseudonym and the real author turns out to be a successful judge, a senator, about to sit on the US Supreme Court.

Wallace and his team had done their obscenity research. The pseudonymous author is a clue; the invented name was, the reader will know, a good Olympia Press convention. Jadway was one of the expatriate American authors in Paris in the 1930s. Wallace provides a checklist of censorship history, with references to John Cleland, Radclyffe Hall, Frank Harris, James Joyce, D. H. Lawrence, Henry Miller, Wallace Smith's *Bessie Cotter*, Sylvia Beach's bookshop and the Marquis de Sade ('I wondered how long it would take for them to drag him in'[3]). The fictional first publisher of Jadway's book in Paris was inspired by Jack Kahane and Obelisk Press to publish a blended portfolio of dirty books and serious sexually explicit literature. The publisher, Christian Leroux, testified in court (paid off by the highest bidder) that *The Seven Minutes* was one of his dirty books rather than one of literary merit: 'I published this filth in order to earn enough to allow me to publish Aubrey Beardsley's *Under the Hill*.'[4] (*Under the Hill*, our reader will again know, was actually published by Olympia in the 1950s.) Leroux is presented reacting favourably to a quote by Maurice Girodias – 'Those of us who've published obscenity and pornography should be honoured'.[5] According to the real Girodias, Wallace visited him in Paris, questioning him about the book trade in preparation for the novel, and then repaid him by caricaturing him and his father Kahane, blended together as the hateful Leroux. He claimed that the author had an unsettling knowledge of the 'Kahane-Girodias dynasty'.[6]

Wallace's characters also invoke the academic porn experts; Steven Marcus is quoted, for example. The publisher Grove Press gets a mention. Wallace even tries his own unsuccessful dirty writing: 'Her pear-shaped breasts heaved, her broad buttock with its strawberry mark trembled, and as she came around once more her hand slipped down below the appendix scar to circle her darkly matted vaginal mound teasingly.'[7]

The fictitious book at the centre of the novel, *The Seven Minutes*, has a bit part in terms of coverage. Only fragments are quoted or described: 'Do you mean when Cathleen says she feels like a cunt all over?'[8] There is a masturbation scene, 'the relentless burning between her thighs', and reference to a passage at the beginning of the invented book where the female protagonist 'thinks of the statues of Priapus that stood on some of the streets of ancient Greece'.[9] But the book remains sketchy. It is clear that it is a woman's experience of sex (the book supposedly relates the author's female lover's sexual life and desires) and that the title refers to a woman's (Cathleen's) explicitly described sexual fantasies and reminiscences during seven minutes of sex. As the enthusiastic bookseller tells the undercover officer: 'Jadway shows us what's in her mind about what's happening to her down below, and what's in her mind about other men she's had or ones she wished she'd had. The way it's done – it's enough to drive you crazy.'[10]

And then along came Maurice. Girodias knew an opportunity when he saw one: *The Seven Minutes* was a sure seller. Wallace had been paid a $500,000 advance and predicted sales were 1.5 million paperback copies. Girodias and the Israeli writer Michael Bernet confected what was purported to be the real *Seven Minutes* or *The Original Seven Minutes*, contracted, but never before published, by Girodias's father, Kahane, in the 1930s, and audaciously billed as 'The last and greatest underground erotic masterpiece ... on which Irving Wallace based his bestselling novel'.[11] Simon and Schuster took prompt action against the Olympia Press. The New York County Supreme Court ordered the destruction of all copies of Girodias's book and forbade Olympia from using their titles or referring to Wallace in any promotional material. Girodias was unperturbed. He scrapped his introduction, which had claimed the book's origins with Kahane, replacing it with material about his own court case, removed the name of the author Jadway and published Bernet's invention as *7 Erotic Minutes*, endorsed, 'with reluctance', by *Publishers' Weekly* as 'terrific, one of the best dirty books ever written'.[12] It is an unapologetically dirty book, with no concession to the supposed literary qualities of Wallace's fictional *Seven Minutes*. Bernet cleverly incorporated the masturbation and Priapus scenes, the few descriptions in Wallace's original. But, of course, everything is new, beginning with a three-man rape (it is unclear whether it is intended as imaginary or real): 'And suddenly they all burst together. Shattering me and splattering me. Drowning me in their flow.'[13] The sex is unrelenting, with supposed experience ('All cocks are delicious, but this one produces raptures'; 'Sometimes I swear I come in my ears. Aural sex'), as well as narrative fantasy ('One day I want to screw a Negro. A real black Negro').[14] The message is that here is a woman who likes sex: 'Fuck one, fuck all; come one come all. In cunt and in mouth and in arse ... Between my knees. Or the back of my knees. Or with my toes. In my armpits. The crook of my elbow. Under my chin. Between my breasts. In my ears. In the hollow of my tooth.'[15] She is a woman from Marcus's previously discussed pornotopia, who is forever wet, 'Wet from desire, wet for longing, wet from waiting, wet from burning in ache for him to come.'[16] However, the reader cannot avoid the conviction that, in reality, this is a *man* writing about a woman who loved to be fucked.

The original fake book in Wallace's novel was supposed to be obscene but with literary purpose that was to be tested in court. The second fake novel of Girodias and Bernet's invention was unadulterated pornography. A running theme of this book has been the relationship between what we have sometimes called serious literature and what is commonly known as pornography, or, if one likes, between high and low erotica. What was the distinction between the dirty books of our title and literature like *Lolita* and *Tropic of Cancer*, or between the two wings of Kahane's and Girodias's respective enterprises, or the fake and the real Millers?

Girodias was clear that in his mind there was a disparity. As he wrote in a letter to the *Times Literary Supplement* in 1966:

> I am responsible for the first publication in English of the formerly outlawed works of Nabokov, Donleavy, Genet, Beckett, Burroughs, Ableman, Miller, Durrell, and many others who would quite probably have been lost to literature, for good and forever, if the Olympia Press had not been alive and active in a time of dark intolerance. By so doing, and *also* by publishing parodies of traditional pornography, I think I have helped in exposing the nocivity [nocivité: harmfulness] of censorship.[17]

Literary commentators have addressed this issue in various ways over the years, often confident that they know the contrast when they see it, but with different opinions about which work fits into which category. John Phillips has separated what he terms 'literary' erotica from 'the popular erotic novel', based on what seems to be the style of the former – 'a sophistication of form which makes them interesting on a textual as well as a sexual level'.[18]

For Anaïs Nin, her erotica was the product of a struggle between poetic, inventive pornography, and the stripped-down, unimaginative hard-core requested by the broker and his client: 'Sex loses all its power and magic when it becomes explicit, mechanical, overdone, when it becomes a mechanistic obsession. It becomes a bore.'[19] Nin was proud of the poetry, writing quite literally produced by poets, talented writers, and she referred explicitly to herself as the madam of 'this snobbish literary house of prostitution, from which vulgarity was excluded'.[20] 'I gather the poets around me, and persuade them to write erotica', she explained in her unexpurgated diary for 1941, 'communicating eroticism and spreading this writing that is usually suppressed, giving them both the poison of disintegration and perhaps a way of purification, for all of us have violent explosions of poetry, and we eject the purely sexual as fervently as if we had taken vows of chastity.'[21] Referring to the commissioning agent for this paid-for pornography, she continues: 'So we enter openly into the secret world of sex, rebelling at the bondage of sex, and exploding into poetry which we have to cut out afterwards. Haunted by the dream which stupid Mr. Ruder forces us to deny ... forced to walk when we would rather dance.'[22]

But this simple binary, encapsulating traditional distinctions between pure *pornography* (dirt for dirt's sake) and sexually explicit *literature* (serious literary endeavour), was not as straightforward as the division implies. At one point, Nin observed that in writing the commissioned pornography, 'with indifference and detachment', as she put it, 'I attained a smoothness and technical perfection I can never attain in my rarefied writing'.[23] She was aware that this writing born of necessity had beneficial results: 'His [Ruder's] rejection of the mystical in the diary pushes me into the human. It is good for me. I possess both powers, but I must strengthen the human. *I was stopped when they clashed.* When I get confused, when they invade each other like my loves, they must be kept separate.'[24]

The collector, we are told, while urging leaving out the poetry and concentrating on the sex, demanded more material: 'all of us concentrating our skills in a *tour de force*, supplying the old man with such an abundance of perverse felicities, that now he begged for more'.[25] Nin, we have seen, was sending him her journals (with sexually explicit material added) as well as her stories, and she also drew from the former to write the latter.[26] Karen Brennan was on the right track when she understood Nin's erotica as a subversive game with her supposed patron, the collector, where she played with the desired pornographic tropes – with exaggeration and parody – while simultaneously exploring the writing of female desire.[27] Similarly, Diane Richard-Allerdyce has proposed that the writer is, on the face of it, providing her commissioner with what he anticipates but also attempting to subvert the genre, playing with notions of voyeurism, for example, which we have seen is core to pornography: 'The voyeur behind the scenes of Nin's erotica project is paying her ... to have fun at his expense.'[28] Nin 'oscillates between prurience and critique'.[29] Presumably this is why one critic felt that two stories in *Delta of Venus* belonged in different categories: 'Pierre' is 'sexual caricature' (though we would disagree), while 'Elena' 'transcends' pornography.[30] The division between pornography and something much more ambitious in Nin's paid-for erotica is somewhat indistinct.

Although we have touched on the matter throughout this book, it is worth summarising the case for the separation of literary and simple pornography. Peter Michelson identified the latter as describing 'stereotypical actions performed by stereotypical actors'.[31] The appeal of such pornography is its predictability, its animality, and the centrality of sex in all motivation and action. 'Thus', he writes, 'hard-core pornography's fictive representation rests on the inventiveness of its descriptions rather than the energy of its imagination', and he cites Maurice Girodias's complaint that modern pornographic writers were 'too "literary", consequently diminishing pornographic focus as they introduce psychic or moral complexities into the narrative'.[32]

To illustrate simple or hard-core pornography, Michelson discusses, interestingly enough, one of Girodias's Olympia New York dirty books, the pseudonymous Frank Newman's (Sam Abrams's) *Barbara* (1968), a book purportedly written in two weeks 'on a pound of cocaine', which he argues is 'maximally inventive' within a predictable framework.[33] The book begins with a man, Max, observing a young couple making love on the beach. He joins them, forcing himself first on the woman and then on the man, with, in a matter of pages, vaginal sex, oral sex, rimming, double penetration and anal sex. Coercion turns to understanding, sexual synchronicity, as the opening scene ends with the threesome introducing themselves: '"I'm Max" ... "My name is Leslie" ... "Tom"'.[34] Already, Abrams has employed many of the tropes of pornography before he even gets to the twelve-year-old 'boy-girl-woman' Barbara: 'She wants to fuck. But she wants to fuck a man, not a boy.'[35] *Barbara* delivers Michelson's framework of pornographic conventions: defloration, group sex, sexual experimentation, forced sex and incest. Max fucks Barbara, Tom and Leslie, and they fuck Max. Max can stay hard and come indefinitely: 'Max could maintain a hard-on. No. His hard-on would maintain itself.'[36] The book concludes with Barbara's family having sex with each other: mother and daughter, son, and father (Barbara and her fourteen-year-old brother had already engaged in incest). *Barbara* is a notch above the normal hard-core product because of its circumscribed ingenuity (there is lot of varied sex) and stylistic proficiency. *Barbara* was 'the very favourite sex book of the Now Generation'.[37] However, it never transcends those hard-core pornographic tropes. It is aimed at the one-handed reader. The sexual scenarios are unrelenting, and the book, Michael Perkins has observed, is totally without humour.[38] All focus is on the masturbatory pay-off.

For what Michelson calls 'artistic or complex pornography', he focuses on the twentieth-century novel, Pauline Réage's *Story of O* (1954), which we have discussed in a previous chapter.[39] *Story of O* employs much of the imagery of sadomasochistic pornography but is far more than its sex. It has the required psychological and moral complexities referred to earlier; it cares about language and form. It is a work of literature that transcends its pornographic elements (domination, submission, bondage, chains, whips). It is a book about love. 'However fictively exaggerated', writes Michelson, 'O's story spreads before us the dark terrors and the nearly nihilistic rewards waiting in the labyrinth of love.'[40]

It could be argued, then, that there is a historical critical consensus that certain books are literature rather than porn, or that some texts contain literary or artistic content that surpassed their obscenity. Susan Sontag and Phillips concurred on the merits of *Story of O*, what Sontag termed 'literature considered as art'.[41] While the book critic of the *New York Times*, Eliot Fremont-Smith, was not convinced of the literary qualities of *Story of O*, he did in 1966 hail its publication as the end of the literature/pornography distinction:

> What 'Story of O' does is to fracture the last rationale of censorship, our late and somewhat desperate distinction between 'literary' pornography and 'hard-core' pornography. It uses – or anyway is a serious attempt to use – erotic fantasies of the most perverted 'hard-core' sort to elicit erotic responses in the reader as a means to traditional literary end: the delineation of character, the exploration of motivation, the elucidation of, in this case, a somewhat mystical philosophy of life and love.[42]

The assessor for Grove Press, in an analysis that Grove did not use as a planned preface to their published edition, called *Story of O* 'a work of art camouflaged as a "dirty book"'. It was pornography:

'its aim is to arouse; if it has any other purpose, it arrives at that purpose only by this route'. However, its elegance of language and style of the imagination ensured its literary credentials.[43]

Some of those directly involved in this history have also been eager to differentiate sexually explicit modernist literature from pornography. We saw in an earlier chapter that Nabokov was anxious that *Lolita* should not be seen as pornographic. 'It depresses me to think that this pure and austere work may be treated by some flippant critic as a pornographic stunt', he wrote to Edmund Wilson in 1955. 'This danger is the more real to me since I realize that *even* you neither understand nor wish to understand the texture of this intricate and unusual production.'[44] Though Colette Colligan has shown that Nabokov was by no means pornographically naive, the author of *Lolita* declared 'no interest whatever in pornography' when he was asked to contribute to a collection of written erotica for Grove Press in 1969.[45] For Nabokov, pornography 'mated' obscenity and 'banality': 'every kind of aesthetic enjoyment has to be entirely replaced by simple sexual stimulation'.[46] 'Thus, in pornographic novels', he continued, 'action has to be limited to the copulation of clichés. Style, structure, imagery should never distract the reader from his tepid lust. The novel must consist of an alternation of sexual scenes. The passages in between must be reduced to sutures of sense, logical bridges of the simplest design, brief expositions and explanations, which the reader will probably skip'.[47] *Lolita* was something far different. 'For me', Nabokov wrote in a companion piece to the first US extract of his beloved novel, 'a work of fiction exists only insofar as it affords me what I shall bluntly call aesthetic bliss, that is a sense of being somehow, somewhere, connected with other states of being where art (curiosity, tenderness, kindness, ecstasy) is the norm.'[48]

How would one characterise Raymond Queneau's *Zazie dans le Métro* (1959), yet another Olympia publication, Number 74 in the Traveller's Companion Series, which has been compared to *Lolita* in terms of its heroine and its cultural impact in France? It is a picaresque tale about Zazie, a young girl (her age is never specified) who is placed in the temporary care of her uncle Gabriel in Paris, where she encounters a range of colourful personalities. It is a playful book. 'That guy, she decides', referring to a recurring character introduced during Zazie's first morning in Paris, 'is not a sex-fiend trying to look like a fake cop, but a real cop trying to look like a fake sex-fiend trying to look like a real cop.'[49] There is a parrot who is given grenadine and continually chirps, 'Yackity, yak yak ... thassall you ever do.'[50] Queneau provides a running gag about confusing the landmarks of Paris: 'That thing couldn't of been the Panthéon 'cause it was the Gare de Lyon'; 'That ain't the Panthéon ... that's the Invalides'.[51] And Zazie never gets to actually experience the Métro of the book's title: it is closed for most of the duration of her stay and when she travels on it at the book's end, she is fast asleep. *Zazie dans le Métro* is even more mischievous in translation, with Turandot, the parrot's owner, rendered as Turdanrot.[52]

Zazie is linguistically precocious, using allegations of sexual misconduct as a weapon: 'this gennulman's been tellin' me dirty dirty things'; 'You're a lousy sex fiend, thasswhat you are'.[53] But her sexual knowledge does not seem to match her paraded worldliness – even though we learn that her mother killed her father while he was molesting Zazie (a dark background to what is essentially a light-hearted romp). There's another continuing joke about Zazie's inability to grasp the concept of homosexuality and whether her uncle falls into that category: 'hormosickchewell', 'homone-sick-chewall', 'hormone-textual', 'hormosomething', 'hollow textual', 'hobosexual', 'homobubble', 'homesick-shawl'.[54] 'By the way, just what is a fruit?' Zazie asks one of her acquaintances. 'And a pansy? A fag? A peterass? A hormosickshall? Do they all mean the same thing?'[55] Zazie has been compared both to Lolita and Alice of *Alice in Wonderland*, but she is neither.[56] Her boyishness, her gender ambiguity, is accentuated by her acquiring blue jeans, something of another continuing theme, and by her short hair and verbal aggressiveness, saying 'my ass' after practically every observation: 'Napoleon my ass ... that jerk gives me a pain, with his bowlegs and his corny hat.'[57] She wants to become a teacher so that 'I can beat the shit outa the brats'.[58] She refers to her late father as getting 'the hots so bad that he'd be ready to screw the cat'.[59]

Her uncle is gender ambivalent too – Gabriel the night watchman turns out to be Gabriella the drag artist – with his cross-dressing, cosmetics and perfume on the one hand, and his bodily bulk and physicality on the other – 'It's a man's perfume, kid'.[60] His nightly trips are not to some building site but to the club Golden Balls, where the outsize cross-dresser performs as Carmen. '"She ain't a she, she's a he", Zazie explains. "I mean, she's my uncle."'[61] Gabriel's female partner, Marceline, it transpires is really Marcel. The 'Sex of Angels' in the originally advertised title may have been meant to signify this gender indeterminacy.

The book is experimental in a number of ways. It combines the written and the visual with cute marginal sketches by the illustrator Jacqueline Duhème on most pages, conveying a visual sense of the characters without undermining their textual presence. It plays with language by running words together: 'Holifart watastink' are the opening words of the book.[62] There is a knowing textual reference to 'them dirty books'.[63] Yet *Zazie dans le Métro* is far from the usual pornographic fare with its references to 'alexandrine', 'monophasic pentasyllable', 'slightly Kantian thomism', 'peremptory

eurekation', 'parabolic parable' and 'percontative'.[64] With its language games, it must have been a challenging book to translate.
It is a risqué comedy with serious purpose. Critics have explained
that Queneau was fascinated by form and challenged realism in his
writing; Susan Bernofsky has concluded that *Zazie dans le Métro*
has achieved a state between anti-realism and realism.[65] *Zazie dans
le Métro* is certainly not a dirty book. Indeed, Nabokov thought it
'quite a masterpiece in its "whimsical" genre'.[66]

Two former Obelisk authors, one of whom was then an
Olympia Press writer, discussed the problem of literature versus
pornography in 1959, when debating a petition against censorship
and the authorities' pursuit of Girodias: 'our protest would cover
quite a lot of garbage, mostly put out by our friend Girodias',
Lawrence Durrell wrote to Richard Aldington. 'The beastly
[Harriet] Daimler stuff for example. But I don't see how the principle of freedom is divisible'.[67] 'How to demarcate between … the
permissible and the other I don't know at all', he continued. 'The
problem really is whether it isn't worth a hundred pornographies
in order to hold the gate open for one *Lady Chatterley* or *Ulysses*.
I rather feel it is.'[68] So Iris Owens (Harriet Daimler), someone we
have praised, was trash, but *Lady Chatterley* and *Ulysses* were literature. In an earlier letter, he told his friend of Girodias's repub-
lishing of Durrell's own *Black Book*, explaining that the publisher
produced 'a certain amount of porn; but some good stuff too,
like Henry [Miller] and Beckett and Genet'.[69] Again there was a
binary assumed by the two acknowledged literary figures: 'porn'
versus 'good stuff'.

Miller, we saw in Chapter 2, said that he abhorred 'smut for
smut's sake'.[70] He was adamant that there was more to the issue
than, as he expressed it, 'a question of the right to use "four-letter
words"'.[71] 'There is the whole question of attitudes towards the

world', he wrote in a letter to the bookseller Barnet Ruder in 1936, 'toward art, towards literature especially'.[72] Miller explained that he wrote mainly for himself: 'I have my own style. The book creates an effect precisely because it disregards the reader *and* the supposed canons of art.' 'Fuck art!' he wrote as if to prove his point, 'I want to live.'[73] Jack Kahane, who had had the courage to publish *Tropic of Cancer*, had wanted to issue a modified version but Miller had persevered and was proven right by the critical response.[74] Durrell has quoted Miller to the effect that the use of obscenity in literature is 'a technical device; the element of the deliberate which is there has nothing to do with sexual excitation, as in pornography. If there is an ulterior motive, it is one that goes far beyond sex. Its purpose is to waken, to usher in a sense of reality'.[75] *Tropic of Cancer* was, Miller wrote to his friend Emil Schnellock as the book was completed in 1933, 'A truly Joycean picture of the cunt'.[76] As Rachel Potter has expressed it, Miller (and Durrell) used 'unsanctioned vocabulary to create aesthetic effects of shock or disruption, techniques that were central to a wide range of modernist texts'.[77] In short, Miller used some of the language of pornography but was producing literature.

The mutual admiration correspondence between Miller and Durrell in the 1930s encapsulated Potter's comment about modernism: 'the damn book has rocked the scales like a quake and muddled up all my normal weights and measures', Durrell wrote of *Tropic of Cancer*, 'I love its guts. I love to see the canons of oblique and pretty emotion mopped up; to see every whim-wham and bagatelle of your contemporaries from Eliot to Joyce dunged under.'[78] Miller returned the compliment in his comments on Durrell's *Black Book*: 'Breaks the boundaries of books, spills over and creates a deluge which is no longer a book but a river of language, the Verb broken into its component elements and running amok. You have written things in this book which nobody has dared to write. It's brutal, obsessive, cruel, devastating, appalling.'[79] 'The whole thing is a poem, a colossal poem', he continued. '*This is the poem*. It's like the black death, by Jesus. I'm stunned.'[80] Miller identified passages that he admired, where what might be called obscenity underscored the power of the prose: '"look, do you think it would damage our relationship if I sucked you off?" That almost tells the whole story of England!' And '"send out to the clitoris for an ice"', which 'beat[s] all the French Surrealists stiff'.[81]

One of the ways that boundaries were debated was through the prosecutions for obscenity in the courts, and especially through the testimonies of literary critics. Elisabeth Ladenson ended her book *Dirt for Art's Sake* (2007) – about what she terms 'acceptable indecency' – with discussions of the works of Sade and John Cleland's *Memoirs of a Woman of Pleasure* (1748–49).[82] They are perceptive choices. In the various trials of *Memoirs of a Woman of Pleasure* in the 1960s, the debate was whether the book was merely an account of 'various acts of sexual perversion', 'arousing' the reader 'to libidinousness', or was it of 'high literary quality', a 'work of literature that has considerable value'?[83] If the former, it was mere pornography, merely obscene, 'dirt for dirt's sake'; if the latter, it was literature.[84] Charles Rembar, the defence attorney for *Memoirs of a Woman of Pleasure*, maintained that '[w]ell written obscenity' was 'a contradiction in terms'.[85]

Familiar tropes of obscenity were rehearsed in the US trials and tribulations of William Burroughs's *Naked Lunch* (1959). It was stated in the Los Angeles trial that 'Fuck, shit, ass, cunt, prick, asshole, cock-sucker' were mentioned 234 times in total in 235 pages. Did the novel, as its defence attorney claimed, 'not only ha[ve] literary, and artistic importance, but sociologic and psychiatric and moral importance'?[86] Alternatively, the prosecution focused on particular (notorious) passages in the novel: the hypostatic union with the Lamb ('then steer a randy old sheep up his ass'); the coprophagia ('Mmmm, that's my rich substance'); 'A.J.'s Annual Party', with its gallows sex ('She bites away Johnny's lips and nose and sucks out his eyes with a pop'); the water pistol ('He used to go about with a water pistol shooting jissom [*sic*] up career women at parties'); the talking anus ('After a while the ass started talking on its own'); and 'Hassan's Rumpus Room' ('My cock spurts soft diamonds in the morning sunlight!').[87] As the lawyer for the Attorney General argued, was there not 'an extraordinary amount of both natural and unnatural sex in this profanity, perversions, references to human excrement? Of what academic interest are these things?'[88] *Naked Lunch* was subject to a range of censorship actions before the US Supreme Court declared in its favour in 1966.[89]

Issues were rehearsed in self-censorship before the matter even reached the courts. Miller was not beyond censoring his own work if the occasion required it. When Grove Press was publishing extracts from Miller's *Sexus* (1957, 1959) for *The Olympia Reader* (1965), the author asked for a long section to be removed at the galley stage: 'I think it's bad taste, cheap, overdone. Sorry.'[90] The piece is worth quoting almost in full:

> We went into a blind fuck, with the cab lurching and careering, our teeth knocking, tongue bitten, and the juice pouring from her like hot soup ... she went into a prolonged orgasm in which I thought she would rub my cock off. Finally she slid off and slumped back into her corner, her dress still up over her knees, I leaned over to embrace her again and as I did so I ran my hand up her wet cunt. She clung to me like a leech, wiggling her slippery ass around in a frenzy of abandon. I felt the hot juice trickling through my fingers. I had all four fingers up her crotch, stirring up the liquid moss which was tingling with electrical spasms.[91]

The passage was cut.[92] Miller had raised his concerns earlier, saying that it was 'too risky, too much explicit sex stuff'. He thought that it was censorable in a volume probably 'packed with censorable material. Why add fuel to the flames?'[93]

In 1970, British publishers commissioned a solicitor's opinion on the potential publication of *Story of O*, and while the solicitor recognised the book's literary qualities, his verdict was that 'the subject matter is depravity of the very deepest dye and I cannot believe that this book would escape the attention of the Director of Public Prosecutions. Nor can I imagine that he would be able to let it be widely circulated in paper back.'[94] (In a memo from one Grove editor to another, Richard Seaver observed to Barney Rosset, 'Reading the solicitor's report, I begin to understand why the sun has set upon the British empire.'[95])

One person's literature was another's pornography. Burroughs was the subject of protracted correspondence in the *Times Literary Supplement* in 1963–64, after a hostile review of his Olympia Press works. Was Burroughs a gifted writer who was exploring 'the limits of style and reality' (John Calder), 'a serious artist trying to extend the boundaries of the novel-form' (Anthony Burgess)?[96] Should his work be judged aesthetically rather than morally, and were his critics allowing the nature of his novels' content to overwhelm assessment of their form, 'their capacity to make purely literary judgments' (Burgess again)?[97] Alternatively, and what seemed to be the prevailing tone of the numerous letters, was Burroughs's writing, as the anonymous John Willett titled his review, simply 'Ugh'?[98] The writer and critic David Lodge, writing elsewhere a few years later, thought both that *Naked Lunch* was 'a very indecent book' and that Burroughs's literary significance had been overestimated.[99]

Although we will argue later that the boundaries between literature and pornography are somewhat problematic, we have continually been drawing on contrasts between the two, making our own
judgements on artistic merit versus mere obscenity. Let us now
turn to two different Olympia publications to explore the matter
in closer textual detail. The books that we want to discuss are
Alexander Trocchi's *Young Adam* (1954) and Aubrey Beardsley and
John Glassco's *Under the Hill* (1959).

We saw in an earlier chapter that Alexander Trocchi, at the
behest of his editor Maurice Girodias, added sexual scenarios to
his novel *Young Adam* in order to cater for the dirty book formula
and the perceived tastes of Olympia's readers, and that he regret-
ted that choice. Intriguingly, however, many of those scenes were
subsequently removed to produce a powerful literary work, and,
still later, *Young Adam* was thoroughly pornified by Masquerade
Books, when not only were the original passages restored but new
ones were added. Dirty book versus literature: the history of one
book provides insight into the relationship between literature and
pornography.

We will be dealing with three published versions of *Young
Adam*: the first version, appearing as Frances Lengel's *Young Adam*
in 1954 in Olympia's Atlantic Library; a 1966 UK edition, under
Trocchi's real name, produced in the manner approved by Trocchi
(with the expurgation of some erotic passages previously added for
Girodias and out of keeping with Trocchi's original manuscript
and intent), printed by the New English Library but first published
by Heinemann in 1961; and a 1991 US Masquerade Books edition
under anonymous authorship, with Trocchi's name removed but
the original edited sections restored and with further embellish-
ments by an unknown contributor (Trocchi was by then dead),
useful here merely for the purposes of comparison.[100]

Girodias had told Trocchi that he admired the 'quality' of the two-thirds of *Young Adam* that he had seen, but that there were not enough erotic scenes. 'I wouldn't like the book to be ruined as a good book', the editor advised his author, 'But it really does lack something still to make it a good sex book, and you can't put it all in the end.' He suggested the insertion of '3 or 4 sexy scenes', the sharpening of the existing sexual encounters and finishing with a flourish: 'I think it is important to finish the book on a sexual crescendo, and make the last section really strong.'[101] We can locate the passages added by Trocchi by comparing the original Paris Olympia edition against the English edition in which the author, removing the dirty book additions, presented his preferred version (pre-Girodias, so to speak). It is not a foolproof method. Trocchi may have left some of the Olympia prose, persuaded, in retrospect, of its worth. He was also doubtless tempted to rework and refine. However, it is a good rough guide.

There are many sections in the 1954 version that disappear from the 1966 edition. Some relate to Jo's lovemaking with Cathie when he first met her:

> She made no effort to resist as I exposed myself and laid my sex in the groove between the hotly bunched flesh of her thighs. A moment later, our lips came together, and I felt myself sucked inwards. She groaned. We rolled over under the shade of the rocks. That was my first experience of Cathie. We were together a long time.[102]

One of the specific suggestions that Girodias made when seeking more sexual content in *Young Adam* related to the scenes between Jo and Ella. Trocchi seems to have responded, with a more detailed description of them having sex in the Olympia edition than in the English-published version, including the sentences, 'I discovered her skin beneath the smock-like nightgown and felt with the side of my fore-finger the urgent little beard of damp that hung downwards between her slid thighs', and 'I moved my hand slowly at the sensitive fork of her torso and rolled inexorably over until her broad front bore my weight like a broken catapult.'[103]

The Olympia *Young Adam* is far more sexualised than its later iteration. Trocchi has a long section on the violence in sex, 'the constant pressure of violence in the sexual act', cut from the later editions.[104] Jo and Cathie intentionally have sex on the gravel path so that it will cut their bodies and add to the pleasure:

> She was rubbing herself against the ground, like a cat does, and I knew she wished to cut herself on the gravel ... Soon she was groaning with pleasure and pain. She stiffened as though she had inflicted a terrible wound and then, suddenly, she turned over on her belly and gouged it against the gravel. A moment later, she pulled me down on top of her, forcing me to get rid altogether of my trousers, and then we fought while we drove our lust at each other.[105]

There is a lengthy segment on twenty-year-old Jacqueline, who does not feature in the revised edition.[106] Indeed she forms the rather menacing ending in the 1954 book where Jo tells her that he was with Cathie when she died and then asks Jacqueline to meet him again: 'On her answer, on perhaps her mere tone of voice, her life depended.'[107] The cut passages include more violent sex: 'Suddenly, I thrust her downwards over the stones so that her sex struck against mine, and, after one cry of pain, I felt her cool hands close around my buttocks and with violent pressure close me to her.'[108] The prose is closer to the tone of the dirty books than in keeping with Trocchi's literary aspirations. 'She uttered a gasp of pain and joy and her teeth sank into my neck as my hard expansion broke through inexorably into her sex', he writes in the Olympia publication (but not in the 1966 edition), 'her young loins burst like a poppy against my riding belly and her whole lithe frame cracked upwards like a sinuous whip. She cried out. Her ankles twisted together, locking away all possibility of retreat, and her voracious young belly, swilling in its own juices, shuddered violently to receive mine.'[109]

The revised Trocchi has sex scenes, including the infamous one with custard ('The custard was dripping off her nipples and mingling already with the short hairs of her sex'), but it is a far tighter, more literary work than Frances Lengel's Olympia book.[110] Still, we have seen that the prose added at the behest of Girodias and later removed by Trocchi for the book's English publication – hard extensions, burst poppies and sinuous whips aside – actually had genuine literary quality. It was the balance between the erotic and the purely literary (that Trocchi had seemingly got right in the first place if the revised version is a guide) that Girodias had tipped in his quest for 'a good sex book'.

Is *Young Adam* literature or pornography? Does the dirty book element subvert its literary status? We would answer no. But if the reader is sceptical, let us conclude by introducing our third version of *Young Adam* by Masquerade Books. Owned by the New York publisher Richard Kasak, Masquerade and his other venture Badboy Books were major producers of pornographic writing in the 1990s (some by amateurs, interestingly enough). Kasak's product, which we have written about elsewhere, included earlier erotic texts to which his anonymous authors added pornographic prose more in keeping with the tastes of the 1990s than those of their original sexual milieu.[111] *Young Adam* is one of many such repurposed texts.

In the anonymously authored *Young Adam* (1991) there are over twenty pages of rather clunky pornography added to the original edition (as well as the passages that Trocchi had originally included but excised from his revised edition). This book has imaginings of what Jo, the narrator, wants to do to Ella: 'I envisioned my rod between those pouting lips ... spurting its seed into the warm, willing mouth, filling it to the brim and beyond with the sweet cream Ella only now dreamed of.'[112] There is an absurd description of erotic potato peeling and nonsense about what Ella may have done with the sausages before they ate them – 'Slippery between her fingers she might have nimbly lifted one at a time from the pan and holding her dress high with the other hand, gently eased them between her spread legs into her waiting warmth.'[113] Anonymous has Ella pleasuring herself on a teapot (of all things): 'Slowly she brought the tip of the spout to her waiting opening. A warm, moist breath of vapor condensed on the hair of her mons.'[114] There is more about what Jo would do to Ella: 'I would ravage her, pressing my face fully into that fleshy wonderland of womanly intricacy, sucking and poking with my tongue, pressing my lips and face and nose at parts unseen even by their possessor, biting at delicate bits'. And Anonymous intensifies the BDSM theme: '"Leash yourself", I said … "I want to fuck you top to bottom, every opening in your body", and her eyes brightened with excitement at the thought.'[115] This was pornography, not literature.

What of Aubrey Beardsley and John Glassco's *Under the Hill*, the story of Venus and Tannhäuser? The first 69 pages were the originals by Beardsley and the next 54 (of 123) were Glassco's additions, with a transition that is not exactly seamless, introducing a flagellation theme, which, until that moment, had not been at all evident ('Cosmé joined in the fun, and whispered to Venus that birch discipline might be in order'), and with Venus exclaiming, in a rather jarring, New York manner, 'Let's go slumming!'[116] A critic in 1904 had called Beardsley's original prose fragment a 'laboured literary indecency', 'so obscene … it was impossible to publish it except in the privately printed ventures of [Leonard] Smithers' underground press' (which it had been in 1907), and described his prose as 'bent only on satisfying every lust in a dandified way that casts but a handsome garment over the basest and most filthy licence'.[117]

However, Beardsley's was a rarefied kind of pornography. Venus has 'little malicious breasts ... full of the irritation of loveliness that can never be entirely comprehended, or ever enjoyed to the utmost'.[118] When Venus is preparing for supper, one of her retinue 'snatched as usual a slipper ... and fitted the foot over his penis, and made the necessary movements'.[119] Strange things happen at supper in the Court of Venus. Sophie becomes 'very intimate with an empty champagne bottle, swore it had made her enceinte [pregnant], and ended by having a mock accouchement [birth] on the top of the table'. 'Spelto offered a prize for whoever should come first, and Spelto won it!' The portly Mrs Marsuple 'slips' her tongue down the respective throats of Venus and Tannhäuser, and 'refused to be quiet at all until she had had a mouthful of the Chevalier [Tannhäuser]'.[120] Then there is the dance where Venus's attendants bring in the creatures of the wood who prove unable to restrain themselves in the face of courtly pleasure: 'They bit at the white thighs and nozzled wildly in the crevices. They sat aside the women's chests and consummated frantically with their bosoms; they caught their prey by the hips and held it over their heads, irru-mating [fucking in the mouth] with prodigious gusto.'[121]

The 'amorous encounter' between Venus and Tannhäuser is described in a short section, usually interpreted as a parody of por-nographic tropes, where the Chevalier falls upon the diaphanously clad Venus. 'It is, I know', relates the narrator, 'the custom of all romancers to paint heroes who can give a lady proof of their valli-ance at least twenty times a night. Now Tannhäuser had no such Gargantuan felicity'.[122] The next day, the Chevalier is joined by a bevy of 'beautiful boys' at his morning bathing: 'He chased the prettiest of them and bit his fesses [buttocks], and kissed him on the perineum till the dear fellow banded like a Carmelite, and its little bald top-knot looked like a great pink pearl under the water.'[123] Then there is a unicorn scene, where Venus feeds her jealous pet with spiced buns and masturbates him:

> Venus caught that stunning member in her hands and laid her cheek along it; but few touches were wanted to consummate the creature's pleasure. The Queen bared her left arm to the elbow, and with the soft underneath of it made amazing movements upon the tightly-strung instrument. When the melody began to flow, the unicorn offered up an astonishing vocal accompaniment. Tannhäuser was amused to learn that the etiquette of the Venusberg compelled everybody to await the outburst of these venereal sounds before they could sit down to déjeuner. Adolphe had been quite profuse that morning. Venus knelt where it had fallen, and lapped her little apéritif.[124]

This was one of the passages that got the US publisher Samuel Roth into trouble with the US courts in 1954 when he was prosecuted over an issue of his publication *American Aphrodite* which contained the story; when the offending extracts were read out to the jury in court, they were presaged with an unambiguous introduction: 'Now I am going to stand here and read to you some of that filth'.[125]

Whether the world created by Beardsley can be described as a queer utopia, though intriguing, is somewhat beside the point for the purposes of this chapter.[126] This is pornography. Ian Fletcher has classified it, along the lines of Steven Marcus's pornotopia, as 'a theatre of continuous sexuality'.[127] Yet, as George Trail has confirmed, the eroticism is far from hard-core: 'It is an orgy of faeries, a never-never land for adults.'[128]

For his part, Glassco arranges a visit to a bagnio, with its erotic panopticon of peep-holes and scenes of masturbation, including a man 'impersonating a cow' and 'being milked, too!'[129] And in this section of the book, the supplemental part, there is frequent flagellation: 'What ravishing contours were exposed, what quiverings, what tremblings and trepidations, what rosy reluctancies'. Young bodies are whipped for the delight of onlookers: 'birch rods were supplanted by long, supple canes, these by limber straps, and these in turn by many-tongued martinets'.[130] Then, while he recalls the scenes of flagellation, Tannhäuser is masturbated and anally manipulated by Mrs Marsuple until his 'adorable member stood like a stalk of fresh asparagus' (a rather disconcerting image), while Venus is cunnilingued by one of her servants, 'smacking his lips like a gourmet'.[131]

What do we make of Beardsley's erotic descriptions? We have been quoting from a text using what is sometimes called the unexpurgated version of the story (the *Venus and Tannhäuser* published originally by Smithers), but there is another edition, referred to as the expurgated version (*Under the Hill*, ironically the title used by Glassco), published in the journal *The Savoy* in 1896 and then again by John Lane in 1904.[132] George Trail has argued (convincingly) that rather than thinking of the so-called expurgated text as censored, it is in fact a more understated version of the more explicit writing (which in itself, we have seen is not exactly hard-core pornography). The *Savoy* version tantalises; the Smithers (Olympia) rendering delivers. Both, Trail suggests, demonstrate Beardsley's skill as a writer of erotica – though the former 'achieves a higher art'.[133] Trail aside, there is a sense in which Glassco, striving to emulate Beardsley's literary art, merely confirmed the superiority of the original.

Linda Dowling has interpreted Beardsley's text as a parody of avant-garde literary and artistic endeavour, aestheticism and decadence, including self-satire and caricatures of his contemporaries (she detects Oscar Wilde, Herbert Horne and Charles Condor among his victims). The very story of Venus and Tannhäuser was a prime target for satire, but Dowling argues that Beardsley's main objective was 'to turn the radical reductiveness of pornography to … expose the sexual underworld which he knew to lie beneath the art and experience of his contemporaries'.[134] It was pornography in the service of criticism.

Parody or not, we are dealing with a literary type of pornographic writing. Allison Pease has shown that Beardsley, the artist, like James Joyce, the writer, introduced pornographic imagery into his work, combining the aesthetic and the pornographic in what she terms the 'aesthetics of the obscene'.[135] Sexual arousal may occur in the aesthetics of the obscene, but it is not the main goal as it is in pornography. Rather, the aesthetics (structure, punctuation or lack of punctuation, form, style, use of parody) distance the reader or viewer from the pornographic aim. One of the ways in which Pease illustrates the aesthetics of the obscene is through a *New Statesman* review of Beardsley's work: 'He is haunted by the male genitals, and … he exaggerates their proportion in a way normally associated with the vulgarest pornography; but they must be among the most refined, meticulous, decorative and reverential drawings of the male genitals ever devised.'[136] Pease does not discuss *Under the Hill* (she was concerned with Beardsley's art), but the book is surely a perfect example of the aesthetics of the obscene. Whatever his intent, there is no doubting Beardsley's literary ability, what Dowling calls 'the pleasurableness of language as language'.[137] For Michelson, Beardsley's *Venus and Tannhäuser* gave pornography 'dimensions of artistic possibility hitherto unexplored'.[138]

The pornographic and the literary interact in these two examples. While we use the classifications to identify certain elements of the writing, the distinction is impossible to maintain. Trocchi's dirty book had literary qualities, more apparent in his preferred version but evident in Girodias's dirty book too – and highlighted by the crudities of Masquerade's additions. Beardsley's pornography was literary. The literature was arguably more refined in the absence of its pornography, but it was literature nonetheless. And, again, a later supplement (Glassco's in this case) emphasised the quality of the original.

The boundaries of which we have been constantly speaking have proven difficult to maintain. In his letter to Aldington, referred to above, in which he distinguished between garbage and literature, Durrell was less sure of the status of his own Obelisk and Olympia publication, *Black Book*: 'I don't really hold with my own Black Book's excesses, but I know that I tackled the subject matter with no thought of doing anyone dirt!'[139] The distinction was not so clear-cut after all. Similarly, Durrell's praise for Miller's *Tropic of Cancer*, noted earlier, turned to an excoriating critique a decade later when it came to the same author's *Sexus* (1949, 1959). Durrell criticised its 'childish explosions of obscenity'; 'The obscenity in it is really unworthy of you.'[140] 'All the wild resonance of *Cancer* and *Black Spring* has gone', he wrote with his earlier commendation obviously in mind, 'and you have failed to develop what is really new in your prose'.[141] Obscenity in the service of literature had become mere obscenity: 'the moral vulgarity of so much of it is *artistically* painful'.[142]

There are many different ways in which the pornographic can become literary. One is through the power of the imagination, and Trocchi's shockingly memorable imagery is a good example of this. In *White Thighs* (1955) a woman with spider tattoos preys on two naked girls, posed as insects with cellophane wings, one with a bottle-blue belly and the other striped like a wasp:

The illusion was magnificent. It was as if two spiders hung there drawing blood, their bloated bodies hard with suck. Below, across the sweep of her teeming white belly, a perfect web was marked, spotted here and there with red, and at her navel another spider clung, grosser, hairier than the others, looking down at the sweeping web to the dark and hairy center at her crotch. Thus her whole muscled front, the thick slabs of the thighs, the great, creamy, hunky abdomen, the hips, supported the web of which the center was the black hole of her sex and upon which crawled three terrible spiders.[143]

In *Thongs* (1956) the young Gertrude Gault finds an outlet for her budding sexuality in the fetish of an anonymous, used condom: 'I laid it against my cheek. All skin with the slimy little clot within it was more than anything else like an oyster, a warm yellow oyster, a gift from an unknown man.' She toys with it, in Trocchi's extended description, sucks it – 'A man's lust in my mouth' – rubs it against her sex, 'Then, with my middle finger, I slipped it into myself up to the knot.'[144] Finally, in the same book, Trocchi provides an inventively teasing account of underskirt oral sex: 'Don't run home to my cunt like a scared rabbit', the narrator urges her lover. 'Smell it out first! See that it is not dangerous first, that you're stronger than it, and then you can take it like a vandal! ... But not now! Not yet!'[145]

While Burroughs's prose surely tested the limits, in ways referenced earlier, what its author called its 'two pornographic sections' ('Hassan's Rumpus Room' and 'A.J.'s Annual Party') contain flashes of imaginative brilliance:

black dust blowing over lean copper bodies ... ragged pants dropped to cracked bleeding bare feet ... (place where vultures fight over fish heads) ... by jungle lagoons, vicious fish snap at white sperm floating on black water, sand flies bite the copper ass howler monkeys like wind in the trees (a land of great brown rivers where whole trees float, bright colored snakes in the branches, pensive lemurs watch

the shore with sad eyes), a red plane traces arabesques in blue substance of sky, a rattlesnake strikes, a cobra rears, spreads, spits white
venom, pearl and opal chips fall in a slow silent rain through air clear
as glycerine.[146]

The American novelist Norman Mailer testified that Burroughs
had 'extraordinary talent. Possibly he is the most talented writer in
America ... he also has an exquisite poetic sense.'[147]

Another way in which the pornographic is rendered literary is
through the agency of the quality of its prose. The delicate, homoerotic writing of Jean Cocteau's *The White Paper* (1957) comple-
ments its fragile drawings – of sailors mainly. The anonymous
author (Cocteau) describes an early sexual memory, seeing a naked
farm boy bathing a horse, with the contrasting whites and browns
of the young man's body, like 'chestnuts splitting out of their
husks'.[148] 'My ears rang. The blood rushed to my head, my face
turned scarlet. The strength drained out of my legs. My heart beat
like the heart of a murderer preparing to kill.'[149] He writes about
Toulon, 'that charming Sodom smitten by hardly very wrathful
heavenly fires in the form of a caressing sun':

> From the four corners of the earth men whose hearts are gone out to
> masculine beauty come to admire the sailors who hang about singly
> or drift in groups, smile in reply to longing's stare, and never refuse
> the offer of love. Some salt or nocturnal potion transforms the most
> uncouth ex-convict, the toughest Breton, the wildest Corsican, into
> these tall whores with their low-necked jumpers, their swaying hips,
> their pompoms, these lithely graceful, colorful whores who like to
> dance and who, without the least sign of awkwardness, lead their
> partners into the obscure little hotels down by the port.[150]

The narrator meets a sailor with 'LOUSY LUCK' tattooed on
his torso. 'I uncapped my fountain pen and crossed out the omi-
nous tattoo. I drew a star and a heart above it.'[151] 'Lousy luck!

Incredible', he exclaims, 'with that mouth, those teeth, those eyes, that belly, those shoulders and cast-iron muscles, those legs, how was it possible? Lousy luck, with that fabulous little undersea plant, forlorn, inert, shipwrecked on the frothy fleece, which then stirs, unwrinkles, develops, rouses itself and hurls its sap afar once it is restored to its element of love.'[152] He would watch young men through a two-way mirror as they pleasured themselves: 'their bodies would spit like furious animals'.[153] He refers to 'liquid drops similar to mistletoe'.[154]

Jean Genet employed poetry in his descriptions of the most banal objects or actions. Thus, spit is 'spun glassware, transparent and fragile'; a cap thrown to the floor becomes 'the carcass of a poor partridge with clipped wings'; an undressed hustler looks 'as white and sunken as an avalanche'; and a tube of phenobarbital on a mantlepiece 'is enough to detach the room from the masoned block of the building, to suspend it like a cage between heaven and earth'.[155] Or take his long disquisition on a tube of Vaseline seized during a police raid, mentholated Vaseline, 'the very sign of abjection', and mirth – 'You take it in the nose?' And yet! 'Now as I write, I muse on my lovers. I would like them to be smeared with my vaseline, with that gentle, slightly mentholated substance; I would like their muscles to bathe in that delicate transparence without which the tool of the handsomest is less lovely.'[156] He performs a similar task with his description of the power of a police badge: 'That metal object had for me the power of a cigarette-lighter in the fingers of a workman, of a belt-buckle, of a safety-catch, of a calliper, objects in which the quality of males is violently concentrated ... His virility was centred in that badge as much as in his prick.'[157]

Genet wrote of what he termed 'the stateliness of abjection' during his life in the 1930s.[158] 'I experienced the giddiness of finally meeting the perfect brute, indifferent to my happiness', he wrote of one object of desire. 'I discovered the softness that could be contained in a thick fleece on torso, belly and thighs and what force it could transmit.'[159] 'If he granted me the favour of sucking his prick occasionally', he wrote of another, 'I felt deeply grateful to him for allowing me to be his slave, but I never worried about whether it was wrong to love a cop.'[160] He recounted an obsession with the policeman Bernardini: 'I would walk beside him in the street, keeping step with him. If it was broad daylight, I would place myself so that he projected his shadow on my body. This simple game filled me with joy.'[161]

Genet wrote the poetics of gender, the multiple masculinities and femininities fashioned, threatened and lost in the streets and prisons of Paris and Europe. 'I shall speak to you about Divine, mixing masculine and feminine as my mood dictates', he writes in *Our Lady of the Flowers* (1957), 'and if, in the course of the tale, I shall have to refer to a woman, I shall manage, I shall find an expedient, a good device, so that there may be no confusion.'[162] When Divine meets Our Lady of the Flowers, a hidden masculinity resurfaces: 'She ran from boy to girl, and the transitions from one to the other – because the attitude was a new one – were made stumblingly.'[163]

Genet's prose, Elizabeth Stephens has observed, is phallotopian.[164] Darling, Divine's lover, is virility personified: 'He rams it in. So hard and calmly that anuses and vaginas slip onto his member like rings on a finger.'[165] '[A]ll the males in this book are handsome, powerful and lithe, and unaware of their grace', Genet writes in a trademark passage of authorial self-reflection.[166] Frequently, the promise is concealed rather than revealed, all the more powerful for its imagining, as in the penises of the police who arrest Divine: 'Their huge cocks are alive and rap sharply or push with desperate and sobbing thrusts against the door of their blue woollen pants.

They bid them open, like the clergy at the closed church door on Palm Sunday.'[167]

Then there is Georges Bataille. Austryn Wainhouse described Bataille's prose as having 'a heavy, raging fervor, almost unique in French and, in English, uncomfortable.' Bataille is, his Olympia translator told Richard Seaver in 1958, 'a very great, an unknown contemporary who probably isn't going to be discovered, even if by some fluke a book or two of his succeeds in America'.[168] His fiction is shockingly transgressive:

> She was seated, she held one leg stuck up in the air: to open her crack yet wider she used her fingers to draw the skin apart. And so Madame Edwarda's 'old rag and ruin' loured at me, hairy and pink, just as full of life as some loathesome squid. 'Why', I stammered in a subdued tone, 'why are you doing that?' 'You can see for yourself', she said: 'I'm GOD.' 'I'm going crazy –' 'No, hey, no, you've got to see, look …' Her harsh, scraping voice mellowed, she became almost childlike in order to say, with a lassitude, with the infinite smile of abandon: 'Oh, listen fellow! The fun I've had …'[169]

This was a sex worker as God. For Bataille, Patrick Ffrench has written, 'truth lies in the excess, fiction must chart the territory of extremity'.[170]

Bataille's *L'Histoire de l'oeil* ('The Story of the Eye'), translated originally into English as *A Tale of Satisfied Desire*, has been described by Peter Michelson as 'nearly immaculate transgression'.[171] Its sexual descriptions are beyond explicit: from the opening scene where Simone sits on a saucer of milk ('Milk is for the pussy, isn't it?') to the finale, where the protagonists rape and strangle a priest, copulate and insert the man's extracted eye into Simone's vagina so that the eye looks back at them ('that dreamy vision of a disastrous sadness').[172] When their friend Marcelle hangs herself, the narrator and Simone fuck next to the corpse and then the young woman urinates over her dead friend. In another scene, they retreat and have sex while watching a bull fight, when the death of a bull arouses them: 'I exposed Simone's cunt, and into her blood-red, slobbery flesh I stuck my fingers, then my penis, which entered that cavern of blood while I tossed off her arse, thrusting my bony middle finger deep inside.'[173] As the narrator explains: 'My kind of debauchery soils not only my body and my thoughts, but also any-thing I may conceive in its course, that is to say, the vast starry uni-verse, which merely serves as a backdrop.'[174] There is no attempt at standard eroticism. With its complicated imagery of eggs, testicles, eyes and milk, this was no 'normal' pornography. It was, Roland Barthes insisted, literature rather than mere writing.[175] 'Bataille's works, better than any others I know of, indicate the aesthetic pos-sibilities of pornography as an art form', Susan Sontag has written, '*Histoire de l'Oeil* being the most accomplished artistically of all the pornographic prose fictions I have read, and *Madame Edwarda* the most original and powerful intellectually.'[176]

Despite the efforts to distinguish pornography from literary mod-ernism, and the strategic utility of such a distinction in the service of analysis, the two were, in truth, intimately connected. First, Obelisk and Olympia used their dirty books to subsidise their more serious endeavours. The publication of books such as *Daffodil* and *The Sexual Life of Robinson Crusoe* paid for the work of Nabokov and Miller. Nabokov's amusing disdain for what he termed Girodias's 'much simpler commercial ventures, such as *Debby's Bidet* or *Tender Thighs*', ignored the economic support underpin-ning *Lolita*'s publication.[177] Second, the genres of serious literature and pornography were blurred in the sense that some of the authors of the former were also writers of the latter: the creator of *Tropic of Cancer* also wrote *Sexus*, and the person responsible for *Winter of*

Artifice penned *Little Birds* and *Delta of Venus*. But the genres were also indistinct because some of even the most pornographic of texts had literary moments and – as Sontag has stressed – pornography itself could demonstrate the originality and 'psychic dislocation' associated with powerful literature; 'there are writings which it seems reasonable to call pornographic – assuming that the stale label has any use at all – which, at the same time, cannot be refused accreditation as serious literature'.[178]

The borders were vague in the sense that obscenity was historically contingent, the previously condemned becoming literary classics, which is what Ladenson's *Dirt for Art's Sake* (2007) is all about. Witness, too, the Penguin editions of *Gordon, Delta of Venus, Zazie, Naked Lunch, Story of the Eye* and *Madame Edwarda*. Furthermore, one person's literature was another's pornography, as we have seen repeatedly. Geoffrey Wagner was convinced that Ed Martin's *Busy Bodies*, though pornographic, had 'definite literary quality', while we have dismissed it as a mere dirty book.[179] Alternatively, while acknowledging that Henry Miller is 'avant-garde and a highly inventive artist', Kate Millett has argued – with full resort to explicit language and description – that 'his most original contribution to sexual attitudes is confined to giving the first full expression to an ancient expression of contempt', 'a complete depersonalization of woman into cunt'.[180] Serious literature and pornography are difficult to separate. Finally, of course, the blurring was reprised with Olympia Press New York and Grove's reprinting of much of Olympia's catalogue in the 1960s, bringing dirty book and modernist text firmly into the sexual revolution.

Conclusion

The motives of the patrons of the young men and women producing pornography from the 1930s to the 1960s were different.
For the anonymous Roy Melisander Johnson, the oil man, it was
purely a case of sex for the sake of sex – though he did, inadvert-
ently, give us the erotica of Anaïs Nin. Maurice Girodias, on
the other hand, had grander aims. His was a war against censorship: 'I look back on a practically unblemished career', he said in
Playboy in 1961, 'one pleasant outcome of which will have been the
dismantling and near destruction of moral censorship in English
speaking countries'.[1]

Although its themes will be familiar by now to readers of this
book, Girodias set out his claimed programme most system-
atically in 'The Changing Guard', a special issue of the *Times
Literary Supplement* in 1964 devoted to the avant-garde. With a
nice inclusion of his father, Jack Kahane, and Obelisk Press in
his outlined history, he emphasised the fight against censorship,
a battle carried out on several fronts. The first was 'to force those
writers who had been suppressed by fear and ignorance past
the censor's eye'; he referenced books by Beckett, Burroughs,
Donleavy, Durrell, Genet, Miller, Nabokov, and Southern and

Hoffenberg.[2] But this was not enough; 'more was required to beat censorship out of existence', and here the second front comes in: 'I decided to be less gentle than my father had been in his time and to push the white-hot brand of pornography down the censor's throat … My friends were disguised under such pseudonyms as Marcus van Heller, Palmiro Vicarion, Carmencita de las Lunas, Miles Underwood, Akbar del Piombo, and we started producing unrestrained pornography on an unprecedented scale.'[3] Girodias was clear that he was working with talented young writers 'who had not yet emerged from obscurity' (this was 1964), naming Bryant, Chester, Hoffenberg, Logue, Lougee, Meeske, Owens, Rubington, Seaver, Stevenson and Wainhouse (Trocchi and Southern had achieved more public recognition).[4] He claimed that this campaign had had the desired outcome: 'The mass effect of that production was exactly what we had aimed for: it broke the spell. There was no mystery any more in obscene literature because it had become easily available; anyone travelling on the continent could buy the books'.[5] The overall outcome was that, 'One after the other, the great outlaw masterpieces were published and rehabilitated, first in the United States, and then in England.'[6] (He named *Lolita, Lady Chatterley's Lover, Tropic of Cancer, Our Lady of the Flowers, The Naked Lunch* and *Memoirs of a Woman of Pleasure*.) Girodias anticipated the heralding of a 'new knowledge', with eroticism as 'a constructive force … more and more an integral part of literature' – sex as 'the first source of art'.[7] He was exaggerating the teleology of intent, his own role, the coherence of the programme, and he neglected to mention any financial motive on his part (he ran a business after all), but it is a helpful, if amplified, summary of the issues at hand. What he did not address, though it has been a striking theme of our book, is the role of women in this battle.

It is surely important that some of the Olympia writers saw themselves – in retrospect – as engaged in the literary vanguard of the sexual revolution. 'We were sexual revolutionaries with a need to shock', Iris Owens told John de St. Jorre, 'and our books were more exploratory than we knew at the time'.[8] Baird Bryant said, 'We regarded ourselves as part of the sexual revolution.'[9] 'I believe modern pornographic writing is the literary accompaniment to the far-reaching changes at present occurring in our sexual morality', Philip Oxman, another dirty book author, claimed in 1965, 'It is, if you like, the tractarian polemical aspect of those changes.' Oxman felt that his book, *The Watcher and the Watched* (1954), 'whatever needs it may originally have satisfied, [had] come to be objectively polemical'.[10] Gregory Stephenson captured the spirit of the time in a reported conversation with Girodias: 'The Olympia Press was a salutary event, I tell him. It was entirely *sui generis*, a kind of Wild West of literature. The pizzazz, the panache, the mad humour, the exuberance. The preposterous noms-de-plumes, the extravagant sexual antics recounted in the "dirty books". Norman Rubington's crazy collage novels.'[11]

Girodias should be remembered for his creative literary and erotic publishing and for being proud of the attribution of pornologist.[12] 'You know what they call you in Tangiers?' the British publisher John Calder reputedly told him: 'The Lenin of the Sexual Revolution. Hah!'[13] Stephenson, who talked to Girodias in 1989, a year before the latter's death, persuaded him (according to Stephenson's telling) that Olympia Press 'was a vital aspect of the postwar cultural revolution, that it not only prefigured but precipitated certain elements of the rebellious 1960s'.[14]

Chris Forster has usefully described Obelisk and Olympia as 'institutions of modernist publishing', as 'halfway houses for modernist obscenity', accommodating the very different literature of

Miller and Nabokov alongside the content of the dirty books.[15] But there was also a link between the projects of Obelisk and Olympia and the new world of the 1960s. Three former Girodias writers who had moved on to success in different spheres (Southern was a famed screenwriter, Seaver a respected publisher and Trocchi had finally achieved recognition as a writer) combined in 1963 to edit *Writers in Revolt*, a literary collection for the 1960s. It was billed as 'an anthology of the most controversial writing in the world today', and they chose several familiar authors from Obelisk and Olympia: Beckett, Burroughs, Durrell, Genet, Miller, Sade, Wainhouse.[16] The 1930s and 1950s were not so distant.

If, as Loren Glass has claimed, Barney Rosset and New York's Grove Press were responsible for mainstreaming avant-garde European literature in the 1960s as part of the sexual revolution, it is noteworthy that many of their titles had been published a decade earlier by the Olympia Press in Paris; Glass has referred to Grove cannibalising Olympia's catalogue.[17] It is notable that most of the books mentioned by S. E. Gontarski as an indication of Rosset's early publishing verve and versatility have Girodias connections: Casement's *Black Diaries*, Miller's *Tropic of Cancer*, Burroughs's *Naked Lunch*, Harris's *My Life and Loves*, *The Story of O*, even *Harriet Marwood, Governess*. As Gontarski admits, 'In Grove's early years the source of much of its most provocative material was Maurice Girodias of the Olympia Press in Paris.'[18] Girodias would have agreed. Grove's claim for discovering the European greats drove the French publisher to distraction, and he outlined his grievances in a long letter to Samuel Beckett, referring to 'all the Olympia authors' Rosset had 'pumped away' from his catalogue, 'all my great authors vanished one by one, in the manner of a classical Agatha Christie novel, only to pop up on Grove's list'.[19] Rosset had, according to Girodias, 'drained

Olympia's backlist to the dregs'.[20] Aury, Beckett, Burroughs, Genet, Sade, Miller, all important Grove authors, were published in English, before Grove, by Girodias – though granted that Grove was negotiating with the Merlinois and Beckett very early in the piece.[21] While we would never deny credit to Rosset and Grove for fighting the great court battles of the twentieth century – for, in effect, ending US literary censorship – it does not hurt to remind readers that among the books being contested were Miller's *Tropic of Cancer* and Burroughs's *Naked Lunch*.

The Story of O, as we have seen, published in the same year in French (by Jean-Jacques Pauvert) and in English by Girodias, would sell 450,000 copies for Grove – claimed, by Amy Wyngaard, as the press's most culturally influential text.[22] Seaver, who translated the Grove edition, cheekily using the name Sabine d'Estrée, criticised an initial translation by a man ('male pride, male superiority'), extolling the virtues of a female translator for a book written by a woman.[23]

Significantly too, Grove's Seaver and Wainhouse, Sade's translators, had worked earlier with Olympia and *Merlin* in Paris. Girodias told Beckett that the poaching of Seaver was because of his Olympia connection.[24] Despite their eventual differences, and what Wainhouse called 'the ice of estrangement, indifference, and utterly impenitent unfeeling', it was to Girodias and Olympia, not Rosset and Grove, that the translator attributed 'the deliverance of the Marquis de Sade from the prison of obscurity'.[25]

Grove also published Sewall's *Sign of the Scorpion* and Legman's *The Oxford Professor Returns*, from the earlier New York combine, and Legman wrote the introduction to Grove's highly successful piece of repurposed pornography, *My Secret Life* (1966), which, in its abridged but uncensored version, sold almost 750,000 copies.[26] (The press also printed a version of the spurious Miller text *Opus Pistorum* (1983), albeit outside our period of interest.) In a sense, both syndicates were writing the sexual revolution before the sexual revolution and are a reminder that the literary wing of this cultural transformation had a long and protracted history.

Notes

Introduction

1 Nina Attwood and Barry Reay, 'Amateur sexology: Gershon Legman and US sexual history', *Journal of the History of Sexuality*, 30:1 (2021), 1–22.

2 Jamie Stoops, *The Thorny Path: Pornography in Early Twentieth-Century Britain* (Montreal: McGill-Queen's University Press, 2018), pp. 97, 100.

3 Rachel Potter, *Obscene Modernism: Literary Censorship and Experiment, 1900–1940* (Oxford: Oxford University Press, 2013), p. 9.

1 Jack Kahan and Obelisk Press

1 Neil Pearson, *Obelisk: A History of Jack Kahane and the Obelisk Press* (Liverpool: Liverpool University Press, 2007), p. 4.

2 Jack Kahane, *Memoirs of a Booklegger* (Newmarket, ON: The Obolus Press, 2010), p. 212. Kahane's book was first published in 1939.

3 Maurice Girodias, *The Frog Prince: An Autobiography* (New York: Crown, 1980), p. 230.

4 Henry Miller to Lawrence Durrell, [*c*. August, 1936], in Ian S. MacNiven (ed.), *The Durrell–Miller Letters, 1935–80* (London: Faber and Faber, 1989), p. 16.

5 Henry Miller to Lawrence Durrell, 8 March 1937, in *ibid.*, p. 56. Emphasis in original.

6 For a complete list of books published by Kahane and Obelisk, see Pearson, *Obelisk*, pp. 79–268.

7   *Ibid.*, p. 215.

8   For the publishing history and censorship of *The Well*, see, for example, Diana Souhami, *The Trials of Radclyffe Hall* (London: Weidenfeld & Nicolson, 1998); Alistair McCleery, 'Banned books and publishers' ploys', *Journal of Modern Literature*, 43:1 (2019), 34–52. For the frequently cited quote, see Souhami, *Trials of Radclyffe Hall*, p. 178.

9   Extract in Vera Brittain, *Radclyffe Hall: A Case of Obscenity?* (London: Femina Books, 1968), p. 107. For publishing numbers, see Richard Dellamora, *Radclyffe Hall: A Life in the Writing* (Philadelphia: University of Pennsylvania Press, 2011), p. 205.

10 Alec Craig, *The Banned Books of England* (London: George Allen & Unwin, 1938), p. 78.

11 Kahane, *Memoirs of a Booklegger*, p. 171.

12 *Ibid.*, p. 174.

13 Girodias, *The Frog Prince*, p. 88. Ellipsis in original.

14 Sylvia Beach, *Shakespeare and Company* (London: Faber and Faber, 1960), p. 140.

15 James Joyce, *Haveth Childers Everywhere* (Paris: Henry Babou and Jack Kahane, 1930), p. 36. For the bibliographic details of these two Joyce books, see Pearson, *Obelisk*, pp. 83–4, 121–3.

16 Girodias, *The Frog Prince*, pp. 113, 114.

17 Kahane, *Memoirs of a Booklegger*, p. 199.

18 Henry Miller to Anaïs Nin, [October 1932], in Henry Miller, *Letters to Anaïs Nin*, ed. and with an introduction by Gunther Stuhlmann (London: Peter Owen, 1965), p. 92. Emphases in original.

19 Henry Miller to Lawrence Durrell, 8 March 1937, in MacNiven, *Durrell–Miller Letters*, p. 56.

20 Alfred Perlès, *My Friend Henry Miller* (London: Neville Spearman, 1955), p. 91.

21 Kahane, *Memoirs of a Booklegger*, p. 175.

22 Cecil Barr [Jack Kahane], *Daffodil or Accidents Will Happen* (no place: Olympia Press, 2015), ebook, loc. 1197. The ebook says 'Olympia Press' but the publisher and place of publication of this edition are unknown. First published as Cecil Barr [Jack Kahane], *Daffodil or Accidents Will Happen* (Paris: Vendome Press, 1931) and then Cecil Barr [Jack Kahane], *Daffodil or Accidents Will Happen* (Paris: The Obelisk Press, 1933).

23 Barr, *Daffodil* (2015), loc. 434.

24 *Ibid.*, loc. 1311.

25 Kahane, *Memoirs of a Booklegger*, p. 176.

26 Cecil Barr [Jack Kahane], *Lady Take Heed!* (Paris: [The Obelisk Press], 1946), p. 46. First published in 1937.

27 *Ibid.*, p. 90.

28 *Ibid.*, p. 31.

29 *Ibid.*, pp. 85, 130.

30 For example, Elena Gorfinkel, *Lewd Looks: American Sexploitation Cinema in the 1960s* (Minneapolis: University of Minnesota Press, 2017), pp. 4, 11; Damon R. Young, *Making Sex Public and Other Cinematic Fantasies* (Durham, NC: Duke University Press, 2018), p. 3.

31 Girodias, *The Frog Prince*, p. 113.

32 Norah C. James, *I Lived in a Democracy* (London: Longmans, Green and Co, 1939), p. 230.

33 *Ibid.*, p. 231.

34 Norah C. James, *Sleeveless Errand* (Paris: Henry Babou and Jack Kahane, 1929), p. 6.

35 *Ibid.*, p. 2.

36 *Ibid.*, p. 42.

37 *Ibid.*, p. 206.

38 *Ibid.*, p. 66.

39 'Seized Novel to be Destroyed', *Manchester Guardian*, 5 March 1929, p. 12.

40 *Ibid.*

41 Chris Forster, *Filthy Material: Modernism and the Media of Obscenity* (New York: Oxford University Press, 2018), pp. 93–5.

42 *Ibid.*, p. 96.

43 Kahane, *Memoirs of a Booklegger*, p. 185.

44 Peter Neagoe, *Storm* (Paris: The Obelisk Press, [1932]), p. 18.

45 *Ibid.*, p. 66.

46 *Ibid.*, pp. 68, 135, 215, 280.

47 Kahane, *Memoirs of a Booklegger*, p. 186.

48 Henry Miller to Lawrence Durrell, 3 March [1935], in MacNiven (ed.), *Durrell–Miller Letters*, p. 13.

49 Cyril Connolly, *The Rock Pool* (New York: New Directions, *c.*1949), p. 15. First published by the Obelisk Press in Paris in 1936.

50 Quoted in Michael Shelden, *Friends of Promise: Cyril Connolly and the World of Horizon* (London: Hamish Hamilton, 1989), p. 21.

51 Philip Larkin, 'Inner Horizons', *Spectator*, 9 July 1983, p. 20.

52 Connolly, *The Rock Pool*, p. 20.

53 *Ibid.*, p. 13.

54 *Ibid.*, p. 93.

55 *Ibid.*, p. 103.

56 *Ibid.*, p. 59.

57 *Ibid.*, p. 187.

58 Gavin Ewart, 'Reputations – VIII: Cyril Connolly', *London Magazine*, 1 December 1963, pp. 35–50, at p. 37.

59 James Armstrong, 'The publication, prosecution, and re-publication of James Hanley's *Boy* (1931)', *Library*, 19:4 (1997), 351–62; Pearson, *Obelisk*, p. 196.

60 Letter from James Hanley to Harold Raymond, 2 September 1935, quoted in Armstrong, 'Publication, prosecution', 359.

61 Anthony Burgess, 'Introduction', in James Hanley, *Boy: A Novel* (New York: Open Road Integrated Media, 2015), ebook, p. 8. This is the edition published in London in 1990.

62 John Fordham, *James Hanley: Modernism and the Working Class* (Cardiff: University of Wales Press, 2002), p. 10.

63 Burgess, 'Introduction', p. 8.

64 James Hanley, *Boy* (Paris: The Obelisk Press, 1946), pp. 21–2. First published by Obelisk in 1935.

65 *Ibid.*, p. 75.

66 *Ibid.*, p. 141. The phrases in square brackets, indicating Obelisk's modifications, are from Hanley, *Boy* (2015), p. 150. The ellipsis is ours.

67 T. E. Lawrence to James Hanley, 2 July 1931, in David Garnett (ed.), *The Letters of T. E. Lawrence* (London: Jonathan Cape, 1938), p. 729.

68 J. W. Lambert and Michael Ratcliffe, *The Bodley Head 1887–1987* (London: The Bodley Head, 1987), p. 243.

69 Hanley, *Boy* (1946), p. 125.

70 *Ibid.*, p. 144. The phrase in square brackets is from Hanley, *Boy* (2015), p. 154, again indicating Obelisk's modifications.

71 Frank Harris to Bernard Shaw, 31 July 1928, in Stanley Weintraub (ed.), *The Playwright and the Pirate: Bernard Shaw and Frank Harris: A Correspondence* (Gerrards Cross: Colin Smythe, 1982), p. 213.

72 Samuel Roth, *The Private Life of Frank Harris* (New York: William Faro, 1931), p. 251. For Clement Wood as the book's ghost-writer, see J. A. Gertzman, *Bookleggers and Smuthounds: The Trade in Erotica 1920–1940* (Philadelphia: University of Pennsylvania Press, 2002), p. 243.

73 Roth, *Private Life of Frank Harris*, p. 242.

74 See Richard Davenport-Hines, 'Harris, James Thomas [Frank]', in H. C. G. Matthew and Brian Harrison (eds), *Oxford Dictionary of*

National Biography (Oxford: Oxford University Press, 2004), https://doi.org/10.1093/ref:odnb/33727.

75 A. I. Tobin and Elmer Gertz, *Frank Harris: A Study in Black and White* (Chicago: Madelaine Mendelsohn, 1931), pp. 73, 253.

76 A letter of 1924, quoted in Tobin and Gertz, *Frank Harris*, p. 324.

77 Beach, *Shakespeare and Company*, pp. 99–100.

78 Colette Colligan, *A Publisher's Paradise: Expatriate Literary Culture in Paris, 1890–1960* (Amherst: University of Massachusetts Press, 2013), p. 170.

79 Frank Harris, *My Life and Loves*, 4 volumes (Paris: The Obelisk Press, 1952), Vol. 1, p. 152. First published by Obelisk in 1934.

80 *Ibid.*, p. 168.

81 Harris, *My Life and Loves*, Vol. 3, p. 22.

82 *Ibid.*, p. 20.

83 See Harris, *My Life and Loves*, Vol. 1, pp. 156, 173; Vol. 2, p. 15.

84 Harris, *My Life and Loves*, Vol. 2, p. 15.

85 Harris, *My Life and Loves*, Vol. 1, pp. 11–12.

86 *Ibid.*, p. 17.

87 Harris, *My Life and Loves*, Vol. 1, pp. 134–5.

88 *Ibid.*, p. 135.

89 *Ibid.*, p. 141.

90 *Ibid.*, p. 173.

91 Harris, *My Life and Loves*, Vol. 2, p. 62.

92 *Ibid.*, p. 66.

93 *Ibid.*, p. 210.

94 Beach, *Shakespeare and Company*, p. 100.

95 George Orwell, 'Some Recent Novels', *New English Weekly*, 24 September 1936, p. 396.

96 Richard Aldington, *Death of a Hero* (London, World Distributors, 1965), p. 56.

97 *Ibid.*, p. 7.

98 See J. H. Willis, 'The censored language of war: Richard Aldington's Death of a Hero and three other war novels of 1929', *Twentieth Century Literature*, 45:4 (1999), 467–87; Pearson, *Obelisk*, pp. 93, 313–18.

99 Richard Aldington, *Life For Life's Sake: A Book of Reminiscences* (London: Cassell, 1968), p. 174. First published 1941.

100 Compare Aldington, *Death of a Hero* (1965), pp. 98–9; Richard Aldington, *Death of a Hero* (New York: Penguin, 2013), ebook, p. 83; and Richard

Aldington, *Death of a Hero: A Novel*, 2 volumes (Paris: Henri Babou and Jack Kahane, 1930), Vol. 1, pp. 98–9.

101 Compare Aldington, *Death of a Hero* (1965), p. 48; Aldington, *Death of a Hero* (2013), p. 35; Aldington, *Death of a Hero* (1930), Vol. 1, p. 42.

102 Compare Aldington, *Death of a Hero* (1965), p. 235; Aldington, *Death of a Hero* (2013), p. 210; Aldington, *Death of a Hero* (1930), Vol. 2, p. 57.

103 Compare Aldington, *Death of a Hero* (1965), p. 233; Aldington, *Death of a Hero* (2013), p. 209; Aldington, *Death of a Hero* (1930), Vol. 2, p. 56.

104 Aldington, *Death of a Hero* (1965), p. 8.

105 *Ibid.*, p. 35.

106 *Ibid.*, p. 24.

107 *Ibid.*, p. 18.

108 Harry Ransom Humanities Research Center, University of Texas at Austin (hereafter HRHRC), Parker Tyler Papers, Box 9, Folder 1, Correspondence with Charles Henri Ford, 1960–61: Charles Henri Ford to Parker Tyler, 15 February 1960. Emphasis in original.

109 HRHRC, Charles Henri Ford Papers, Box 3.1: Charles Henri Ford, 'I Will Be What I Am', p. 200.

110 *Ibid.*, p. 235.

111 Charles Henri Ford and Parker Tyler, *The Young and Evil*, with an Introduction by Steven Watson (New York: Masquerade Books, 1996), p. 11. The novel was first published by the Obelisk Press in Paris in 1933.

112 *Ibid.*, p. 16.

113 *Ibid.*, p. 56.

114 Steven Watson, 'Introduction', in Ford and Tyler, *Young and Evil*, no pagination.

115 Ford and Tyler, *Young and Evil*, p. 124.

116 *Ibid.*, p. 74. Emphasis in original.

117 Joseph Allen Boone, *Libidinal Currents: Sexuality and the Shaping of Modernism* (Chicago, 1998), p. 258. Emphasis in original.

118 *Ibid.*, p. 255.

119 Ford and Tyler, *Young and Evil*, pp. 75, 150, 184. Emphasis in original.

120 Sam See, 'Making modernism new: queer mythology in "The Young and Evil"', *ELH*, 76:4 (2009), 1073–105, at 1080.

121 Juan A. Suárez, *Pop Modernism: Noise and the Reinvention of the Everyday* (Urbana: University of Illinois Press, 2007), pp. 179–207, at p. 195.

122 Ford, 'I Will Be What I Am', pp. 333–4. Emphasis in original.

123 See the recent exhibition and catalogue, Jarret Earnest (ed.), *The Young and Evil: Queer Modernism in New York, 1930–1955* (New York: David Zwirner Books, 2019).

124 'Indecent book withdrawn', *The Times*, 11 April 1935, p. 4.

125 Wallace Smith, *Bessie Cotter* (Paris: The Obelisk Press, 1946), p. 79. First published by Obelisk in 1936.

126 Elisabeth Ladenson, 'After Jix (1930–1945)', in David Bradshaw and Rachel Potter (eds), *Prudes on the Prowl: Fiction and Obscenity in England, 1850 to the Present* (Oxford: Oxford University Press, 2013), pp. 111–37, at p. 130.

127 Smith, *Bessie Cotter*, p. 11.

128 *Ibid.*, pp. 17, 21, 28, 103, 142.

129 Pearson, *Obelisk*, pp. 200–4.

130 See G. W. Stonier, 'Current literature: books in general', *New Stateman and Nation*, 9 April 1938, p. 616.

131 *Ibid.* Emphasis in original.

132 Publication details in Pearson, *Obelisk*, pp. 227–31.

133 Kahane, *Memoirs of a Booklegger*, pp. 205–6.

134 Stonier, 'Current literature: books in general', p. 616. The ellipses are ours.

135 Graham Greene, 'Vengeance of Jenny's case', *New Statesman and Nation*, 21 November 1953, pp. 642, 644. For Matthews' authorship and his relationship with Greene, see Pearson, *Obelisk*, pp. 342–6; and Ladenson, 'After Jix', pp. 133–4. The quote comes from Sheila Cousins [Ronald Matthews], *To Beg I Am Ashamed* (London: The Richards Press, 1953), p. 238. Obelisk first published the book in 1938.

136 Cousins, *To Beg I Am Ashamed*, p. 110.

137 *Ibid.*, p. 8.

138 *Ibid.*, pp. 138, 238.

139 *Ibid.*, p. 241.

140 Pearson, *Obelisk*, p. 459.

141 Marika Norden [Mirjam Vogt], *The Gentle Men* (Paris: The Obelisk Press, 1935), p. 17.

142 *Ibid.*, p. 21.

143 *Ibid.*, p. 98.

144 *Ibid.*, p. 301.

145 Pearson, *Obelisk*, p. 475.

146 Richard Thoma, *Tragedy in Blue* (no place: Elektron Ebooks, 2012), ebook, loc. 343. First published by the Obelisk Press in 1936.

147   *Ibid.*, locs 635, 645. Ellipsis in original.

148   HRHRC, Parker Tyler Papers, Box 8, Folder 2: Correspondence with Charles Henri Ford, 1930–31, Charles Henri Ford to Parker Tyler, 18 July 1931.

149   See Wambly Bald, *On the Left Bank, 1929–1933*, ed. Benjamin Franklin (Athens, OH: Ohio University Press, 1987), pp. 73–4; Pearson, *Obelisk*, p. 475 (for the 'baffling' comment).

150   Bald, *On the Left Bank*, p. 73. From Bald's column of 19 August 1931.

151   Henry Miller, *The Books in My Life* (New York: New Directions Publishing Company, 1969), p. 16.

152   Bald, *On the Left Bank*, pp. 85–6.

153   *Ibid.*, p. 133.

154   Anaïs Nin, *Nearer the Moon: From 'A Journal of Love', the Unexpurgated Diary of Anaïs Nin, 1937–1939* (London: Peter Owen, 1996), p. 370.

155   For the omission of 'Djuna', see Benjamin Franklin, 'Introduction', in Anaïs Nin, *The Winter of Artifice: A Facsimile of the Original 1939 Paris Edition* (New York: Blue Sky Press, 2007), pp. ix–xxii, at p. xvi.

156   Sharon Spencer, 'Beyond therapy: the enduring love of Anaïs Nin for Otto Rank', in Suzanne Nalbantian (ed.), *Anaïs Nin: Literary Perspectives* (New York: St. Martin's Press, 1996), pp. 97–111.

157   Anaïs Nin, *Fire: From 'A Journal of Love', the Unexpurgated Diary of Anaïs Nin, 1934–1937* (New York: Harcourt, Inc., 1995), p. 44.

158   *Ibid.*, pp. 44, 56, 242, 372.

159   Anaïs Nin, *Incest: From 'A Journal of Love': The Unexpurgated Diary of Anaïs Nin, 1932–1934* (New York: Harcourt Brace & Company, 1992), p. 280.

160   Anaïs Nin, *Mirages: The Unexpurgated Diary of Anaïs Nin 1939–1947*, ed. Paul Herron (Athens, OH: Ohio University Press, 2013), p. 76.

161   Nin, *Incest*, p. 260.

162   Spencer, 'Beyond therapy', pp. 104, 105, 106.

163   Nin, *Winter of Artifice*, p. 15. Ellipsis and emphasis in original.

164   *Ibid.*, p. 48. Emphasis in original but the ellipsis is ours.

165   Witness: Anaïs Nin, *Henry and June* (London: Penguin, 2017); Nin, *Incest*.

166   Nin, *Winter of Artifice*, p. 125. Ellipsis in original.

167   *Ibid.*, p. 144.

168   *Ibid.* For the diary, see Nin, *Fire*, p. 168.

169   Nin, *Winter of Artifice*, p. 202.

170   *Ibid.*, p. 253.

171 *Ibid.*, p. 203.

172 *Ibid.*, p. 266.

173 Nin, *Fire*, p. 302.

174 *Ibid.*, p. 160; Nin, *Winter of Artifice*, p. 197.

175 For the account, see Nin, *Incest*, pp. 373–85.

176 For the diary, see *ibid.*, pp. 208–15, 287–8, quote at p. 209. Ellipsis in original.

177 See George Craig, Martha Dow Fehsenfeld, Daniel Gunn and Lois More Overbeck (eds), *The Letters of Samuel Beckett, Volume 1: 1929–1940* (Cambridge: Cambridge University Press, 2009), pp. 604, 607, 610.

178 Amy S. Wyngaard, 'Translating Sade: the Grove Press editions, 1953–1968', *Romantic Review*, 104:3–4 (2013), 313–31.

179 James Laughlin to Tennessee Williams, 18 December 1948, in Peggy L. Fox and Thomas Keith (eds), *The Luck of Friendship: The Letters of Tennessee Williams and James Laughlin* (New York: W. W. Norton, 2018), pp. 110–13, quote at p. 112.

2 The syndicate: pornography for the private collector

1 For a recent biography of Legman, see Susan Davis, *Dirty Jokes and Bawdy Songs: The Uncensored Life of Gershon Legman* (Champaign: University of Illinois Press, 2019). See also, Nina Attwood and Barry Reay, 'Amateur sexology: Gershon Legman and US sexual history', *Journal of the History of Sexuality*, 30:1 (2021), 1–22.

2 Gershon Legman, 'Introduction', in Patrick J. Kearney, *The Private Case: An Annotated Bibliography of the Private Case Erotica Collection in the British (Museum) Library* (London: Humanities Press, 1981), p. 35.

3 See the useful summaries in 'The Celebrated Stable of Clandestine Erotica Writers Part 1: The Man, His Plan', *FineBooks & Collections*, 26 May 2009: www.finebooksmagazine.com/blog/celebrated-stable-clandestine-erotica-writers-part-i-man-his-plan; and 'The Celebrated Stable of Clandestine Erotica Writers Part 2: The Perp Walk', *FineBooks & Collections*, 29 May 2009: https://www.finebooksmagazine.com/blog/celebrated-stable-erotica-writers-part-ii-perp-walk.

4 Gershon Legman, *World I Never Made: Book Three of Peregrine Penis* (Scotts Valley: Createspace, 2017), pp. 40–2. Barnet Ruder appears as Rudolph Bernays in Legman's autobiography: see *ibid.*, pp. 33, 40–2.

5 For the collaboration, see *ibid.*, pp. 86–9.

6 Clifford J. Scheiner, *The Essential Guide to Erotic Literature*, 2 volumes (Ware: Wordsworth Classics, 1996), Vol. 2, p. 195.

7 Legman, 'Introduction', p. 53.

8 *Ibid.*, pp. 52–3.

9 Legman, *World I Never Made*, p. 52. The quote is from L. Erectus Mentulus [Gershon Legman], *The Oxford Professor Returns* (New York: Grove Press, 1971), p. 3.

10 Gershon Legman, *Mooncalf: Book Two of Peregrine Penis* (Scotts Valley: Createspace, 2017), pp. 487–8; and Legman, *World I Never Made*, pp. 123–35.

11 For Tice, see Marie T. Keller, 'Clara Tice, "Queen of Greenwich Village"', in Naomi Sawelson-Gorse (ed.), *Women in Dada: Essays on Sex, Gender, and Identity* (Cambridge, MA: MIT Press, 1998), pp. 414–41. For *My Secret Life*, see Legman, *Mooncalf*, p. 486.

12 Legman, *Mooncalf*, pp. 479, 485, 487.

13 Gershon Legman, *Musick to My Sorrow: Book Four of Peregrine Penis* (Scotts Valley, CA: Createspace, 2018), p. 191.

14 Gershon Legman, 'On faking Henry Miller' (n.p., 1983), p. 4. This is a typescript of a proposed preface to Grove Press's edition of *Opus Pistorum* (more of which later), which was not used. We obtained this copy from Susan Davis.

15 Legman, *Mooncalf*, p. 487.

16 Peter Long [Gene Fowler], *The Demi-Wang* (Atlanta: Pendulum Books, 1968).

17 Legman, *Mooncalf*, p. 485.

18 *The Loves of Lord Roxboro (In Six Complete Volumes) … by Sir Walter Bone … (written 1898)* (London: Locus Elm Press, 2014). Locus Elm Press is an erotica publisher.

19 Gore Vidal, 'Pornography', in his *Collected Essays, 1952–1972* (London: Heinemann, 1974), pp. 219–33, at p. 222. The review originally appeared in the *New York Review of Books* in 1966.

20 For Walsh and the male brothel scandal, see Hugh Ryan, *When Brooklyn Was Queer* (New York: St. Martin's Griffin, 2020), pp. 209–11.

21 Department of Special Collections (hereafter DSC), Charles E. Young Research Library, UCLA, Anaïs Nin Papers, Box 21, Folder 1: Anaïs Nin, Diary 63, Mon Journal: House of Death & Escape, 8 December 1940 – 1 November 1941, pp. 1–7: 'This is the way it began'. This is a seven-page typescript at the beginning of Nin's diary.

22 Yale Collection of American Literature, Beinecke Rare Book and Manuscript Library (hereafter BRBML), Henry Miller Letters to Barnet Ruder, Box 1, Folder 6: Henry Miller to Barnet Ruder, 12 April [1936].

23 *Ibid.*, Folder 2: Henry Miller to Barnet Ruder, undated [May 1941].

24 Nin, 'This is the way it began', p. 2.

25 *Ibid*, p. 4.

26 See David L. Ulin, 'The inadvertent pornographer', *LA Weekly*, 15 September 1999: www.laweekly.com/the-inadvertent-pornographer/.

27 Nin, 'This is the way it began', p. 7.

28 Anaïs Nin, 'Preface', *Delta of Venus* (London: Penguin, 2000), pp. xi–xii. First published in 1977.

29 Anaïs Nin, *Mirages: The Unexpurgated Diary of Anaïs Nin 1939–1947*, ed. Paul Herron (Athens, OH: Ohio University Press, 2013), p. 84.

30 Anaïs Nin, *The Journals of Anaïs Nin: Vol. 3: 1939–1944* (London: Quartet Books, 1976), p. 73.

31 Nin, 'This is the way it began', p. 8.

32 *Ibid.*, p. 7.

33 Nin, *Journals, Vol. 3*, p. 61.

34 *Ibid.*, p. 81.

35 *Ibid.*, pp. 81–5; Nin, *Delta of Venus:* 'The Basque and Bijou'.

36 Daniel R. Barnes, 'Nin and traditional erotica', *Seahorse: The Anaïs Nin/ Henry Miller Journal*, 1:1 (1982), 1–5.

37 Quoted in Lisa Jarnot, *Robert Duncan: The Ambassador from Venus: A Biography* (Berkeley and Los Angeles: University of California Press, 2012), p. 78.

38 Bernard Wolfe, *Memoirs of a Not Altogether Shy Pornographer*, selected by J. Lethem (New York: Counterpoint, 2016), p. 103. First published in 1972. Emphasis in original.

39 *Ibid.*, p. 84.

40 *Ibid.*, p. 111.

41 *Ibid.*, p. 116.

42 *Ibid.*, p. 244.

43 Anaïs Nin, *Little Birds* (New York: Pocket Books, 1979), p. 8.

44 Nin, *Journals, Vol. 3*, p. 157.

45 Nin, *Mirages*, p. 42.

46 Henry Miller to Anaïs Nin, [January 1941], in Gunther Stuhlmann (ed.), *A Literate Passion: Letters of Anaïs Nin and Henry Miller, 1932–1953* (Orlando: Harcourt Brace Jovanovich, 1987), p. 325.

47 BRBML, Henry Miller Letters to Barnet Ruder, Box 1, Folder 8: Henry Miller to Barnet Ruder, 6 January 1941.

48 Nin, 'This is the way it began', p. 3.

49 *Ibid.*, p. 6.

50 Nin, *Mirages*, p. 42. For *Henry and June*, see Anaïs Nin, *Henry and June* (London: Penguin, 2017). For the dates for specific diaries, see Finding Aid for the Anais Nin Papers, *c.*1910–1977: http://oac.cdlib.org/findaid/ark:/13030/kt3489p4x9. *Henry and June* is based on diaries 32 to 36.

51 DSC, Nin, Diary 63, 14 December 1941, p. 28.

52 *Ibid.*, 4 January 1941, p. 62. Nin, *Mirages*, p. 44 prints this passage, but the wording is slightly different.

53 DSC, Nin, Diary 63, 10 January 1941, p. 79.

54 Nin, *Mirages*, p. 48.

55 Nin, *Journals, Vol. 3*, p. 61.

56 DSC, Nin, Diary 63, 13 February 1941, pp. 135–6.

57 *Ibid.*, 3 March 1941, p. 144.

58 *Ibid.*, p. 145.

59 *Ibid.*, 8 March 1941, pp. 148, 149, 150.

60 *Ibid.*, 15 April 1941, p. 176.

61 *Ibid.*, 1 June 1941, p. 220.

62 *Ibid.*, p. 223.

63 *Ibid.*, 10 June 1941, p. 226.

64 *Ibid.*, 13 June 1941, p. 229.

65 Nin, *Henry and June*, p. 53.

66 *Ibid.*, p. 91.

67 Nin, *Mirages*, p. 50.

68 *Ibid.*, p. 82.

69 *Ibid.*, p. 55. Emphasis in original.

70 Legman, *World I Never Made*, p. 41.

71 Nin, *Journals, Vol. 3*, p. 75.

72 *Ibid.*, p. 61.

73 See '82 Erotic Typescripts', Between the Covers Rare Books Inc: www.betweenthecovers.com/pages/books/381515/82-e; and 'Roy Melisander Johnson Erotic Typescripts, 1830–2012', Southern Illinois University Special Collections Research Center: https://archives.lib.siu.edu/index.php?p=collections/findingaid&id=3439&q=roy+melisander+johnson.

74 Legman, *World I Never Made*, pp. 37–8.

75   Gershon Legman, 'The Bibliography of Prohibited Books: Pisanus Fraxi', in his *The Horn Book: Studies in Erotic Folklore and Bibliography* (New York: University Books, 1966), p. 35.

76   *Ibid.*, pp. 35–6.

77   John Ferrone, 'The making of *Delta of Venus*', *A Café in Space: The Anaïs Nin Literary Journal*, 7 (2010), 53–60, at 57.

78   Legman, *World I Never Made*, pp. 34, 40, 72–3.

79   Legman, 'Bibliography of Prohibited Books', p. 36.

80   *Ibid.*; Legman, *World I Never Made*, p. 72; Legman, *Musick to My Sorrow*, p. 167.

81   Legman, *World I Never Made*, pp. 72–3. See also Legman, 'On faking Henry Miller', pp. 19–21.

82   Clifford J. Scheiner, 'Introduction', in Anaïs Nin and Friends, *White Stains* (London: Delectus Books, 1995), pp. iii–xi, at p. ix.

83   See https://iucat.iu.edu/kinsey?utf8=%E2%9C%93&search_field=all_field&q=oxford+thesis+on+love.

84   Legman, 'On faking Henry Miller', p. 12a.

85   Erectus Mentulus, *Oxford Professor Returns*, pp. 31, 41.

86   *Ibid.*, p. 41. For other examples of (supposedly) historic erotic texts see pp. 54, 60, 70, 161.

87   Legman, *World I Never Made*, p. 265.

88   Erectus Mentulus, *Oxford Professor Returns*, pp. 99, 161, 101.

89   Legman, 'On faking Henry Miller', p. 20.

90   Erectus Mentulus, *Oxford Professor Returns*, pp. 137–8.

91   *Ibid.*, p. 108.

92   Eberhard and Phyllis Kronhausen, *Pornography and the Law: The Psychology of Erotic Realism and Hard Core Pornography* (New York: Ballantine Books, 1964).

93   Anonymous [Robert Sewall], *The Sign of the Scorpion: An Erotic Mystery Story* (New York: Grove Press, 1981), p. 60.

94   *Ibid.*, p. 77.

95   *Ibid.*, p. 83.

96   *Ibid.*, p. 121.

97   *Ibid.*, p. 135. Ellipses in original.

98   *Ibid.*, pp. 71–2.

99   Legman, *World I Never Made*, pp. 159, 175.

100 See 'Epilogue', in Henry Miller, *Opus Pistorum* (New York: Star, 1984), pp. 287–8.

101 Noël Riley Fitch, *Anaïs: The Erotic Life of Anaïs Nin* (Boston and New York: Little, Brown, 1993), p. 249.

102 Jay Martin, 'Historical truth and narrative reliability: three biograph-ical stories', in Frederick R. Karl (ed.), *Biography and Source Studies* (New York: AMS Press, 1994), pp. 25–72, at p. 39.

103 Legman, *World I Never Made*, pp. 72–5, 83.

104 *Ibid.*, pp. 86–8.

105 *Ibid.*, p. 69. For the Tania passage, see Henry Miller, *Tropic of Cancer* (New York: Grove Press, 1970), p. 6. First published in 1934.

106 Legman, *World I Never Made*, p. 71.

107 *Ibid.*, p. 70.

108 Legman, 'On faking Henry Miller', p. 14.

109 *Ibid.*, p. 18. Emphasis in original.

110 *Ibid.*, p. 14.

111 *Ibid.*, p. 15.

112 *Ibid.*, p. 14.

113 Miller, *Opus Pistorum*, p. 158.

114 Legman, 'On faking Henry Miller', p. 15.

115 *Ibid.*; Legman, *World I Never Made*, p. 70.

116 Miller, *Opus Pistorum*, pp. 11, 14, 15. See also, for example, pp. 26, 32, 37, 45, 61, 129, 153, 183, 198, 265.

117 Legman, *World I Never Made*, p. 70.

118 Editor's note in Richard Clement Wood (ed.), *Collector's Quest: The Correspondence of Henry Miller and J. Rives Childs, 1947–1965* (Charlottesville: University Press of Virginia, 1968), p. 34; Roger Jackson, '*Opus Pistorum* and Henry Miller', in Lawrence J. Shifreen and Roger Jackson (eds), *Henry Miller: A Bibliography of Primary Sources* (Ann Arbor: self-published, 1993), pp. 931–8. All of these manuscript type-scripts are in the Kinsey Library: Kinsey Institute, University of Indiana, Bloomington.

119 Kinsey Institute: Toby Hackett [attributed to Henry Miller], 'Some Paris Nights' (1940), p. 3.

120 Fitch, *Anaïs*, p. 249.

121 Henry Miller to J. Rives Childs, 21 July 1950, in Wood, *Collector's Quest*, pp. 39–41.

122 *Ibid.*

123 Jackson, '*Opus Pistorum* and Henry Miller'.

124 DSC, Nin, Diary 63, 8 March 1941, p. 150; 24 May 1941, p. 219; 4 June 1941, p. 225.

125 See Paul Herron, 'Introduction', in Anaïs Nin, *Auletris: Erotica by Anaïs Nin* (San Antonio: Sky Blue Press, 2016), p. 11.

126   *Ibid.*, p. 10; Miller, *Opus Pistorum*, pp. 287–8.

127   Herron, 'Introduction', p. 10.

128   *Ibid.*, p. 11.

129   Henry Miller to J. Rives Childs, 21 July 1950, in Wood, *Collector's Quest*, pp. 39–41.

130   Legman, *World I Never Made*, p. 74.

131   Miller, *Opus Pistorum*, p. 118. Ellipses in original.

132   *Ibid.*, p. 29. Ellipses in original.

133   Robert Ferguson, *Henry Miller: A Life* (London: Hutchinson, 1991), p. 277.

134   Miller, *Opus Pistorum*, p. 15.

135   *Ibid.*, p. 31. Ellipsis in original.

136   *Ibid.*, p. 32.

137   For the 'John Thursday' information, see Legman, *World I Never Made*, p. 70.

138   Ferguson, *Henry Miller*, p. 277.

139   Fitch, *Anaïs*, p. 249.

140   See Herron, 'Introduction'.

141   Nin, *Little Birds*, p. 91.

142   For a list of the original typescripts at UCLA, see Finding Aid for the Anais Nin Papers, *c.*1910–1977: http://oac.cdlib.org/findaid/ark:/13030/kt3489p4x9. For the Kinsey Institute, see https://iucat.iu.edu/kinsey?f%5Bformat%5D%5B%5D=Manuscript&q=anais+nin&search_field=all_field.

143   Nin, *Journals, Vol. 3*, p. 69.

144   *Ibid.*, p. 73.

145   *Ibid.*, p. 87.

146   *Ibid.*, p. 102.

147   *Ibid.*, p. 122.

148   Ferrone, 'The making of *Delta of Venus*', 55.

149   Nin, *Delta of Venus*, p. 70.

150   *Ibid.*

151   *Ibid.*, p. 71.

152   *Ibid.*, p. 75.

153   *Ibid.*, p. 77.

154   *Ibid.*, p. 78.

155   *Ibid.*, p. 79.

156   *Ibid.*, pp. 79, 80–1.

157   *Ibid.*, p. 78.

158 *Ibid.*, p. 76.

159 *Ibid.*, p. 78.

160 Legman, *World I Never Made*, p. 26.

161 Scheiner, 'Introduction', pp. x, iii, vi, xi.

162 *Ibid.*, p. x.

163 Anaïs Nin and Friends, *White Stains*, pp. 27, 33, 32, 28, 61, 53.

164 *Ibid.*, p. 101.

165 *Ibid.*, p. 107.

166 Scheiner, 'Introduction', p. xi.

167 Nin, *Journals, Vol. 3*, p. 177.

168 Legman, 'Introduction', p. 59.

169 Nin, *Journals, Vol. 3*, p. 148.

170 See Herron, 'Introduction', p. 9.

171 Ferrone, 'The making of *Delta of Venus*', 55.

172 Nin, *Delta of Venus*, p. xiii.

173 Erectus Mentulus, *Oxford Professor Returns*, pp. 178–9; Nin, *Delta of Venus*, p. 77.

174 Nin, *Delta of Venus*, pp. 77–8.

175 Nin, *Delta of Venus,* p. 129.

176 *Ibid.*, p. xiii; Herron, 'Introduction', p. 9.

177 Legman, *World I Never Made*, p. 41.

3 Olympia, Paris

1 Gershon Legman, *World I Never Made: Book Three of Peregrine Penis* (Scotts Valley: Createspace, 2017), p. 79.

2 *Ibid.*, p. 80.

3 Richard Seaver, *The Tender Hour of Twilight*, ed. Jeannette Seaver (New York: Farrar, Straus and Giroux, 2012), p. 196.

4 Gregory Stephenson, 'Tête-à-tête with the Frog Prince: conversations with Maurice Girodias', in his *Points of Intersection* (Thy, Denmark: Eyecorner Press, 2018), pp. 114–34, at p. 122.

5 Maurice Girodias, 'Introduction', in Maurice Girodias (ed.), *The Olympia Reader* (New York: Grove Press, 1965), pp. 11–29, at p. 20.

6 Stephenson, 'Tête-à-tête with the Frog Prince', p. 122.

7 Austryn Wainhouse, 'On translating Sade', *Evergreen Review*, 10:42 (1966), 50–6 and 87, quote at 56.

8 *Ibid.*

9   Barry Miles, *The Beat Hotel: Ginsberg, Burroughs, and Corso in Paris, 1958–1963* (New York: Grove Press, 2000), pp. 21–2; John Calder, *The Garden of Eros: The Story of the Paris Expatriates and the Post-War Literary Scene* (London: Calder Publications, 2013), pp. 108–9, 112–17; John de St. Jorre, *Venus Bound: The Erotic Voyage of the Olympia Press and Its Writers* (New York: Random House, 1994), p. 71.

10 Colette Colligan, *A Publisher's Paradise: Expatriate Literary Culture in Paris, 1890–1960* (Amherst: University of Massachusetts Press, 2013), pp. 141–84.

11 Maurice Girodias, *The Frog Prince: An Autobiography* (New York: Crown, 1980), p. 224.

12 *Ibid.*, p. 273.

13 On the modernist texts, see Lise Jaillant, *Cheap Modernism: Expanding Markets, Publishers' Series and the Avant-Garde* (Edinburgh: Edinburgh University Press, 2017), pp. 48–70. It was before Girodias's time, but, as we know, his father was a publisher.

14 For the complex story of this loss, see Calder, *Garden of Eros*, pp. 5–38.

15 University Museums and Special Collections Service, University of Reading (hereafter UMSCS), Maurice Girodias Collection: Maurice Girodias to Frederick Warburg, 2 January 1963.

16 Patrick J. Kearney, *A Bibliography of the Publications of the New York Olympia Press* (Santa Rosa: privately printed, 1988), p. xviii.

17 Special Collections Research Center, Syracuse University Libraries (hereafter SCRC), Austryn Wainhouse Papers, Correspondence, Box 3, Richard Aldington: Austryn Wainhouse to John Berger, 15 April 1955. (The letter is presumably misfiled in the Aldington box.)

18 Richard Seaver, 'Introduction', in Alexander Trocchi, *Cain's Book* (New York: Grove Press, 1992), pp. xi–xx, at p. xi.

19 Justin Beplate discusses the relationship in his 'Samuel Beckett, Olympia Press and the Merlin Juveniles', in Mark Nixon (ed.), *Publishing Beckett* (London: The British Library, 2011), pp. 97–109.

20 SCRC, Austryn Wainhouse Papers, Correspondence, Box 6, Richard Seaver: Austryn Wainhouse to Richard Seaver, 25 February 1955.

21 *Ibid.*

22 SCRC, Austryn Wainhouse Papers, Diaries, Box 9: Austryn Wainhouse Diary, 16 January 1955.

23 Richard Seaver, 'Samuel Beckett', in Girodias, *Olympia Reader*, pp. 220–5, at p. 225.

24 UMSCS, Maurice Girodias Collection: Maurice Girodias to Frederick Warburg, 2 January 1963.

25 Seaver, *Tender Hour of Twilight*, p. 197.

26 Christopher Logue, *Prince Charming: A Memoir* (London: Faber and Faber, 1999), pp. 141–2; Calder, *Garden of Eros*, p. 67.

27 James Campbell, 'The Olympia Press', *Times Literary Supplement*, 14 February 1992, pp. 17–18, at p. 17.

28 For the Broughton description, see James Broughton, *Coming Unbuttoned*, with a foreword by Mark Thompson ([San Francisco]: Query Books, 2016), p. 152.

29 Austryn Wainhouse, *Hedyphagetica* (Champaign: Dalkey Archive Press, 2007), p. 19. First published by the Olympia Press in 1954.

30 Austryn Wainhouse, 'Of the clandestine', in Terry Southern, Richard Seaver and Alexander Trocchi (eds), *Writers in Revolt: An Anthology* (New York: Berkeley Publishing Corporation, 1965), pp. 41–61, at p. 43. The essay was first published in *Merlin* in 1953.

31 SCRC, Austryn Wainhouse Papers, Correspondence, Box 5, Christopher Logue: Christopher Logue to Austryn Wainhouse, 2 July 1956. Bertolt Brecht died a month after Logue wrote this letter.

32 Beplate, 'Samuel Beckett, Olympia Press and the Merlin Juveniles', p. 97.

33 Richard Seaver, 'Introduction', in Richard Seaver (ed.), *I Can't Go On, I'll Go On: A Selection from Samuel Beckett's Work* (New York: Grove Press, 1976), pp. x–xlviii, at p. x.

34 *Ibid.*, p. xi.

35 Richard Seaver, 'On translating Beckett', in James and Elizabeth Knowlson (eds), *Beckett Remembering: Remembering Beckett: Uncollected Interviews with Samuel Beckett and Memories of Those Who Knew Him* (London: Bloomsbury, 2006), pp. 100–7, at p. 102.

36 For the errors, see Seaver, 'Introduction', p. xvii.

37 Patrick Bowles, 'How to fail: notes on talks with Samuel Beckett', *PN Review*, 20:4 (1994), 24–38, at 24.

38 *Ibid.*, 33.

39 *Ibid.*, 27.

40 See Samuel Beckett to George Reavey, 12 May 1953, in George Craig, Martha Dow Fehsenfeld, Daniel Gunn and Lois More Overbeck (eds), *The Letters of Samuel Beckett, Volume 2: 1941–1956* (Cambridge: Cambridge University Press, 2011), p. 376.

41 Patrick J. Kearney, *The Paris Olympia Press*, ed. Angus Carroll (Liverpool: Liverpool University Press, 2007), pp. 35–6.

42 *Ibid.*, pp. 35, 161–2; Amy S. Wyngaard, 'The Austryn Wainhouse Papers', *Translation Review*, 92:1 (2015), 99–106, at 101.

43 These works are all catalogued in Kearney, *Paris Olympia Press* (2007), pp. 26–9, 37–9, 169–86.

44 *Ibid.*, pp. 39–41, 229–31.

45 *Ibid.*, pp. 176–7.

46 *Ibid.*, pp. 52–3; Wyngaard, 'Austryn Wainhouse Papers', 101.

47 SCRC, Austryn Wainhouse Papers, Correspondence, Box 7, Mary [Muffie] Wainhouse: Austryn Wainhouse to Muffie Wainhouse, 28 September 1957, 7 October 1957 (for the quote), 9 December 1957.

48 Wyngaard, 'Austryn Wainhouse Papers', 100; Wainhouse, 'On translating Sade', 52.

49 Wainhouse, 'On translating Sade', 51.

50 SCRC, Austryn Wainhouse Papers, Correspondence, Box 6, Richard Seaver: Austryn Wainhouse to Richard Seaver, 19 January 1967.

51 Wainhouse, 'On translating Sade', 51.

52 Seaver, *Tender Hour of Twilight*, pp. 59–61, 186.

53 Wainhouse, 'On translating Sade', 54.

54 SCRC, Austryn Wainhouse Papers, Diaries, Box 9: Austryn Wainhouse Diary, 2 April 1953.

55 For the nineteenth century, see Will McMorran, 'The Marquis de Sade in English, 1800–1850', *Modern Language Review*, 112:3 (2017), 549–66.

56 Alyce Mahon, *The Marquis de Sade and the Avant-Garde* (Princeton: Princeton University Press, 2020), pp. 125–33.

57 *Ibid.*, pp. 88–123.

58 Yale Collection of American Literature, Beinecke Rare Book and Manuscript Library, Henry Miller Letters to Barnet Ruder, Box 1, Folder 2: Henry Miller to Barnet Ruder, undated [May 1941?].

59 Edmund Wilson, 'The vogue of the Marquis de Sade', *New Yorker*, 18 October 1952, pp. 144–56.

60 Wainhouse, 'Of the clandestine', pp. 42–3.

61 Wyngaard, 'Austryn Wainhouse Papers', 100.

62 Logue, *Prince Charming*, p. 141.

63 Girodias, 'Introduction', p. 19.

64 Logue, *Prince Charming*, pp. 147–8.

65 Marilyn Meeske, 'Memoirs of a female pornographer', *Esquire*, April 1965, pp. 112–15, at p. 115. Emphasis in original.

66 For the rejections, see Harry Ransom Humanities Research Center, University of Texas at Austin (hereafter HRHRC), Marilyn Meeske Collection, Folder 1.

67 Quoted in de St. Jorre, *Venus Bound*, p. 75.

68 Maurice Girodias to Samuel Beckett, 17 September 1986, in Barney Rosset, *Dear Mr. Beckett: The Samuel Beckett File*, ed. Louis Oppenheim (Tuxedo Park: Opus, 2017), pp. 351–60, at p. 353.

69 Patrick J. Kearney, *The Paris Olympia Press: An Annotated Bibliography* (London: Black Spring Press, 1987), p. 14.

70 Kearney, *Paris Olympia Press* (2007), p. 53.

71 Georges Bataille, 'Preface', in Pierre Angélique [Georges Bataille], *The Naked Beast at Heaven's Gate*, trans. Audiart [Austryn Wainhouse], with a preface by Georges Bataille (Paris: The Olympia Press, 1956), pp. 11–21, at p. 14.

72 Seaver, *Tender Hour of Twilight*, p. 302.

73 Terry Southern, 'Flashing on Gid', *Grand Street*, 37 (1991), 226–34, at 231.

74 *Ibid.*, 232.

75 William S. Burroughs to Allen Ginsberg, 5 September 1959, in William S. Burroughs, *The Letters of William S. Burroughs, 1945–1959*, ed. Oliver Harris (New York: Viking, 1993), p. 423.

76 Seaver, *Tender Hour of Twilight*, p. 197.

77 Andrew Murray Scott, *Alexander Trocchi: The Making of a Monster* (Kilkerran: Kennedy & Boyd, 2012), p. 81. First published in 1991.

78 Seaver, *Tender Hour of Twilight*, p. 197.

79 Chester Himes, *My Life of Absurdity: The Autobiography of Chester Himes* (New York: Thunder's Mouth Press, 1976), p. 221. It should be noted that *Pinktoes* is bawdy but not sexually explicit. It is also very funny.

80 J. P. Donleavy, *The Ginger Man* (New York: The Atlantic Monthly Press, 1988), pp. 95–6. For the Brophy comment, see Brigid Brophy, 'Onto the cart', *New Statesman*, 2 August 1963, p. 147.

81 Brophy, 'Onto the cart', p. 147.

82 See Robert A. Corrigan, 'The artist as censor: J. P. Donleavy and the *Ginger Man*', *Midcontinent American Studies Journal*, 8:1 (1967), 60–72.

83 J. P. Donleavy, *The History of The Ginger Man: An Autobiography* (Dublin: Lilliput Press, 2011), ebook, loc. 7952. For the numbering, see Kearney, *Paris Olympia Press* (1987), pp. 65–8.

84 Apart from the fact that he did not know who Nabokov was: Donleavy, *History of The Ginger Man*, locs 8402–7.

85 Vladimir Nabokov, 'Lolita and Mr. Girodias', *Evergreen Review*, 11:45 (1967), 37–41, at 38. For Nabokov and Girodias, see Brian Boyd, *Vladimir Nabokov: The American Years* (Princeton: Princeton University Press, 1991); de St. Jorre, *Venus Bound*, pp. 116–54.

86 Vladimir Nabokov, 'On a book entitled *Lolita*', *Anchor Review*, 2 (1957), 105–12, at 108–9.

87 Vladimir Nabokov to Maurice Girodias, 18 July 1955, in Dimitri Nabokov and Matthew J. Bruccoli (eds), *Vladimir Nabokov: Selected Letters 1940–1977* (London: Weidenfeld and Nicolson, 1990), p. 175.

88 Vladimir Nabokov, *Lolita* (New York: Vintage, 1997), p. 20. First published by the Olympia Press in Paris in 1955.

89 De St. Jorre, *Venus Bound*, p. 151.

90 Vladimir Nabokov to Graham Greene, 31 December 1956, in Nabokov and Bruccoli, *Vladimir Nabokov: Selected Letters*, p. 198.

91 John Hollander, 'The perilous magic of nymphets', *Partisan Review*, 23:4 (1956), 557–60, at 557.

92 Alfred Appel, 'Backgrounds of *Lolita*', *TriQuarterly*, 17 (1970), 17–40, at 19.

93 HRHRC, Philip O'Connor Collection, Maurice Girodias to Philip O'Connor, 3 February 1960, 4 March 1960, and 8 June 1960.

94 For his life, see Andrew Barrow, *Quentin and Philip: A Double Portrait* (London: Macmillan, 2002).

95 Philip O'Connor, *Steiner's Tour* (no place: Olympia Press, 2004), ebook, loc. 12. The ebook says 'Olympia Press' but the publisher and place of publication of this edition are unknown. First published as Philip O'Connor, *Steiner's Tour* (Paris: The Olympia Press, 1960).

96 O'Connor, *Steiner's Tour*, loc. 691. Emphasis in original.

97 Paul Ableman, 'Faith at the first', *Guardian*, 10 July 1990, p. 39.

98 Philip Toynbee, 'Paul Abelman', in Girodias, *Olympia Reader*, p. 59; Paul Abelman, 'I Can Hear Voices', in Girodias, *Olympia Reader*, pp. 44–58, at p. 44. *I Can Hear Voices* was published by the Olympia Press in 1957.

99 HRHRC, Parker Tyler Papers, Box 9, Folder 1, Correspondence with Charles Henri Ford, 1960–61: Charles Henri Ford to Parker Tyler, 5 March 1960.

100 *Ibid.*, Charles Henri Ford to Parker Tyler, 26 March 1960.

101 HRHRC, Parker Tyler Papers, Box 12, Folder 1, Correspondence Obelisk and Olympia Press: contract with Olympia Press, 25 April 1960.

102 HRHRC, Parker Tyler Papers, Box 10, Folder 2, Olympia Press Correspondence: Maurice Girodias to Parker Tyler, 17 January 1961.

103 SCRC, Grove Press Records, Olympia Reader Files: Note from Gregory Corso to Grove editors, [*c*.10 August 1965]; Miles, *Beat Hotel*, p. 250 (for the quote).

104 Miles, *Beat Hotel*, p. 251.

105 *Ibid.*, p. 250; Gregory Corso, *The American Express* (no place: Olympia Press, 2005), ebook, loc. 497 (for the quote). The ebook says 'Olympia Press' but the publisher and place of publication of this edition are unknown. First published as Gregory Corso, *The American Express* (Paris: The Olympia Press, 1961).

106 SCRC, Grove Press Records, Olympia Press Files: Maurice Girodias to Barney Rosset, no date [1960].

107 William S. Burroughs, *The Ticket That Exploded: The Restored Text*, ed. and with an introduction by Oliver Harris (London: Penguin Books, 2014), p. 52. First published by the Olympia Press in Paris in 1962.

108 Miles, *Beat Hotel*, pp. 218–19.

109 Peter Parker, *Ackerley: A Life of J. R. Ackerley* (New York: Farrar, Straus and Giroux, 1989), p. 349.

110 Ableman, 'Faith at the first', p. 39.

111 SCRC, Austryn Wainhouse Papers, Correspondence, Box 7, Mary [Muffie] Wainhouse: Maurice Girodias to Muffie Wainhouse, 18 July [1956].

112 Alexander Trocchi, *The Fifth Volume of Frank Harris's My Life and Loves: An Irreverent Treatment by Alexander Trocchi* (London: The New English Library, 1966), p. 14. This edition, published during Girodias's brief association in England with the New English Library, and with some of its erotic content removed, has the distinct green cover and design of the Olympia Press Traveller's Companion Series; it is named as No. 108 in that series. The book was first published as Frank Harris [Alexander Trocchi], *My Life and Loves, Vol. 5* (Paris: The Olympia Press, 1954) in the Atlantic Library series, and then again in 1955, 1958 and 1959 in the Traveller's Companion Series (in which it was No. 10). For bibliographic details, see Kearney, *Paris Olympia Press* (2007), pp. 98–9, 121–3.

113 Frances Lengel [Alexander Trocchi], 'Foreword to Vol. 5 of Frank Harris' *Memoirs*' [for the Brandon House edition of the book, 1966], in Alexander Trocchi, *Invisible Insurrection of a Million Minds: A Trocchi Reader*, ed. Andrew Murray Scott (Edinburgh: Polygon, 1991), pp. 113–14, 222.

114 Frank Harris, *My Life and Loves*, ed. and with an introduction by John F. Gallagher (New York: Grove Press, 1976). First published in 1963.

115   Frank Harris [Alexander Trocchi], *My Life and Loves, Vol. 5* (Paris: The Olympia Press, 1959), p. 54.

116   *Ibid.*, pp. 61–3.

117   Humphrey Richardson [Michel Gall], *The Sexual Life of Robinson Crusoe* (New York: The Traveller's Companion INC., 1967), pp. 52, 66, 156. First published by the Olympia Press in Paris in 1955 and as *The Secret Life of Robinson Crusoe* in 1962. See Kearney, *Paris Olympia Press* (2007), pp. 125–6.

118   Ed [Edgar A.] Martin, *Busy Bodies* (no place: Olympia Press, 2015), ebook, loc. 202. The ebook says 'Olympia Press' but the publisher and place of publication of this edition are unknown. First published as Ed [Edgar A.] Martin, *Busy Bodies* (Paris: The Olympia Press, 1963, 1965). See also, Kearney, *Paris Olympia Press* (2007), pp. 242–3.

119   Gregory Stephensen, *Alias Akbar del Piombo: Annotations to the Life and Work of Norman Rubington* (Heidelberg: Ober-Limbo Verlag, 2022), p. 38; HRHRC, Marilyn Meeske Collection, Folder 25: Miriam Worms to Marilyn Meeske, 29 May [1965]. Ellipsis in original.

120   De St. Jorre, *Venus Bound*, p. 86; Calder, *Garden of Eros*, pp. 123, 126, 133, 143, 145, 161, 199, 200, 215; John Calder, *Pursuit: The Uncensored Memoirs of John Calder* (London: Calder publications, 2001), p. 342. One of the sources for Calder's *Garden of Eros* was the second volume of Girodias's autobiography *Les Jardins d'Eros* (Calder stole the book's title too), so the sexual bragging may be Girodias's; nonetheless, the preoccupation reads oddly.

121   SCRC, Austryn Wainhouse Papers, Correspondence, Box 7, Mary [Muffie] Wainhouse: Muffie Wainhouse to Christopher Logue, 20 May 1956.

122   Quoted in James Campbell, *Exiled in Paris: Richard Wright, James Baldwin, Samuel Beckett, and Others on the Left Bank* (New York: Scribner, 1995), pp. 158, 159.

123   Wainhouse, 'On translating Sade', 54.

124   Michael Fraenkel and Walter Lowenfels, *Anonymous: The Need for Anonymity* (Paris: Carrefour Press, 1930), p. 11.

125   Vladimir Nabokov to Carl R. Proffer, 26 September 1966, in Nabokov and Bruccoli, *Vladimir Nabokov: Selected Letters*, p. 391.

126   De St. Jorre, *Venus Bound*, p. 89.

127   *Ibid.*, pp. 52–86.

128   Kearney, *Paris Olympia Press* (2007), p. 120.

129   *Ibid.*, p. 111.

130 Maurice Girodias, 'Henry Jones', in Girodias, *Olympia Reader*, p. 388; Julian Barnes, 'One famous writer brought him a piece and was told it might serve as cat litter', *Guardian*, 17 April 1999: https://www.theguard ian.com/books/1999/apr/17/julianbarnes; Kearney, *Paris Olympia Press* (2007), p. 135.

131 SCRC, Grove Press Records, Olympia Reader Files: John Coleman to Harry Braverman, 10 December 1964.

132 Kearney, *Paris Olympia Press* (2007), p. 382.

133 Homer & Associates [Michel Gall], *A Bedside Odyssey* (London: The New English Library, 1966), p. 41. First published by the Olympia Press in Paris in 1962. The reader of the book's foreword, familiar with *Lolita*, should have been alerted by the involvement of a Colonel Humbert in the discovery.

134 B[ernhardt] Von Soda [Robert Waltz], *Abandon* (Paris: Ophelia Press, 1958); Kearney, *Paris Olympia Press* (2007), p, 389 (for the quote).

135 For the quote, William Talsman, *The Gaudy Image* (no place: Olympia Press, 2004), ebook, loc. 48. The ebook says 'Olympia Press' but the publisher and place of publication of this edition are unknown. First published by the Olympia Press in Paris in 1958.

136 SCRC, Grove Press Records, Olympia Reader Files: Correspondence between Harry Braverman and Ross Beckerman, 8 and 10 December 1964. For Kearney, see Kearney, *Paris Olympia Press* (2007), p. 387.

137 SCRC, Grove Press Records, Olympia Press Files: Maurice Girodias to Barney Rosset, 24 February 1959.

138 Kearney, *Paris Olympia Press* (2007), p. 94.

139 Count Palmiro Vicarion [Christopher Logue], *Count Palmiro Vicarion's Grand Grimoire of Bawdy Ballads and Limericks* (no place: Olympia Press, 2015), ebook, pp. 19, 107. The ebook says 'Olympia Press' but the publisher and place of publication of this edition are unknown. This edition combines the *Ballads* and *Limericks* books.

140 For the bibliographic details, see Kearney, *Paris Olympia Press* (2007), pp. 41–5, 47–52.

141 Gershon Legman, *The Horn Book* (New Hyde Park, NY: University Books, 1964), p. 450.

142 Kearney, *Paris Olympia Press* (2007), pp. 61–2, 269–70; Brian Busby, *A Gentleman of Pleasure: One Life of John Glassco, Poet, Memoirist, Translator, and Pornographer* (Montreal: McGill-Queen's University Press, 2011), pp. 158–61.

143 Willie Baron [Baird Bryant], *Play This Love With Me* (Cazador: Double N, 2019), p. 23. First published by the Olympia Press in Paris in 1955; Kearney, *Paris Olympia Press* (2007), pp. 110–11.

144 Kearney, *Paris Olympia Press* (2007), pp. 371–2.

145 De St. Jorre, *Venus Bound*, pp. 64–5.

146 Maurice Girodias, 'Hamilton Drake', in Girodias, *Olympia Reader*, pp. 369–73; Kearney, *Paris Olympia Press* (2007), pp. 398–9.

147 Niles Southern, *The Candy Men: The Rollicking Life and Times of the Notorious Novel Candy* (New York: Arcade Publishing, 2014), p. 112.

148 Kearney, *Paris Olympia Press* (1987), p. 42; Kearney, *Paris Olympia Press* (2007), p. 387.

149 Sandy P. Klein, 'The ragged-trousered pornographers', Nabokov-L listserv archives, The Nabokovian: International Vladimir Nabokov Society, 30 June 2003: https://thenabokovian.org/index.php/node/26066.

150 *Ibid.*

151 Kearney, *Paris Olympia Press* (2007), pp. 139–40, 146–7, 159–60, 212–14, 224, 227–8, 295–9. For Rubington as an artist, see Santa Bannon Fine Art Gallery, 'Norman Rubington full documentary produced by Santa Bannon Fine Art Gallery' [video], YouTube (uploaded 1 December 2016): https://www.youtube.com/watch?v=a4w35-g10f4.

152 Stephenson, 'Tête-à-tête with the Frog Prince', p. 128.

153 See Lisa Tremper Hanover, 'Norman Rubington (1921–1991) – Full Circle: New York, Paris, Rome, London, New York, July 14 – October 9, 2005', Traditional Fine Arts Organization: http://www.tfaoi.com/aa/6aa/6aa19.htm.

154 Alexander Trocchi, 'Postscript', in Alexander Trocchi, *Helen and Desire*, introduction by Jack Hirschman (North Hollywood: Brandon House, 1967), pp. 207–8, at p. 208.

155 Stephenson, 'Tête-à-tête with the Frog Prince', p. 128.

156 For Pearson, see Kearney, *Paris Olympia Press* (1987), pp. 59, 63; Kearney, *Paris Olympia Press* (2007), pp. 314, 317. For the quotes, see Meeske, 'Memoirs of a female pornographer', p. 113; Greta X [John Millington-Ward], *Whipsdom* (Paris: The Olympia Press, 1962), p. 54; Ruth Lesse [John Millington-Ward], *Lash* (Paris: The Olympia Press, 1962), p. 78.

157 De St. Jorre, *Venus Bound*, pp. 66–7; Kearney, *Paris Olympia Press* (2007), p. 380.

158 Meeske, 'Memoirs of a female pornographer', p. 112.

159 *Ibid.*

160 Harriet Sohmers Zwerling, *Abroad: An Expatriate's Diaries 1950–1959* (New York: Spuyten Duyvil, 2014), ebook, loc. 3952.

161 *Ibid.*, loc. 3977.

162 For Chester, see Norman Glass, 'The decline and fall of Alfred Chester', *Paris Review*, 71 (1977), 89–125; Edward Field, *The Man Who Would Marry Susan Sontag* (Madison: University of Wisconsin Press, 2005).

163 Sohmers Zwerling, *Abroad*, loc. 3977.

164 Harriet Daimler [Iris Owens] and Henry Crannach [Marilyn Meeske], *The Pleasure Thieves* (Covina: Collectors Publications, 1967), p. 136; Lisa Zeidner, 'Sex and the single woman: rediscovering the novels of Iris Owens', *American Scholar*, 30 November 2011: https://theameri canscholar.org/sex-and-the-single-woman/#.XnmciFBS9-U; Harriet Daimler [Iris Owens], *The New Organization* (Paris: The Olympia Press, 1962), p. 173.

165 Susan Sontag, *Reborn: Journals and Notebooks 1947–1963*, ed. D. Rieff (New York: Farrar, Straus and Giroux, 2008), p. 162.

166 Girodias, 'Introduction', p. 23.

167 Seaver, *Tender Hour of Twilight*, p. 12.

168 HRHRC, Marilyn Meeske Collection, Folder 25: Miriam Worms to Marilyn Meeske, 1 July [1961].

169 Claire Rabe, 'Sicily Enough', *Olympia, a Bimonthly Review from Paris*, 4 (1963), pp. 64–89, at p. 80.

170 Outlined in a letter, dated 1996, quoted in Kearney, *Paris Olympia Press* (2007), p. 239.

171 De St. Jorre, *Venus Bound*, pp. 90–1; Calder, *Garden of Eros*, pp. 133–6, 138–9, 143; S. E. Gontarski, 'Olympia and Grove: an interview with Maurice Girodias', *Review of Contemporary Fiction*, 10:3 (1990), 124–7, at 126.

172 J. P. Donleavy to A. K. Donoghue, 1 November 1955, in Bill Dunn (ed.), *The Ginger Man Letters: Correspondence by J. P. Donleavy, Gainor Crist, and A. K. Donoghue* (Dublin: Lilliput Press, 2018), p. 94.

173 SCRC, Austryn Wainhouse Papers, Correspondence, Box 7, Mary [Muffie] Wainhouse: Muffie Wainhouse to Austryn Wainhouse, 15 July 1958.

174 *Ibid.*, Muffie Wainhouse to Austryn Wainhouse, 3 April 1957.

175 Kearney, *Paris Olympia Press* (1987), pp. 43, 66.

176 Maurice Girodias, 'Ataullah Mardaan', in Girodias, *Olympia Reader*, pp. 304–5; de St. Jorre, *Venus Bound*, p. 63. The quote from *Kama Houri* is from Ataullah Mardaan, 'Kama Houri', in Girodias, *Olympia Reader*,

pp. 293–304, at p. 303. There is no record of her name in the permissions files in SCRC, Grove Press Records, Olympia Press Files.

177 De St. Jorre, *Venus Bound*, p. 84.

178 Peter Singleton-Gates and Maurice Girodias, *The Black Diaries* (Paris: The Olympia Press, 1959). This edition included Casement's 1911 cash ledger (misleadingly called a diary) but not the actual 1911 diary, which was later published by Jeffrey Dudgeon, *Roger Casement: The Black Diaries* (Belfast: Belfast Press, 2019), pp. 375–439 (first published in 2002).

179 Singleton-Gates and Girodias, *The Black Diaries*, p. 555.

180 John Sparrow, 'The end of Casement', *Times Literary Supplement*, 26 February 1960, pp. 121–3, at p. 121.

181 Maurice Girodias, 'Preface', in Maurice Girodias (ed.), *The Best of Olympia* (London: The New English Library, 1966), pp. vii–xii, at p. vii.

182 *Ibid.*, p. xi.

183 These examples come from *The New Olympia*, Number 3 (London: The Olympia Press, 1962); *Olympia*, Number 4 (Paris: The Olympia Press, 1963); and Girodias, *Best of Olympia*. For the magazine, see Maarten van Gageldonk, 'The representation of literary and cultural Paris in *Olympia Review* (1961–1963)', *L'Esprit Créateur*, 58:4 (2018), 15–30.

184 HRHRC, Marilyn Meeske Collection, Folder 2: Iris Owens to Marilyn Meeske, 12 February 1963.

185 HRHRC, Marilyn Meeske Collection, Folder 47: Lenny Bruce to Marilyn Meeske, 28 June 1962.

186 Gilbert Millstein, 'Something for the Hip Pocket', *New York Times*, 14 January 1962, pp. 28–9.

187 See Gregory Stephenson, 'Mutinous Jester: The Collage Novels of Akbar del Piombo', *Empty Mirror*, 31 January 2020: https://www.emptymirror books.com/literature/collage-novels-akbar-del-piombo.

188 Akbar del Piombo [Norman Rubington], *Fuzz Against Junk: The Saga of the Narcotics Brigade* (New York and Paris: The Citadel Press and the Olympia Press, 1961), no pagination.

189 Kearney, *Paris Olympia Press* (1987), pp. 31–2.

190 Maurice Girodias, 'John Cleland', in Girodias, *Olympia Reader*, pp. 255–7, at p. 257.

191 Kearney, *Paris Olympia Press* (2007), p. 53.

192 *Ibid.*, pp. 269–70; Busby, *Gentleman of Pleasure*, pp. 195–6.

193 SCRC, Austryn Wainhouse Papers, Diaries, Box 9: Austryn Wainhouse Diary, 21 July 1954.

194 Kearney, *Paris Olympia Press* (2007), p. 333. His Appendix A (pp. 329–49) deals with the bans.

195 Maurice Girodias, 'Pauline Réage', in Girodias, *Olympia Reader*, pp. 289–92, at p. 292.

196 *Ibid.*

197 Michael Barry Goodman, *Contemporary Literary Censorship: The Case History of Burroughs' Naked Lunch* (Metuchen: The Scarecrow Press, 1981), p. 106.

198 *Ibid.*, pp. 106–7.

199 Michael Barry Goodman, 'The customs' censorship of William S. Burroughs' *Naked Lunch*', *Critique*, 1 January 1980, pp. 92–104.

200 Rare Book and Manuscript Library, Columbia University Library (hereafter RBML), Barney Rosset Papers, Box 24, Folder 12, Subject Files: Maurice Girodias, Naked Lunch: Judith Schmidt to Edward Gross and Geoffrey Gunn, 26 October 1960.

201 The National Archives, Kew (hereafter NA), Home Office Papers, Supplementary, HO 302/4: Obscene Publications Bill 1955, Select Committee on Obscene Publications Evidence, Folder IPN 9/1/3 Memorandum of Evidence, Memo to C. F. Payne of Postal Services Department, 17 April 1957.

202 NA, Customs and Excise, CUST 49/4712, Folder 21721, Memo to House of Commons Select Committee on Obscene Publications Bill, 4 July 1957.

203 *Ibid.*, 'List of obscene matter seized [in] 1956'.

204 *Ibid.*, Memo to House of Commons Select Committee on Obscene Publications Bill, *c.*20 May 1957.

205 NA, Home Office Papers, HO 302/4, Folder IPN 9/1/3, 'Confidential: Olympia Press publications which have come to Home Office notice – October 1956: Travellers Companion Series' and 'Other Works'.

206 NA, Customs and Excise, CUST 49/4712, Folder 21721, Memo to House of Commons Select Committee on Obscene Publications Bill, *c.*20 May 1957.

207 See NA, Home Office Papers, HO 302/4, Folder IPN 9/1/3, House of Commons Select Committee on Obscene Publications Bill, Brief for Sir Frank Newsam on his Appearance before the Committee on Monday, 20th May [1957] (for the quote); Folder IPN 9/1/11, House of Commons Select Committee on Obscene Publications Bill, Supplementary Evidence, 'Details of communications between the Home Office and the French Central Authority in connection with the Olympia Press, Paris' [1957].

208   The best description of this venture is in de St. Jorre, *Venus Bound*, pp. 257–62.

209   See the discussion in Chapter 6 of this volume.

210   For Donleavy's revenge, see de St. Jorre, *Venus Bound*, pp. 281–9.

211   RBML, Barney Rosset Papers, Box 24, Folder 15, Subject Files: Maurice Girodias, Olympia Press: Barney Rosset to Maurice Girodias, 20 July 1965.

212   For some detail, see Girodias, 'Introduction', p. 26.

213   HRHRC, Marilyn Meeske Collection, Folder 2: Iris Owens to Marilyn Meeske, no date [1965].

214   HRHRC, Marilyn Meeske Collection, Folder 25: Miriam Worms to Marilyn Meeske, no date [1965].

215   Maurice Girodias, 'Commentary', in Maurice Girodias (ed.), *The New Olympia Reader* (New York: Black Watch, 1970), pp. 852–91, at p. 861. Ellipsis in original.

4 Repurposed pornography: the role of erotic classics

1   Patrick J. Kearney, *The Paris Olympia Press*, ed. Angus Carroll (Liverpool: Liverpool University Press, 2007), pp. 260–1.

2   *Ibid.*, pp. 94–5, 129–31.

3   *Ibid.*, p. 34; Alfred Musset, *Gamiani* (no place: E-Bookarama, 2020), ebook, loc. 25.

4   Kearney, *Paris Olympia Press* (2007), pp. 61–2; Brian Busby, *A Gentleman of Pleasure: One Life of John Glassco, Poet, Memoirist, Translator, and Pornographer* (Montreal: McGill-Queen's University Press, 2011), pp. 158–61.

5   Aubrey Beardsley and John Glassco, *Under the Hill* (Paris: The Olympia Press, 1959), p. 19.

6   Anonymous, *Teleny or The Reverse of the Medal* (Paris: The Olympia Press, 1958), p. 112. First published in 1893.

7   *Ibid.*, p. 104.

8   *Ibid.*, pp. 115–16.

9   See Colette Colligan, *A Publisher's Paradise: Expatriate Literary Culture in Paris, 1890–1960* (Amherst: University of Massachusetts Press, 2013), pp. 212–44.

10   *Ibid.*, p. 228. For some discussions of *Teleny* and its authorship, see John McRae, 'Introduction', in Oscar Wilde and Others, *Teleny*, ed. John

McCrae (London: GMP Publishers, 1986), pp. 7–24; Robert Gray and Christopher Keep, '"An uninterrupted current": homoeroticism and collaborative authorship in *Teleny*', in Marjorie Stone (ed.), *Couplings: Writing Couples, Collaborators, and the Construction of Authorship* (Madison: University of Wisconsin Press, 2006), pp. 193–208; John D. Stratford, '*Teleny* – Wilde or not?', *The Wildean*, 48 (2016), 104–21; Will Visconti, '*Teleny*: a tale of two cities', in Leila Kassir and Richard Espley (eds), *Queer Between the Covers: Histories of Queer Publishing and Publishing Queer Voices* (London: University of London Press, 2012), pp. 61–75.

11 Kearney, *Paris Olympia Press* (2007), pp. 33, 208–10.

12 Richard Seaver, *The Tender Hour of Twilight*, ed. Jeannette Seaver (New York: Farrar, Straus and Giroux, 2012), p. 198.

13 Quoted by Andrew Murray Scott, *Alexander Trocchi: The Making of a Monster* (Kilkerran: Kennedy & Boyd, 2012), p. 55.

14 Kearney, *Paris Olympia Press* (2007), pp. 29–31, 208–10.

15 *Ibid.*, pp. 256–8, 384.

16 Lynn Hunt, 'Introduction: obscenity and the origins of modernity, 1500–1800', in Lynn Hunt (ed.), *The Invention of Pornography: Obscenity and the Origins of Modernity, 1500–1800* (New York: Zone Books, 1993), pp. 9–45, at p. 10.

17 Robert Darnton, 'Sex for thought', in Kim M. Phillips and Barry Reay (eds), *Sexualities in History: A Reader* (New York: Routledge, 2002), pp. 203–21, at p. 203. For pornography before pornography, see Kim M. Phillips and Barry Reay, 'Before pornography', in *Sex before Sexuality* (Cambridge: Polity, 2011), pp. 112–33.

18 Darnton, 'Sex for thought', p. 214.

19 Marquis de Sade, *120 Days of Sodom*, trans. and with an introduction by Will McMorran and Thomas Wynn (London: Penguin Classics, 2016), p. 319.

20 Randolph Trumbach describes the book as 'principally aimed at sexually arousing [its] reader' and establishing 'in England the modern pornographic genre': Randolph Trumbach, 'Erotic fantasy and male libertinism in Enlightenment England', in Hunt, *Invention of Pornography*, pp. 253–82, at p. 253. For *pornographe*, see Walter Kendrick, *The Secret Museum: Pornography in Modern Culture* (New York: Viking, 1987), p. 17. Discussion of the pornographic nature of *Memoirs of a Woman of Pleasure* will occur later.

21 Maurice Girodias, 'Introduction', in Maurice Girodias (ed.), *The Olympia Reader* (New York: Grove Press, 1965), pp. 11–29, at p. 18.

22 *Ibid.*, pp. 19–20.

23 Alyce Mahon, *The Marquis de Sade and the Avant-Garde* (Princeton: Princeton University Press, 2020), p. 5.

24 Quoted in *ibid.*, p. 93.

25 Marquis de Sade, *Justine, Philosophy in the Bedroom and Other Writings*, compiled and trans. by Richard Seaver and Austryn Wainhouse (New York: Grove Press, 1965), p. 496 (*Justine*).

26 *Ibid.*, pp. 241, 272 (*Philosophy in the Bedroom*).

27 Sade, *120 Days of Sodom*, p. 178.

28 Sade, *Justine, Philosophy in the Bedroom and Other Writings*, pp. 229–30 (*Philosophy in the Bedroom*).

29 *Ibid.*, p. 191 (*Philosophy in the Bedroom*).

30 *Ibid.*, pp. 207–8 (*Philosophy in the Bedroom*).

31 Beauregard de Farniente, *The Adventures of Father Silas* (Paris: Ophelia Press, 1958), p. 47.

32 John Cleland, *Memoirs of a Woman of Pleasure*, ed. with an introduction and notes by Peter Sabor (Oxford: Oxford University Press, 2008), p. 131. First published in London, 1748–9.

33 Sade, *Justine, Philosophy in the Bedroom and Other Writings*, p. 273 (*Philosophy in the Bedroom*).

34 Farniente, *Adventures of Father Silas*, pp. 120–1.

35 Darnton, 'Sex for thought', p. 213.

36 Musset, *Gamiani*, loc. 696.

37 Sade, *Justine, Philosophy in the Bedroom and Other Writings*, p. 488 (*Justine*).

38 Cleland, *Memoirs of a Woman of Pleasure*, pp. 11–12.

39 *Ibid.*, pp. 11, 76, 77, 82, 116.

40 *Ibid.*, pp. xix, 26, 33, 40, 76, 116.

41 Scott J. Juengel, 'Doing things with Fanny Hill', *ELH*, 76:2 (2009), 419–46, at 425.

42 Cleland, *Memoirs of a Woman of Pleasure*, pp. 42–3.

43 *Ibid.*, p. 91.

44 Quoted in Charles Rembar, *The End of Obscenity: The Trials of Lady Chatterley, Tropic of Cancer and Fanny Hill* (New York: Random House, 1968), p. 291.

45 Marquis de Sade, *Juliette*, trans. Austryn Wainhouse (New York: Grove Press, 1968), p. 1006.

46 *Ibid.*, p. 662.

47 Kathryn Norberg, 'The libertine whore: prostitution in French pornography from Margot to Juliette', in Hunt, *Invention of Pornography*, pp. 225–52, at p. 250.

48 Angela Carter, *The Sadeian Woman: An Exercise in Cultural History* (London: Virago Press, 1979), p. 27.

49 Peter Lewys [Pierre Louÿs], *The She-Devils* (Paris: The Olympia Press, 1965), p. 38. It was published under the Ophelia Press imprint.

50 *Ibid.*, pp. 129–30.

51 *Ibid.*, p. 149.

52 John Phillips, *Forbidden Fictions: Pornography and Censorship in Twentieth-Century French Literature* (London: Pluto Press, 1999), p. 43.

53 Jean Marie Goulemot, *Forbidden Texts: Erotic Literature and its Readers in Eighteenth-Century France*, trans. James Simpson (Philadelphia: University of Pennsylvania Press, 1994), p. 42.

54 Guillaume Apollinaire, *Two Novels by Guillaume Apollinaire* (Paris: The Olympia Press, 1959), pp. 165–6 (*Memoirs of a Young Rakehell*).

55 Sade, *120 Days of Sodom*, p. 270.

56 Musset, *Gamiani*, loc. 436.

57 Steven Marcus, *The Other Victorians: A Study of Sexuality and Pornography in Mid-Nineteenth-Century England* (New York: Basic Books, 1966), p. 270.

58 Sade, *120 Days of Sodom*, p. 87.

59 *Ibid.*, p. 86.

60 Sade, *Justine, Philosophy in the Bedroom and Other Writings*, pp. 570, 620 (*Justine*). Ellipsis in original.

61 Carter, *Sadeian Woman*, p. 50.

62 Sade, *Justine, Philosophy in the Bedroom and Other Writings*, p. 233 (*Philosophy in the Bedroom*). Ellipsis in original.

63 *Ibid.*, p. 257 (*Philosophy in the Bedroom*).

64 Apollinaire, *Two Novels*, p. 8 (*The Debauched Hospodar*).

65 Lewys, *She-Devils*, p. 49.

66 *Ibid.*, p. 50.

67 Sade, *120 Days of Sodom*, p. 135.

68 Restif de La Bretonne, *Pleasures and Follies of a Good-Natured Libertine: Being an English Rendering of L'Anti Justine* (Paris: Olympia Press, 1956), p. 37.

69 Sade, *Justine, Philosophy in the Bedroom and Other Writings*, p. 618 (Justine).

70 Apollinaire, *Two Novels*, p. 118 (*The Debauched Hospodar*).

71 Sade, *Justine, Philosophy in the Bedroom and Other Writings*, p. 277 (*Philosophy in the Bedroom*) and p. 512 (Justine). Ellipsis in original.

For libertinism and sodomy, see James A. Steintrager, *The Autonomy of Pleasure: Libertines, License, and Sexual Revolution* (New York: Columbia University Press, 2016), pp. 128–69.

72 Sade, *120 Days of Sodom*, p. 48.

73 Apollinaire, *Two Novels*, p. 44 (*The Debauched Hospodar*).

74 Frans Amelinckx, 'Apollinaire's *Les Onze Mille Verges*: humor and pornography', *West Virginia Philological Papers*, 29 (1983) 8–15, at 10.

75 Apollinaire, *Two Novels*, p. 25 (*The Debauched Hospodar*).

76 Sade, *Justine, Philosophy in the Bedroom and Other Writings*, p. 202 (*Philosophy in the Bedroom*).

77 Lewys, *She-Devils*, p. 210.

78 *Ibid.*

79 See the ebook version, Pierre Louÿs, *The She-Devils* (New York: Elektron Books, 2012). In the ebook 'cornholing' is rendered as 'buttfucking'.

80 Sade, *Justine, Philosophy in the Bedroom and Other Writings*, p. 257 (*Philosophy in the Bedroom*). Ellipsis in original.

81 Lewys, *She-Devils*, p. 169.

82 Steintrager, *Autonomy of Pleasure*, p. 171. He discusses the role of the clitoris in libertine literature on pp. 170–99.

83 Sade, *Justine, Philosophy in the Bedroom and Other Writings*, pp. 204, 248 (*Philosophy in the Bedroom*).

84 Sade, *120 Days of Sodom*, p. 57.

85 Musset, *Gamiani*, loc. 590.

86 Apollinaire, *Two Novels*, pp. 23, 62–3 (*The Debauched Hospodar*).

87 Sade, *120 Days of Sodom*, p. 342.

88 Farniente, *Adventures of Father Silas*, p. 67.

89 Apollinaire, *Two Novels*, p. 204 (*Memoirs of a Young Rakehell*).

90 Quoted in Amy S. Wyngaard, *Bad Books: Rétif de la Bretonne, Sexuality, and Pornography* (Newark: University of Delaware Press, 2013), p. 62. She discusses incest on pp. 61–3.

91 La Bretonne, *Pleasures and Follies of a Good-Natured Libertine*, p. 19.

92 *Ibid.*, p. 21.

93 Sade, *120 Days of Sodom*, p. 60.

94 Cleland, *Memoirs of a Woman of Pleasure*, p. 162; Rembar, *End of Obscenity*, p. 260.

95 Sade, *Justine, Philosophy in the Bedroom and Other Writings*, p. 265 (*Philosophy in the Bedroom*).

96 Sade, *120 Days of Sodom*, pp. 60, 67.

97 Apollinaire, *Two Novels*, pp. 20, 85, 113 (*The Debauched Hospodar*).

98 Sade, *Justine, Philosophy in the Bedroom and Other Writings*, p. 269 (*Philosophy in the Bedroom*). Ellipses in original.

99 Lewys, *She-Devils*, p. 54. Ellipsis in original.

100 Sade, *120 Days of Sodom*, p. 40.

101 Apollinaire, *Two Novels*, p. 52 (*The Debauched Hospodar*).

102 *Ibid.*, p. 19 (*The Debauched Hospodar*).

103 Goulemot, *Forbidden Texts*, p. 72.

104 Sade, *120 Days of Sodom*, p. 41.

105 Lewys, *She-Devils*, pp. 51–2.

106 Sade, *Juliette*, p. 1007.

107 Harriet Daimler [Iris Owens], *The New Organization* (Paris: The Olympia Press, 1962), pp. 105, 150.

108 Sade, *120 Days of Sodom*, p. 80.

109 Lewys, *She-Devils*, p. 91.

110 Goulemot, *Forbidden Texts*, p. 66.

111 Sade, *Juliette*, p. 1186.

112 Amelinckx, 'Apollinaire's *Les Onze Mille Verges*', 13.

113 Peter Michelson, *Speaking the Unspeakable: A Poetics of Obscenity* (Albany: State University of New York Press, 1993), p. 13.

114 Lewys, *She-Devils*, p. 72.

115 *Ibid.*, p. 68.

116 Edmund Wilson, 'The documents on the Marquis de Sade', *New Yorker*, 18 September 1965, pp. 175–97, 201–24, quote at p. 176.

117 Lucienne Frappier-Mazur, 'Truth and the obscene word in eighteenth-century French pornography', in Hunt, *Invention of Pornography*, pp. 203–21, at p. 206.

118 Wyngaard, *Bad Books*, p. 62.

119 All discussed in Frappier-Mazur, 'Truth and the obscene word'.

120 Goulemot, *Forbidden Texts*, pp. 110–11.

121 Apollinaire, *Two Novels*, pp. 60–1 (*The Debauched Hospodar*). Ellipses in original.

122 Goulemot, *Forbidden Texts*, p. 43.

123 *Ibid.*, pp. 30–50.

124 *Ibid.*, pp. 36–41.

125 La Bretonne, 'Introduction', in *Pleasures and Follies of a Good-Natured Libertine*, no page number. Ellipsis in original.

126 Sade, *120 Days of Sodom*, p. 86.

127 Apollinaire, *Two Novels*, p. 16 (*The Debauched Hospodar*).

128 *Ibid.*, p. 104.

129 Sade, *Juliette*, p. 582.

130 Sade, *120 Days of Sodom*, pp. 124–5. Ellipsis in original.

131 *Ibid.*, p. 342.

132 *Ibid.*, p. 271.

133 *Ibid.*, p. 280. Ellipsis in original.

134 *Ibid.*, pp. 156, 158, 161, and quotes at p. 296.

135 Phillips, *Forbidden Fictions*, p. 34.

136 *Ibid.*, p. 43.

137 Goulemot, *Forbidden Texts*, p. 91.

138 Lucienne Frappier-Mazur, *Writing the Orgy: Power and Parody in Sade*, trans. Gillian C. Gill (Philadelphia: University of Pennsylvania Press, 1996), p. 2.

139 Susan Sontag, 'The pornographic imagination', in Susan Sontag, *Essays of the 1960s & 70s*, ed. David Rieff (New York: The Library of America, 2013), pp. 320–52, at p. 334.

140 Darnton, 'Sex for thought', p. 221.

141 Hunt, 'Introduction', p. 21.

142 Apollinaire, *Two Novels*, p. 10 (*The Debauched Hospodar*).

143 Phillips, *Forbidden Fictions*, p. 2.

144 Annie Le Brun, *Sade: A Sudden Abyss*, trans. Camille Naish (San Francisco: City Light Books, 1990), p. 9. First published in French in 1986.

145 Sade, *Juliette*, pp. 544–5.

146 Mahon, *Marquis de Sade and the Avant-Garde*, p. 17. Mahon also cites the case of the heart.

147 Sade, *120 Days of Sodom*, p. 84.

148 The point about children is also made by the editors of the Penguin edition: *Ibid.*, p. 23.

149 Roger Shattuck, 'The Divine Marquis', in his *Forbidden Knowledge from Prometheus to Pornography* (New York: St. Martin's Press, 1996), pp. 227–99, quotes at pp. 268, 299.

150 Carter, *Sadeian Woman*, p. 19.

151 Michelson, *Speaking the Unspeakable*, p. 129.

152 Figures from Shattuck, 'Divine Marquis', p. 283.

153 Steintrager, *Autonomy of Pleasure*, p. 280.

5 Dirty books

1   Anaïs Nin, 'Preface', *Delta of Venus* (London: Penguin, 2000), p. xiv. First published in 1977.

2   Michael Perkins, *The Secret Record: Modern Erotic Literature* (New York: William Morrow, 1976), p. 75.

3   Alexander Trocchi, 'Postscript', in Alexander Trocchi, *Helen and Desire* (North Hollywood: Brandon House, 1967), pp. 207–8, at p. 208. First published as Frances Lengel [Alexander Trocchi], *Helen and Desire* (Paris: The Olympia Press, 1954, 1962).

4   Gregory Stephenson, 'Tête-à-tête with the Frog Prince: conversations with Maurice Girodias', in his *Points of Intersection* (Thy, Denmark: Eyecorner Press, 2018), pp. 114–34, at p. 121.

5   Peter O'Neil, *The Corpse Wore Grey* (Paris: The Olympia Press, 1962), pp. 34, 35.

6   Marcus van Heller [John Stevenson], *Adam and Eve* (no place: Olympia Press, 2015), ebook, loc. 704. The ebook says 'Olympia Press' but the publisher and place of publication of this edition are unknown. First published by the Olympia Press in Paris in 1961.

7   Marcus van Heller [John Stevenson], *Kidnap* (no place: Olympia Press, 2003), ebook, p. 109. The ebook says 'Olympia Press' but the publisher and place of publication of this edition are unknown. First published by the Olympia Press in Paris in 1961.

8   John de St. Jorre, *Venus Bound: The Erotic Voyage of the Olympia Press and Its Writers* (New York: Random House, 1994), p. 76.

9   Patrick J. Kearney, *A Bibliography of the Publications of the New York Olympia Press* (Santa Rosa: privately printed, 1988), pp. 60–1

10 De St. Jorre, *Venus Bound*, p. 76.

11 Marcus van Heller, *The House of Borgia. Two Volumes in One* (North Hollywood: Brandon House, 1967). First published by the Olympia Press in Paris in 1957 (vol. 1) and 1958 (vol. 2).

12 Maurice Girodias, 'Marcus van Heller', in Maurice Girodias (ed.), *The Olympia Reader* (New York: Grove Press, 1965), pp. 97–8.

13 De St. Jorre, *Venus Bound*, p. 76.

14 *Ibid.*, p. 83.

15 Marcus van Heller, *The Loins of Amon* (New York: Carroll & Graf, 1983). First published by the Olympia Press in Paris in 1955. For the donkey scene, see pp. 139–45; for the sacred baboons, see pp. 6–10 and 186–7; for the quote, see p. 9.

16   Count Palmiro Vicarion [Christopher Logue], *Lust* (no place: Olympia Press, 2015), ebook, loc. 386. The ebook says 'Olympia Press' but the publisher and place of publication of this edition are unknown. First published by the Olympia Press in Paris in 1954.

17   *Ibid.*, loc. 524.

18   *Ibid.*, loc. 617.

19   *Ibid.*, loc. 632.

20   *Ibid.*, locs 535, 627.

21   Robert Desmond [Robert Desmond Thompson], *Iniquity* (no place: Olympia Press, 2004), ebook, p. 17. The ebook says 'Olympia Press' but the publisher and place of publication of this edition are unknown. First published by the Olympia Press in Paris in 1958.

22   *Ibid.*, p. 23.

23   *Ibid.*, p. 123.

24   Robert Desmond [Robert Desmond Thompson], *Without Violence* (Paris: The Olympia Press, 1962), p. 115.

25   Robert Desmond [Robert Desmond Thompson], *An Adult's Story* (no place: Olympia Press, 2015), ebook, loc. 1132. The ebook says 'Olympia Press' but the publisher and place of publication of this edition are unknown. First published by the Olympia Press in Paris in 1954. For Desmond's real name, see Patrick J. Kearney, *The Paris Olympia Press*, ed. Angus Carroll (Liverpool: Liverpool University Press, 2007), p. 119.

26   Desmond, *Iniquity*, p. 211.

27   Willie Baron [Baird Bryant], *Play This Love With Me* (Cazador: Double N, 2019), pp. 11, 14, 21. First published by the Olympia Press in Paris in 1955.

28   *Ibid.*, p. 33.

29   *Ibid.*, pp. 54–5.

30   *Ibid.*, p. 64.

31   Steven Marcus, *The Other Victorians: A Study of Sexuality and Pornography in Mid-Nineteenth-Century England* (New York: Basic Books, 1966), p. 279.

32   Van Heller, *Kidnap*, p. 109.

33   *Ibid.*, p. 37.

34   Van Heller, *Adam and Eve*, loc. 1384.

35   Van Heller, *Kidnap*, p. 37.

36   Van Heller, *Adam and Eve*, loc. 182.

37   Van Heller, *Kidnap*, pp. 37–8.

38   Marcus, *Other Victorians*, pp. 272–3.

39 B[ernhardt] Von Soda [Robert Waltz], *The Beaten and the Hungry* (Paris: The Olympia Press, 1962), pp. 7, 24.

40 *Harriet Marwood, Governess* was published by Grove in the guise of an anonymous Victorian novel: Anonymous, *Harriet Marwood, Governess* (New York: Grove Press, 1967).

41 This publishing history is outlined in Brian Busby, *A Gentleman of Pleasure: One Life of John Glassco, Poet, Memoirist, Translator, and Pornographer* (Montreal: McGill-Queen's University Press, 2011), pp. 159–70.

42 John Glassco, *The English Governess*, with an introduction by Michael Gnarowski (Ottawa: The Golden Dog Press, 2000), p. 5. Originally published as Miles Underwood, *The English Governess* (Paris: The Olympia Press, 1960), and *Under the Birch: The Story of an English Governess* (Paris: Ophelia Press, 1965). See Kearney, *Paris Olympia Press* (2007), pp. 269–70. The Ottawa version is based on the 1965 Ophelia Press edition: see Michael Gnarowski, 'Introduction', Glassco, *English Governess*, loc. 138.

43 Glassco, *English Governess*, pp. 12–13.

44 *Ibid.*, p. 24.

45 *Ibid.*, p. 48.

46 *Ibid.*, p. 28.

47 *Ibid.*, p. 31.

48 *Ibid.*, p. 56.

49 *Ibid.*, p. 127.

50 *Ibid.*, p. 131.

51 *Ibid.*, p. 128.

52 Busby, *Gentleman of Pleasure*, p. 161.

53 Thomas Peacham [Philip Oxman], *The Watcher and the Watched* (New York: The Olympia Press, 1967), p. 118. First published by the Olympia Press in Paris in 1954.

54 *Ibid.*, p. 175.

55 *Ibid.*, pp. 90, 92.

56 *Ibid.*, p. 166.

57 *Ibid.*, pp. 134, 197.

58 Marcus, *Other Victorians*, p. 273.

59 Diane Bataille, *The Whip Angels* (New York: Elektron Books, 2013), ebook, loc. 631. First published as XXX [Diane Bataille], *The Whip Angels* (Paris: The Olympia Press, 1955).

60 *Ibid.*, locs 366–71.

61   Edith Templeton, *Gordon* (London: Penguin Books, 2012), p. 17. First published as Louise Walbrook [Edith Templeton], *Gordon* (London: The New English Library, 1966).

62   *Ibid.*, p. 20.

63   *Ibid.*, pp. 56, 102.

64   *Ibid.*, p. 58.

65   *Ibid.*, p. 176.

66   *Ibid.*, p. 58.

67   *Ibid.*, p. 59.

68   Maria Russo, 'Remembrance of flings past', *New York Times Magazine*, 17 February 2002, pp. 46–9, at p. 48.

69   Templeton, *Gordon*, p. 66.

70   *Ibid.*, p. 146.

71   Russo, 'Remembrance of flings past', p. 48.

72   From an excerpt of Harriet Daimler [Iris Owens] and Henry Crannach [Marilyn Meeske], *The Pleasure Thieves*, in Girodias, *Olympia Reader*, pp. 169–77, at p. 176.

73   John Ferrone, 'The making of *Delta of Venus*', *A Café in Space: The Anaïs Nin Literary Journal*, 7 (2010), 53–60, at 54.

74   *Ibid.*, 55–6.

75   *Ibid.*, 56; Nin, *Delta of Venus*, p. v: Table of contents. For a list of the original typescripts at UCLA, see Finding Aid for the Anais Nin Papers, *c.*1910–1977: http://oac.cdlib.org/findaid/ark:/13030/kt3489p4x9.

76   Ferrone, 'Making of *Delta of Venus*', 56.

77   Anaïs Nin, *Auletris: Erotica by Anaïs Nin* (San Antonio: Sky Blue Press, 2016), pp. 27, 36, 38, 24, 42.

78   *Ibid.*, p. 18. Ellipsis in original.

79   *Ibid.*

80   Smaro Kamboureli, 'Discourse and intercourse, design and desire in the erotica of Anaïs Nin', *Journal of Modern Literature*, 11:1 (1984), 143–58, at 152.

81   *Ibid.*

82   *Ibid.*, 151.

83   Anaïs Nin, *Henry and June* (London: Penguin, 2017) p. 49. First published in 1986.

84   Anna Powell, 'Heterotica: The 1000 tiny sexes of Anaïs Nin', in Frida Beckman (ed.), *Deleuze and Sex* (Edinburgh: Edinburgh University Press, 2011), pp. 50–68, at p. 63. See also Sonya Blades, 'The feminine erotic: écriture feminine in Anaïs Nin's erotica', *A Café in Space: The Anaïs Nin Literary Journal*, 8 (2011), 38–56, at 45–7.

85   Nin, *Delta of Venus*, p. xiii.

86   Nin, *Henry and June*, p. 92.

87   *Ibid.*, p. 109.

88   Department of Special Collections, Charles E. Young Research Library, UCLA, Anaïs Nin Papers, Box 21, Folder 1: Anaïs Nin, Diary 63, Mon Journal: House of Death & Escape, 8 December 1940 – 1 November 1941, 13 November 1940, p. 39. (Although the diary ostensibly begins in December 1940, the November dating is correct.)

89   Anaïs Nin, *Fire: From 'A Journal of Love', the Unexpurgated Diary of Anaïs Nin, 1934–1937* (New York: Harcourt, Inc., 1995), p. 245.

90   *Ibid.*, p. 230.

91   *Ibid.*

92   *Ibid.*, p. 231.

93   *Ibid.*, p. 214.

94   Nin, *Auletris*, p. 23.

95   Nin, *Delta of Venus*, pp. 19, 20.

96   Nin, *Auletris*, pp. 27–8. Ellipsis in original.

97   From 'Pierre' in Nin, *Delta of Venus*, p. 216.

98   Angela M. Carter, 'Feminist smut(?): a study of Nin's erotica', *A Café in Space: The Anaïs Nin Literary Journal*, 6 (2009), 92–108, at 107.

99   Powell, 'Heterotica', pp. 50–68.

100 Edmund Miller, 'Erato throws a curve: Anaïs Nin and the elusive feminine voice in erotica', in Suzanne Nalbantian (ed.), *Anaïs Nin: Literary Perspectives* (London: Palgrave Macmillan, 1997), pp. 164–84.

101 Kamboureli, 'Discourse and intercourse', 156, 158.

102 Richard Seaver, *The Tender Hour of Twilight*, ed. Jeannette Seaver (New York: Farrar, Straus and Giroux, 2012), p. 357.

103 Special Collections Research Center, Syracuse University Libraries, Grove Press Records, Story of O Files: Eric Larrabee, 'Apropos D'O' [1965].

104 Pauline Réage and Régine Deforges, *Confessions of O: Conversations with Pauline Réage by Régine Deforges*, trans. Sabine d'Estrée (New York: The Viking Press, 1979), p. 73.

105 John de St. Jorre, 'The Unmasking of O', *New Yorker*, 1 August 1994, pp. 42–50, at p. 43.

106 *Ibid.*, p. 45.

107 Pauline Réage, *Story of O Part Two*, preceded by 'A Girl in Love', trans. Sabine d'Estrée (London: Transworld Publishers, n.d.), ebook, pp. 9–10 ('A Girl in Love'). The book was first published in English as *Return to*

the *Château: Story of O Part II* (New York: Grove Press, 1971). It was written at the same time as *Story of O* but published later (1969). *A Girl in Love* was written in 1968.

108 Quoted in de St. Jorre, *Venus Bound*, p. 225. Emphasis in original.

109 Alyce Mahon, *The Marquis de Sade and the Avant-Garde* (Princeton: Princeton University Press, 2020), pp. 124–79: '*Story of O*: Slave and Suffragette of the Whip', quote at p. 134.

110 Jean Paulhan, 'A slave's revolt: an essay on *The Story of O*', in Pauline Réage, *Story of O* (London: Corgi Books, 1995), pp. 265–87, at p. 270.

111 Réage, *Story of O*, pp. 237–8.

112 *Ibid.*, pp. 63, 116, 246.

113 *Ibid.*, p. 146.

114 *Ibid.*, p. 118.

115 *Ibid.*, p. 117.

116 John Phillips, *Forbidden Fictions: Pornography and Censorship in Twentieth-Century French Literature* (London: Pluto Press, 1999), p. 103.

117 Réage, *Story of O*, p. 25.

118 Mahon, *Marquis de Sade and the Avant-Garde*, p. 126.

119 Réage, *Story of O*, p. 200.

120 Réage, *Story of O Part Two*, p. 10.

121 Réage, *Story of O*, p. 48.

122 *Ibid.*, p. 240.

123 Réage and Deforges, *Confessions of O*, p. 144.

124 For Aury and Thomas, see Dorothy Kaufmann, 'The story of two women: Dominique Aury and Edith Thomas', *Signs*, 23:4 (1998), 883–905.

125 *Ibid.*, 892.

126 Réage, *Story of O*, p. 234.

127 *Ibid.*, p. 251.

128 *Ibid.*, p. 130.

129 *Ibid.*, pp. 57, 149.

130 Susan Sontag, 'The pornographic imagination', in Susan Sontag, *Essays of the 1960s & 70s*, ed. David Rieff (New York: The Library of America, 2013), pp. 320–52, at pp. 340, 348.

131 Réage and Deforges, *Confessions of O*, p. 140.

132 Phillips, *Forbidden Fictions*, pp. 95–7.

133 Stephenson, 'Name upon name: encountering Pauline Réage/Dominique Aury/Anne Desclos', in his *Points of Intersection*, pp. 82–103, quote at p. 85.

134 Réage, *Story of O Part Two*, p. 11.

135 Malcolm Nesbit [Alfred Chester], *The Chariot of Flesh* (Paris: The Olympia Press, 1961), p. 23. First published in 1955.

136 *Ibid.*, p. 24.

137 *Ibid.*, p. 22.

138 *Ibid.*, p. 75. Ellipsis in original.

139 *Ibid.*, p. 66.

140 Marcus, *Other Victorians*, pp. 194–6, 277–81.

141 Nesbit, *Chariot of Flesh*, pp. 89, 95, 118–19, 151.

142 Nile Southern, *The Candy Men: The Rollicking Life and Times of the Notorious Novel Candy* (New York: Arcade Publishing, 2014), p. 237.

143 Lee Server, 'Introduction: an interview with Terry Southern', in Nile Southern and Josh Alan Friedman (eds), *Now Dig This: The Unspeakable Writings of Terry Southern 1950–1995* (New York: Grove Press, 2001), pp. 1–14, at p. 1.

144 *Ibid.* Emphasis in original.

145 Southern, *Candy Men*, p. 238.

146 Terry Southern and Mason Hoffenberg, *Candy* (New York: Grove Press, 1994), p. 93. First published as Maxwell Kenton [Terry Southern and Mason Hoffenberg], *Candy* (Paris: The Olympia Press, 1958).

147 Kearney, *Bibliography of the Publications of the New York Olympia Press*, p. vi.

148 Marilyn Meeske, 'Memoirs of a female pornographer', *Esquire*, April 1965, pp. 112–15, at p. 115.

149 Eberhard and Phyllis Kronhausen, *Pornography and the Law: The Psychology of Erotic Realism and Hard Core Pornography* (New York: Ballantine Books, 1964), pp. 379–84.

150 Akbar del Piombo [Norman Rubington], *Who Pushed Paula?* (Paris: The Olympia Press, 1967), p. 12. First published in 1955. Also published as *Paula the Piquôse*: see Akbar del Piombo [Norman Rubington], *The Fetish Crowd: Three Novels* (Paris: The Olympia Press, 1965).

151 Del Piombo, *Who Pushed Paula?*, p. 74.

152 *Ibid.*, pp. 144–5.

153 Akbar del Piombo [Norman Rubington], *The Traveller's Companion* (Paris: The Olympia Press, 1957) was also published as *The Double-Bellied Companion*, in del Piombo, *The Fetish Crowd*.

154 Akbar del Piombo [Norman Rubington], *The Double-Bellied Companion*, p. 39.

155 *Ibid.*, p. 32.

156 Marcus, *Other Victorians*, pp. 277, 281.

157   Calculated from Akbar del Piombo [Norman Rubington], *The Traveller's Companion (The Double-Bellied Companion)* (no place: Olympia Press, 2003), ebook. The ebook says 'Olympia Press' but the publisher and place of publication of this edition are unknown.

158   James Sherwood, *Stradella* (London: The New English Library, 1966), pp. 13, 14, 17. First published by the Olympia Press in Paris in 1962.

159   This history is outlined in a letter, dated 1996, quoted in Kearney, *Paris Olympia Press* (2007), pp. 237–9.

160   Maurice Girodias to Samuel Beckett, 17 September 1986, in Barney Rosset, *Dear Mr. Beckett: The Samuel Beckett File*, ed. Louis Oppenheim (Tuxedo Park: Opus, 2017), pp. 351–60, at p. 354.

161   Maurice Girodias, 'Letters to the editor: freedom of expression', *Times Literary Supplement*, 9 June 1966, p. 515.

162   J. S. Atherton, 'The maternal instinct', *Times Literary Supplement*, 7 July 1978, p. 756. He is referring to the story 'Mathilde', in *Delta of Venus*.

163   Anaïs Nin, *The Journals of Anaïs Nin: Vol. 3: 1939–1944* (London: Quartet Books, 1976), p. 73.

164   *Ibid.*, p. 103.

165   Nin, *Delta of Venus*, p. 241.

166   *Ibid.*

167   *Ibid.*, p. 242.

168   *Ibid.*, pp. 242–3.

169   Alfred Perlès, *My Friend Henry Miller* (London: Neville Spearman, 1955), p. 99.

170   John Hollander, 'The perilous magic of nymphets', *Partisan Review*, 23:4 (1956), 557–60, at 560.

171   Girodias to Beckett, 17 September 1986, in Rosset, *Dear Mr. Beckett*, p. 354.

172   Trocchi, *Helen and Desire*, p. 27.

173   *Ibid.*, pp. 61, 62.

174   *Ibid.*, p. 24.

175   Allan Campbell and Tim Niel (eds), *A Life in Pieces: Reflections on Alexander Trocchi* (Edinburgh: Rebel Inc., 1997), p. 211.

176   Alexander Trocchi, *Thongs*, introduction by Robert Creeley (North Hollywood: Brandon House, 1967). First published as Carmencita de las Lunas [Alexander Trocchi], *Thongs* (Paris: The Olympia Press, 1956).

177 James Campbell, 'Alexander Trocchi: the biggest fiend of all', *Antioch Review*, 50:3 (1992), 458–71, at 466; Guy Stevenson, 'Alexander Trocchi (1925–1984)', in Jay Parini (ed.), *British Writers, Supplement 25* (New York: Charles Scribner's Sons, 2018), pp. 255–70, at p. 267.

178 Campbell and Niel, *A Life in Pieces*, p. 227.

179 Harriet Daimler [Iris Owens], *Woman* (Paris: The Olympia Press, 1965), p. 22. First published in 1958 as *The Woman Thing*.

180 George Steiner, 'Night words: high pornography and human privacy', *Encounter*, 25:4 (1965), 14–19, at 17.

181 Daimler, *Woman*, p. 126.

182 Owens was involved in a long affair with Trocchi, the 'Macdonald' in her novels: Emily Gould, 'Stephen Koch on Iris Owens' [blog], *Emily Books*, 18 October 2013: https://emilybooks.com/2013/10/18/stephen-koch-on-iris-owens/.

183 Daimler, *Woman*, p. 41.

184 *Ibid.*, p. 27.

185 *Ibid.*, p. 70.

186 Gerald Howard, 'Not that innocent: Iris Owens's quality-lit pornography', *Artforum International*, 55:10 (2017), S34.

187 Meeske, 'Memoirs of a female pornographer', p. 113.

188 *Ibid.*, p. 114.

189 Perkins, *Secret Record*, pp. 82–3; Mason Hoffenberg, *Sin for Breakfast* (London: Grafton Books, 1989), p. 41. First published as Hamilton Drake [Mason Hoffenberg], *Sin for Breakfast* (Paris: The Olympia Press, 1957).

6 Sexual revolution: Olympia, New York

1 The count is based on the titles listed in Patrick J. Kearney, *A Bibliography of the Publications of the New York Olympia Press* (Santa Rosa: privately printed, 1988).

2 Ed Martin [Edgar A. Martin], *Frankenstein '69* (no place: Olympia Press, 2005), ebook, loc. 1317 (for the quote). The ebook says 'Olympia Press' but the publisher and place of publication of this edition are unknown. First published by the Olympia Press, New York, 1969.

3 Akbar del Piombo [Norman Rubington], *Into the Harem* (no place: Olympia Press, 2014), ebook, loc. 425. The ebook says 'Olympia Press' but the publisher and place of publication of this edition are unknown. First published by the Olympia Press, New York, 1970.

4   *Ibid.*, loc. 2123.
5   Maurice Girodias, 'Commentary', in Maurice Girodias (ed.), *New Olympia Reader* (New York: Black Watch, 1970), pp. 852–91, at p. 890.
6   Special Collections Research Center, Syracuse University Libraries (hereafter SCRC), Grove Press Records, Maurice Girodias Files: Maurice Girodias to Barney Rosset, 7 May 1959.
7   Maurice Girodias and Barney Rosset, 'Our Lady of the Flowers', *eI22*, 4:5 (2005): https://efanzines.com/EK/eI22/#flowers. The details can be found in SCRC, Grove Press Records, Olympia Press Files.
8   Peter Singleton-Gates and Maurice Girodias, *The Black Diaries* (New York: Grove Press, 1959).
9   Ted Morgan, *Literary Outlaw: The Life and Times of William S. Burroughs* (New York: Henry Holt and Company, 1988), p. 328. The Grove edition was not published until 1962.
10 SCRC, Grove Press Records, Olympia Press Files: Maurice Girodias to Barney Rosset, 27 October 1958; Barney Rosset to Maurice Girodias, 1 December 1958; and Barney Rosset to Maurice Girodias, undated letter [late December 1958: 'Grove Press Books … Olympia Distributors'].
11 SCRC, Grove Press Records, Olympia Press Files: Maurice Girodias to Barney Rosset, 14 November 1958; and Barney Rosset to Maurice Girodias, 18 November 1958.
12 SCRC, Grove Press Records, Olympia Press Files: Maurice Girodias to Judith Schmidt, 4 January 1960; and Judith Schmidt to Maurice Girodias, 29 January 1960.
13 SCRC, Grove Press Records, The Black Diaries Files: Barney Rosset to Maurice Girodias, 6 February 1959.
14 SCRC, Grove Press Records, Olympia Press Files: Maurice Girodias to Barney Rosset, 30 January 1959.
15 SCRC, Grove Press Records, Olympia Press Files: Barney Rosset to Diners Club de France, 6 July 1964, and Barney Rosset to Maurice Girodias, 15 September 1966.
16 Rare Book and Manuscript Library, Columbia University Library (hereafter RBML), Barney Rosset Papers, Box 24, Folder 12, Subject Files: Maurice Girodias, Naked Lunch: Barney Rosset to Maurice Girodias, 6 December 1961.
17 The argument can be followed in SCRC, Grove Press Records, Story of O Files.
18 Girodias touches on this in a letter to Samuel Beckett: Maurice Girodias to Samuel Beckett, 17 September 1986, in Barney Rosset, *Dear*

Mr. Beckett: The Samuel Beckett File, ed. Louis Oppenheim (Tuxedo Park: Opus, 2017), pp. 351–60.

19 See Amy S. Wyngaard, 'Translating Sade: the Grove Press editions, 1953–1968', *Romantic Review*, 104:3–4 (2013), 313–31, at 320–1.

20 See SCRC, Austryn Wainhouse Papers, Correspondence, Box 6, Richard Seaver: Maurice Girodias to Austryn Wainhouse, 22 February 1966 (first quote); Austryn Wainhouse to Maurice Girodias, 23 February 1966 (second quote); Austryn Wainhouse to Richard Seaver, 19 January 1967; and Richard Seaver to Austryn Wainhouse, 20 January 1967.

21 The first was published in Grove's magazine *Evergreen Review*; Grove passed on the latter: SCRC, Austryn Wainhouse Papers, Correspondence, Box 6, Richard Seaver: Austryn Wainhouse to Richard Seaver, 21 July 1964; Austryn Wainhouse to Barney Rosset, 4 September 1964.

22 This story is set out in SCRC, Austryn Wainhouse Papers, Correspondence, Box 6, Richard Seaver, in correspondence between Seaver and Wainhouse in letters dated 23 February 1968, 9 March 1968, 9 April 1968, 12 April 1968 and 23 October 1968.

23 SCRC, Austryn Wainhouse Papers, Correspondence, Box 6, Richard Seaver: Austryn Wainhouse to Richard Seaver, 9 April 1968.

24 RBML, Barney Rosset Papers, Box 24, Folde 7, Subject Files: Maurice Girodias, Correspondence: Barney Rosset to Ian Ballantine, 30 January 1967.

25 RBML, Barney Rosset Papers, Box 24, Folder 14, Subject Files: Maurice Girodias, Olympia Press: Maurice Girodias to Barney Rosset, 17 July 1965.

26 See SCRC, Grove Press Records, Olympia Press Files: unsigned contracts of January 1966 and 21 January 1966; and Maurice Girodias to Barney Rosset, 18 March 1966.

27 SCRC, Grove Press Records, Olympia Press Files: Barney Rosset to Henry Ledwig-Rowohlt, 31 July 1968.

28 Peter Collier, 'Pirates of pornography', *Ramparts*, August 1968, pp. 17–23, at p. 19.

29 *Ibid.*, p. 23.

30 Margaret A. Harrell, 'Maurice Girodias – a bit of adventure – the sixties' [blog]: https://margaretharrell.com/2017/02/maurice-girodias-a-bit-of-adventure-the-sixties/.

31 Gerald Williams, 'Olympia's demise: 7 meetings with Maurice Girodias', *Harvard Review*, 15 (1998), 105–13, at 107.

32 Anthony Haden Guest, 'The Porn£roker', *Other Scenes*, January 1968, p. [8].

33 Jenny Fabian, 'Jung Hearts Run Free', *Guardian*, 21 April 2000: https://www.theguardian.com/film/2000/apr/21/4.

34 The Henry W. and Albert A. Berg Collection of English and American Literature, New York Public Library (hereafter BCEAL), William S. Burroughs Papers, Box 75, Folder 8, Correspondence C-14 Olympia Press/Maurice Girodias File: Maurice Girodias to William Burroughs, 24 March 1969.

35 Harry Ransom Humanities Research Center, University of Texas at Austin (hereafter HRHRC), Philip O'Connor Collection: undated [1968/69] memo from Olympia Press, Inc. New York.

36 Lithlibido, 'Creeming of America', *Berkeley Barb*, 4–10 December 1970, pp. 5, 12.

37 William Levy, 'Enter Mister Maurice: a memoir of Maurice Girodias', *RealityStudio*, 5 May 2014: https://realitystudio.org/biography/enter-mister-maurice/.

38 Counted from Kearney, *Bibliography of the Publications of the New York Olympia Press*.

39 Girodias, *New Olympia Reader*.

40 RBML, Barney Rosset Papers, Box 24, Folder 2, Subject Files: Maurice Girodias, Correspondence: Grove Press Accounting to Olympia Press, 31 January 1969.

41 RBML, Barney Rosset Papers, Box 24, Folder 2, Subject Files: Maurice Girodias, Correspondence: Irwin Berger, Memo, 2 April 1970.

42 Harvey Hornwood, 'Maurice and me', *eI27*, 5:4 (2006): https://efanzines.com/EK/eI27/index.htm#maurice. Originally published in 1997.

43 Collier, 'Pirates of pornography', p. 19.

44 HRHRC, Marilyn Meeske Collection, Folder 20: Maurice Girodias to Marilyn Meeske, 12 May 1969. *Honey Finger* was the only one of these used if Kearney's *Bibliography* is a guide.

45 HRHRC, Marilyn Meeske Collection, Folder 20: Maurice Girodias to Marilyn Meeske, 8 May [1970].

46 HRHRC, Marilyn Meeske Collection, Unnumbered Folder: Meeske/Girodias.

47 HRHRC, Marilyn Meeske Collection, Folder 23.

48 HRHRC, Marilyn Meeske Collection, Unnumbered Folder: Meeske/Girodias.

49 Kearney, *Bibliography of the Publications of the New York Olympia Press*, p. 61.

50 Collier, 'Pirates of pornography', p. 19.

51 *Ibid.*

52 D. A. Latimer, 'Decomposition', *East Village Other*, 7 July 1971, p. 10.

53 Diane di Prima, *Memoirs of a Beatnik* (New York: Penguin, 1998), pp. 191, 193. First published in 1969.

54 *Ibid.*, p. 124.

55 George Kimball, *Only Skin Deep*, introduction by James Grauerholz (Bloomington: iUniverse, 2011), p. 3. First published by Olympia New York, 1968.

56 Hunter Thompson to George Kimball, 17 November 1968, in Hunter S. Thompson, *Fear and Loathing in America: The Brutal Odyssey of an Outlaw Journalist*, ed. Douglas Brinkley (London: Bloomsbury, 2001), p. 144.

57 Victor J. Banis, 'A virgin anew', *eI22*, 4:5 (2005): https://efanzines.com/EK/eI22/#virgin.

58 *Ibid.*

59 Earl Kemp, 'Maurice … the gangster of love …', *eI22*, 4:5 (2005): https://efanzines.com/EK/eI22/#love.

60 For Turner, see Steve Aldous, *The World of Shaft: A Complete Guide to the Novels, Comic Strip, Films and Television Series* (Jefferson: McFarland and Co., 2015), pp. 39–40.

61 Robert Turner, *Pretty Thing* (New York: The Olympia Press, 1968), p. 157. Emphases in original.

62 K. K. Klein, *The Sex of Angels* (no place: Olympia Press, 2005), ebook, loc. 63. The ebook says 'Olympia Press' but the publisher and place of publication of this edition are unknown. First published by the Olympia Press, New York, 1968.

63 Norman Singer, *The Pornographer* (New York: Ophelia Press, 1968), p. 200.

64 *Ibid.*, p. 26.

65 Jay A. Gertzman, 'Porno noir, 1968–1974', *eI48*, 9:1 (2010): https://efanzines.com/EK/eI48/index.htm#noir.

66 *Ibid.*

67 Charles Platt, *An Accidental Life: Volume 3, 1970–1979: The Improvident Years* (Las Vegas: independently published, 2020), p. 76.

68 *Ibid.*, p. 99.

69 For this censorship episode, see Christopher Hilliard, *A Matter of Obscenity: The Politics of Censorship in Modern England* (Princeton: Princeton University Press, 2021), p. 127.

70 Benjamin Grimm [Spencer Lambert], *Sir Cyril Black* (New York: The Olympia Press, 1969), p. 226. Ellipses in original.

71 Girodias, quoted in Michael Palin, *Diaries 1969–1979: The Python Years* (London: Weidenfeld & Nicolson, 2006), pp. 236–7 (entry 24 May 1975).

72 Benjamin Grimm [Spencer Lambert], *Nightland Spell* (no place: Olympia Press, 2005), ebook, loc. 2028 (for the quote). The ebook says 'Olympia Press' but the publisher and place of publication of this edition are unknown. First published by the Olympia Press, New York, 1969.

73 *Ibid.*, locs 2046, 2069–73.

74 *Ibid.*, loc. 2107.

75 *Ibid.*, locs 3648–53.

76 'Benjamin Grimm', in Girodias, *New Olympia Reader*, p. 463.

77 Sybah Darrich [Richard Ashby], *Love on a Trampoline* (no place: Olympia Press, 2015), ebook, loc. 405. The ebook says 'Olympia Press' but the publisher and place of publication of this edition are unknown. First published by the Olympia Press, New York, 1968.

78 Rene Auden [Uta West], *The Party* (no place: Olympia Press, 2005), ebook, loc. 33. The ebook says 'Olympia Press' but the publisher and place of publication of this edition are unknown. First published by the Olympia Press, New York, 1971.

79 *Ibid.*, loc. 98.

80 Rene Auden [Uta West], *High Thrust* (no place: Olympia Press, 2005), ebook, loc. 348. The ebook says 'Olympia Press' but the publisher and place of publication of this edition are unknown. First published by the Olympia Press, New York, 1971.

81 *Ibid.*, loc. 1088.

82 *Ibid.*, locs 798–802.

83 *Ibid.*, locs 1559–64.

84 See the full-page advertisement at the end of Frank Newman [Sam Abrams], *Barbara* (New York: The Olympia Press, 1970), p. 179.

85 This and what follows comes from email and phone conversations with Sharon Rudahl, 10–12 November 2021. We are grateful to her for permission to quote from those conversations.

86 Hornwood, 'Maurice and me'; Sharon Rudahl, phone conversation, 12 November 2021.

87 Mary Sativa [Sharon Rudahl], *Acid Temple Ball* (no place: Olympia Press, 2005), ebook, locs 198, 371. The ebook says 'Olympia Press' but

the publisher and place of publication of this edition are unknown. First published by the Olympia Press, New York, 1969.

88 *Ibid.*, loc. 772.

89 *Ibid.*, loc. 213.

90 *Ibid.*, locs 788, 799.

91 Michael Perkins, *The Secret Record: Modern Erotic Literature* (New York: William Morrow, 1976), p. 95.

92 Sharon Rudahl, email, 11 November 2021.

93 Mary Sativa [Sharon Rudahl], *The Lovers' Crusade* (no place: Olympia Press, 2005), ebook, locs 71–6. The ebook says 'Olympia Press' but the publisher and place of publication of this edition are unknown. First published by the Olympia Press, New York, 1971.

94 *Ibid.*, loc. 406.

95 *Ibid.*, locs 582–7.

96 *Ibid.*, loc. 1736.

97 *Ibid.*, locs 602–14.

98 Sharon Rudahl, email 11 November 2021.

99 Deneen Peckinpah, *Ceremonies of Love* (New York: The Olympia Press, 1970), p. 123.

100 *Ibid.*, pp. 33–4. Ellipsis in original.

101 *Ibid.*, pp. 16, 17, 66.

102 Perkins, *Secret Record*, p. 157.

103 For her identity and the date of her death, see the later edition of Michael Perkins, *The Secret Record* (New York: Masquerade Books, 1992), p. 195.

104 Lela Seftali, *Ride a Cock-Horse* (no place: Olympia Press, 2006), ebook, locs 404, 517, 566, 635, 667, 762, 858, 953. The ebook says 'Olympia Press' but the publisher and place of publication of this edition are unknown. First published by the Olympia Press, New York, 1970.

105 *Ibid.*, loc. 1675.

106 *Ibid.*, loc. 49.

107 *Ibid.*, locs 27–36.

108 *Ibid.*, loc. 53.

109 *Ibid.*, loc. 83.

110 *Ibid.*, loc. 157.

111 *Ibid.*, loc. 57.

112 *Ibid.*, locs 79, 83.

113 *Ibid.*, loc. 247.

114 *Ibid.*, loc. 399.

115 *Ibid.*, loc. 1041.

116 *Ibid.*, loc. 1616.

117 Perkins, *Secret Record* (1976), p. 154.

118 Maurice Girodias, 'Preface', in Valerie Solanas, *The S. C. U. M. Society for Cutting Up Men Manifesto* (New York: Olympia Press, 1968), pp. 11–27, quote at p. 15.

119 Valerie Solanas, *SCUM Manifesto*, with a foreword by Michelle Tea (Edinburgh: AK Press, 2013), p. 74.

120 *Ibid.*, p. 54.

121 Breanne Fahs, *Valerie Solanas* (New York: The Feminist Press, 2014), p. 113. Fahs provides the best account of Solanas, including her relationship with Girodias.

122 John de St. Jorre, *Venus Bound: The Erotic Voyage of the Olympia Press and Its Writers* (New York: Random House, 1994), p. 294.

123 Marco Vassi, *A Driving Passion*, ed. Martin Shepard, with a preface by Norman Mailer (Sag Harbor, New York: The Permanent Press, 1992), p. 76.

124 *Ibid.*, p. 78.

125 Jerry Stahl, 'Marco Vassi: interviewed by Jerry Stahl', *Transatlantic Review*, 58/59 (1977), 110–13, at 112.

126 Marco Vassi, *Mind Blower* (New York: Open Road Integrated Media, 2014), ebook, locs 1637–42. First published by the Olympia Press in New York in 1970.

127 Marco Vassi, *Metasex, Mirth & Madness: Erotic Tales of the Absurdly Real* (New York: Penthouse Press, 1975), p. 207.

128 Perkins, *Secret Record* (1992), pp. 238, 247.

129 *Ibid.*, pp. 245–6.

130 Marco Vassi, *The Gentle Degenerates* (New York: Open Road Integrated Media, 2014), p. 8. First published by the Olympia Press in New York in 1970.

131 Marco Vassi, *The Saline Solution* (New York: Open Road Integrated Media, 2014), p. 129. First published by the Olympia Press in New York in 1971.

132 Vassi, *Mind Blower*, locs 529–34.

133 Vassi, *The Gentle Degenerates*, pp. 21–2.

134 Marco Vassi, *Contours of Darkness* (New York: Open Road Integrated Media, 2014), p. 133. First published by the Olympia Press in New York in 1972.

135 *Ibid.*, p. 205.

136 Vassi, *Mind Blower*, loc. 1109. Emphasis in original.

137   See for example *The Gentle Degenerates*, p. 24; *The Saline Solution*, p. 72;
      The Gentle Degenerates, p. 61; and for just two of many examples of the
      use of poppers (amyl nitrate), see *The Gentle Degenerates*, pp. 65–9, and
      The Saline Solution, p. 133.

138   Vassi, *The Gentle Degenerates*, p. 61.

139   Vassi, *The Saline Solution*, p. 13. See also p. 94.

140   Norman Mailer, 'Preface', in Vassi, *A Driving Passion*, pp. 9–12, at p. 10.

141   Peter Michelson, 'Preface to *Street of Stairs*', *Chicago Review*, 20:4–21:1
      (1969), 201–11, at 211 (for the Joyce and Burroughs comparison); Ronald
      Tavel, 'Street of Stairs', *Chicago Review*, 16:4 (1964), 73–94, at 80.

142   Ronald Tavel, 'From *Street of Stairs*', *Chicago Review*, 42:3/4 (1996),
      72–8.

143   Peter Rabbit, 'Never piss-fight with a skunk', in Girodias, *New Olympia
      Reader*, pp. 802–8, at p. 805.

144   Barry Malzberg, *Screen* (London: The Olympia Press, 1970), p. 17. First
      published by the Olympia Press in New York in 1968.

145   *Ibid.*, p. 19.

146   *Ibid.*, p. 26.

147   Barry N. Malzberg, 'Repentance, desire and Natalie Wood', *eI22*, 4:5
      (2005): https://efanzines.com/EK/eI22/#wood.

148   *Ibid.*

149   BCEAL, William S. Burroughs Papers, Box 75, Folder 8, Correspondence
      C-14 Olympia Press/Maurice Girodias File: Maurice Girodias to William
      Burroughs Junior, 10 July 1969 and 29 August 1969.

150   RBML, Barney Rosset Papers, Box 24, Folder 13, Subject Files: Maurice
      Girodias, Naked Lunch: Grove Internal Memo to Richard Seaver, 9 June
      1968.

151   For the article, see William Burroughs Jr, 'Life with Father', *Esquire*,
      1 September 1971, pp. 113–15, 140–1, 144, quote at p. 113.

152   BCEAL, William S. Burroughs Papers, Box 75, Folder 8, Correspondence
      C-14 Olympia Press/Maurice Girodias File: Maurice Girodias to William
      Burroughs Junior, 29 August 1969.

153   William S. Burroughs Jr., *Speed and Kentucky Ham*, foreword by Ann
      Charters (New York: Overlook, 1993), p. 163. *Speed* was first published
      by the Olympia Press in New York in 1970.

154   These endorsements are on the respective covers of the two editions of
      the book: Clarence Major, *All Night Visitors* (New York: The Olympia
      Press, 1970), first published in 1969; and Clarence Major, *All Night
      Visitors* (Boston: Northeastern University Press, 1998).

155   Major, *All Night Visitors* (1970), p. 5. Emphases in original.

156   Larry McCaffery and Jerzy Kutnik, '"I follow my eyes": an interview with Clarence Major', *African American Review*, 28:1 (1994), 121–38, at 136.

157   Major, *All Night Visitors* (1970). Ellipses in original.

158   *Ibid.*, p. 4.

159   McCaffery and Kutnik, 'I follow my eyes', 136.

160   Major, *All Night Visitors* (1970), p. 8.

161   *Ibid.*, pp. 4, 7, 9, 10, 11, 12, 14, 20, 27, 28, 29, 47, 85, 86, 98, 99, 102, 103, 105, 108, 110, 129, 131, 137, 138, 172.

162   Eliot Fremont-Smith, 'Books of the Times: on erotica', *New York Times*, 7 April 1969, p. 41.

163   Jerome Klinkowitz, 'Clarence Major: an interview with a post-contemporary author', *Black American Literature Forum*, 12:1 (1978), 32–7, at 33.

164   *Ibid.*, 32.

165   Matt Dube, 'Reviews: Clarence Major, *All-Night Visitors*', *Literary Review: An International Journal of Contemporary Writing*, 43:4 (2000), 605–7, at 605.

166   Keith E. Byerman, *The Art and Life of Clarence Major* (Athens, GA: University of Georgia Press, 2012), p. 42.

167   Samuel R. Delany, 'The Making of *Hogg*', in his *Shorter Views: Queer Thoughts & the Politics of the Paraliterary* (Hanover, NH: University Press of New England, 1999), pp. 298–310, at p. 301.

168   Latimer, 'Decomposition', p. 10.

169   Rosset, *Dear Mr. Beckett*, p. 358.

170   Collier, 'Pirates of pornography', p. 20.

171   Earl Kemp, 'Hot for Harriet or The Woman Thing', *eI39*, 7:4 (2008): https://efanzines.com/EK/eI39/#hot. Ellipsis in original.

172   Earl Kemp and Barry Malzberg, 'Dialogue', *eI22*, 4:5 (2005): https://efanzines.com/EK/eI22/#dial.

173   Kemp, 'Maurice … the gangster of love'.

174   Collier, 'Pirates of pornography', p. 18.

175   Patrick J. Kearney, *The Paris Olympia Press: An Annotated Bibliography* (London: Black Spring Press, 1987). The 164 does not include reissues of the same works.

176   Perkins, *Secret Record* (1992), p. 138.

177   Delany, 'Making of *Hogg*', p. 299.

178   Collier, 'Pirates of pornography', p. 19.

179 Allan Campbell and Tim Niel (eds), *A Life in Pieces: Reflections on Alexander Trocchi* (Edinburgh: Rebel Inc., 1997), p. 211.

180 Andrew Murray Scott, *Alexander Trocchi: The Making of a Monster* (Kilkerran: Kennedy & Boyd, 2012), p. 203. First published in 1991.

181 RBML, Barney Rosset Papers, Box 24, Folder 15, Subject Files: Maurice Girodias, Olympia Press: Barney Rosset to Maurice Girodias, 28 July 1965.

182 SCRC, Austryn Wainhouse Papers, Correspondence, Box 6, Richard Seaver: Richard Seaver to Austryn Wainhouse, 20 January 1967.

183 Scott, *Alexander Trocchi*, p. 205.

184 Williams, 'Olympia's demise', 107.

185 In a letter quoted by Fahs, *Valerie Solanas*, p. 204.

7 Literature of pornography?

1 Irving Wallace, *The Seven Minutes* (New York: Pocket Books, 1970), p. 4. First published in 1969.

2 *Ibid.*, pp. 126–7.

3 *Ibid.*, p. 458.

4 *Ibid.*, pp. 371–2.

5 *Ibid.*, p. 385.

6 Patrick J. Kearney, *A Bibliography of the Publications of the New York Olympia Press* (Santa Rosa, CA: Privately Printed, 1988), pp. 42–6, quote at p. 43.

7 Wallace, *Seven Minutes*, p. 263.

8 *Ibid.*, p. 233.

9 *Ibid.*, pp. 424, 483.

10 *Ibid.*, p. 8.

11 Kearney, *Bibliography of the Publications of the New York Olympia Press*, p. viii. Ellipsis in original.

12 Anonymous [Michael Bernet], *7 Erotic Minutes* (New York: The Olympia Press, 1971), p. 9. First published in 1970.

13 *Ibid.*, p. 14.

14 *Ibid.*, pp. 17, 41, 56.

15 *Ibid.*, p. 107.

16 *Ibid.*, p. 15.

17 Maurice Girodias, 'Letters to the editor: freedom of expression', *Times Literary Supplement*, 9 June 1966, p. 515. Emphasis in original.

18   John Phillips, *Forbidden Fictions: Pornography and Censorship in Twentieth-Century French Literature* (London: Pluto Press, 1999), p. 2.

19   Anaïs Nin, *Delta of Venus* (London: Penguin Books, 2000), p. xii.

20   *Ibid.*, p. xi.

21   Anaïs Nin, *Mirages: The Unexpurgated Diary of Anaïs Nin 1939–1947*, ed. Paul Herron (Athens, OH: Ohio University Press, 2013), p. 81.

22   *Ibid.* Ellipsis in original.

23   *Ibid.*, p. 80.

24   *Ibid.*, p. 48. Emphasis in original.

25   Nin, *Delta of Venus*, p. xi.

26   Smaro Kamboureli is interesting on this: Smaro Kamboureli, 'Discourse and intercourse, design and desire in the erotica of Anaïs Nin', *Journal of Modern Literature*, 11:1 (1984), 143–58, at 147–8.

27   Karen Brennan, 'Anaïs Nin: author(iz)ing the erotic body', *Genders*, 14 (1992), 66–86.

28   Diane Richard-Allerdyce, 'Anaïs Nin's "poetic porn": problematizing the gaze', in Anne T. Salvatore (ed.), *Anaïs Nin's Narratives* (Gainesville: University Press of Florida, 2001), pp. 17–36, at p. 30.

29   *Ibid.*, p. 32.

30   Peter Michelson, *Speaking the Unspeakable: A Poetics of Obscenity* (Albany: State University of New York Press, 1993), pp. 205, 206, 209.

31   *Ibid.*, p. 42.

32   *Ibid.*, p. 44. The words are Michelson's; there is no citation for Girodias's complaint.

33   *Ibid.*, p. 45. For the cocaine story, see D. A. Latimer, 'Decomposition', *East Village Other*, 7 July 1971, p. 10.

34   Frank Newman [Sam Abrams], *Barbara* (New York: The Olympia Press, 1970), p. 7. First published in 1968.

35   *Ibid.*, p. 10.

36   *Ibid.*, p. 38.

37   Latimer, 'Decomposition', p. 10.

38   Michael Perkins, *The Secret Record: Modern Erotic Literature* (New York: William Morrow, 1976), p. 94.

39   Michelson, *Speaking the Unspeakable*, p. 44.

40   *Ibid.*, p. 64.

41   Susan Sontag, 'The pornographic imagination', in Susan Sontag, *Essays of the 1960s & 70s*, ed. David Rieff (New York: The Library of America, 2013), pp. 320–52, at p. 320.

42 Eliot Fremont-Smith, 'Books of the times: the uses of pornography', *New York Times*, 2 March 1966, p. 39.

43 Special Collections Research Center, Syracuse University Libraries (hereafter SCRC), Grove Press Records, Story of O Files: Eric Larrabee, 'Apropos D'O' [1965].

44 Vladimir Nabokov to Edmund Wilson, 24 November 1955, in *The Nabokov–Wilson Letters: Correspondence Between Vladimir Nabokov and Edmund Wilson, 1940–1971*, ed., Simon Karlinsky (New York: Harper Colophon Books, 1980), p. 296. Emphasis in original.

45 For Colligan, see Colette Colligan, *A Publisher's Paradise: Expatriate Literary Culture in Paris, 1890–1960* (Amherst: University of Massachusetts Press, 2013), pp. 245–77; for the quote, Vladimir Nabokov to Kenneth Tynan, 12 July 1969, in Dimitri Nabokov and Matthew J. Bruccoli (eds), *Vladimir Nabokov: Selected Letters 1940–1977* (London: Weidenfeld and Nicolson, 1990), p. 455. The Grove collection was never published.

46 Vladimir Nabokov, 'On a book entitled *Lolita*', *Anchor Review*, 2 (1957), 105–12, at 107.

47 *Ibid.*, 108.

48 *Ibid.*, 109.

49 Raymond Queneau, *Zazie dans le Métro*, trans. Akbar del Piombo [Norman Rubington] and Eric Kahane (Paris: The Olympia Press, 1959), p. 62. The illustrations are by Jacqueline Duhème and the book was first published in French in 1959. The title was previously announced as 'Zazie or the Sex of Angels'.

50 *Ibid.*, p. 21.

51 *Ibid.*, pp. 13, 91.

52 A direction not taken in the later Penguin translation: Raymond Queneau, *Zazie in the Metro*, trans. Barbara Wright, with an introduction by Gilbert Adair (New York: Penguin Books, 2001).

53 Queneau, *Zazie dans le Métro*, pp. 35, 37.

54 *Ibid.*, pp. 93, 101, 107, 112, 113, 135, 139, 211.

55 *Ibid.*, p. 146.

56 For the comparisons, see Susan Bernofsky, 'Zazie in Wonderland: Queneau's reply to the realist novel', *Romantic Review*, 85:1 (1994), 113–24, at 118–22.

57 Queneau, *Zazie dans le Métro*, p. 13.

58 *Ibid.*, p. 23.

59 *Ibid.*, p. 55.

60 *Ibid.*, p. 9.

61 *Ibid.*, p. 116.

62 *Ibid.*, p. 7.

63 *Ibid.*, p. 36.

64 *Ibid.*, pp. 8, 11, 129, 142.

65 Bernofsky, 'Zazie in Wonderland', 124.

66 Vladimir Nabokov to Edmund Wilson, 5 April 1960, in *The Nabokov–Wilson Letters*, p. 330.

67 Letter from Lawrence Durrell to Richard Aldington [August? 1959], in Ian S. MacNiven and Harry T. Moore (eds), *Literary Lifelines: The Richard Aldington – Lawrence Durrell Correspondence* (London: Faber and Faber, 1981), p. 100.

68 *Ibid.*, p. 101.

69 Lawrence Durrell to Richard Aldington [*c.*25–30 May 1959], in *ibid.*, p. 92.

70 Henry Miller to J. Rives Childs, 21 July 1950, in Richard Clement Wood (ed.), *Collector's Quest: The Correspondence of Henry Miller and J. Rives Childs, 1947–1965* (Charlottesville: University Press of Virginia, 1968), p. 39.

71 Yale Collection of American Literature, Beinecke Rare Book and Manuscript Library, Henry Miller Letters to Barnet Ruder, Box 1, Folder 5: Henry Miller to Barnet Ruder, 13 October 1936.

72 *Ibid.*

73 *Ibid.* Emphasis in original.

74 *Ibid.*

75 Lawrence Durrell, 'On Henry Miller', in Terry Southern, Richard Seaver and Alexander Trocchi (eds), *Writers in Revolt: An Anthology* (New York: Berkeley Publishing Corporation, 1965), pp. 147–62, at pp. 153–4. Ellipsis in original. The essay was first published in 1949.

76 Henry Miller, *Letters to Emil*, ed. George Wickes (New York: New Directions, 1989), p. 114.

77 Rachel Potter, *Obscene Modernism: Literary Censorship and Experiment, 1900–1940* (Oxford: Oxford University Press, 2013), p. 142.

78 Lawrence Durrell to Henry Miller, [August 1935], in Ian S. MacNiven (ed.), *The Durrell–Miller Letters, 1935–80* (London: Faber and Faber, 1989), p. 2.

79 Henry Miller to Lawrence Durrell, 8 March 1937, in *ibid.*, p. 55.

80 *Ibid.*, p. 56. Emphasis in original.

81 Henry Miller to Lawrence Durrell, [10 May 1937], in *ibid.*, p. 77.

82 Elisabeth Ladenson, *Dirt for Art's Sake: Books on Trial from Madame Bovary to Lolita* (Ithaca: Cornell University Press, 2007), pp. 221–36, quote at p. 222.

83 Charles Rembar, *The End of Obscenity: The Trials of Lady Chatterley, Tropic of Cancer and Fanny Hill* (New York: Random House, 1968), pp. 251, 297, 436.

84 *Ibid.*, p. 300.

85 *Ibid.*, p. 436.

86 'The Boston trial of *Naked Lunch*', *Evergreen Review*, 36 (1965), 40–9, at 42; Michael Barry Goodman, *Contemporary Literary Censorship: The Case History of Burroughs' Naked Lunch* (Metuchen: The Scarecrow Press, 1981), p. 179.

87 Goodman, *Contemporary Literary Censorship*, pp. 183, 187, 193, 201, 204. The quotes come from William Burroughs, *Naked Lunch: The Restored Text*, ed. James Grauerholz and Barry Miles (London: Penguin Books, 2015), pp. 24, 33, 64, 82, 93, 111. *Naked Lunch* was first published as William Burroughs, *The Naked Lunch* (Paris: The Olympia Press, 1959). It is Number 76 in the Traveller's Companion Series.

88 Goodman, *Contemporary Literary Censorship*, p. 205.

89 Outlined by Goodman, *Contemporary Literary Censorship*.

90 SCRC, Grove Press Records, Olympia Reader Files: a sheet near a letter from Harry Braverman to Henry Miller, 22 January 1965.

91 *Ibid.*

92 The changed section appears in Henry Miller, 'Sexus', in Maurice Girodias (ed.), *The Olympia Reader* (New York: Grove Press, 1965), pp. 641–51, change at p. 649.

93 SCRC, Grove Press Records, Olympia Reader Files: Henry Miller to Harry Braverman, 14 January 1965.

94 SCRC, Grove Press Records, Story of O Files: copy of an English solicitor's report on potential publication of *Story of O*, 27 January 1970.

95 SCRC, Grove Press Records, Story of O Files: Memo from Richard Seaver to Barney Rosset, 12 February 1970.

96 John Calder, 'Letters to the editor: ugh', *Times Literary Supplement*, 16 January 1964, p. 53; Anthony Burgess, 'Letters to the editor: ugh', *Times Literary Supplement*, 2 January 1964, p. 9.

97 Burgess, 'Letters to the editor', p. 9.

98 [John Willett], 'Ugh', *Times Literary Supplement*, 14 November 1963, p. 919.

99 David Lodge, 'Objections to William Burroughs', *Critical Quarterly*, 8:3 (1966), 203–12, at 204.

100 The versions used in this analysis are: Frances Lengel [Alexander Trocchi], *Young Adam* (Paris: The Olympia Press, 1954); Alexander Trocchi, *Young Adam* (London: The New English Library, 1966), first published in England by Heinemann in 1961; Anonymous, *Young Adam* (New York, Masquerade Books, 1991). For a summary of the Trocchi texts, see Andrew Murray Scott, *Alexander Trocchi: The Making of a Monster* (Kilkerran: Kennedy & Boyd, 2012), pp. 82, 231.

101 Scott, *Alexander Trocchi*, p. 81.

102 Lengel, *Young Adam* (1954), pp. 44–5. Compare Trocchi, *Young Adam* (1966), p. 43.

103 Lengel, *Young Adam* (1954), pp. 80–1. Compare Trocchi, *Young Adam* (1966), p. 81.

104 Lengel, *Young Adam* (1954), pp. 89–90, quote at p. 90.

105 Lengel, *Young Adam* (1954), pp. 98–9. Compare Trocchi, *Young Adam* (1966), p. 91.

106 Lengel, *Young Adam* (1954), pp. 171–90.

107 *Ibid.*, p. 190. Compare the totally different ending in Trocchi, *Young Adam* (1966), p. 160, which ends in the courtroom.

108 Lengel, *Young Adam* (1954), p. 187.

109 *Ibid.*

110 Trocchi, *Young Adam* (1966), p. 137.

111 Nina Attwood and Barry Reay, 'ANONYMOUS and Badboy Books: a 1990s moment in the history of pornography', *Porn Studies*, 3:3 (2016), 255–75.

112 Anonymous, *Young Adam* (1991), p. 16.

113 *Ibid.*, pp. 17–18, 58–9 (for the quote).

114 *Ibid.*, p. 78.

115 *Ibid.*, p. 170.

116 Aubrey Beardsley and John Glassco, *Under the Hill* (Paris: The Olympia Press, 1959), pp. 70, 71.

117 Quoted by Glassco in *ibid.*, p. 11.

118 *Ibid.*, p. 27.

119 *Ibid.*, p. 28.

120 All these examples are from *ibid.*, p. 36.

121 *Ibid.*, p. 43.

122 *Ibid.*, p. 48.

123 *Ibid.*, pp. 54–5.

124 *Ibid.*, p. 58.

125 Edward de Grazia, 'I'm just going to feed Adolphe', *Cardozo Studies in Law and Literature*, 3:1 (1991), 127–51, quote at 137–8.

126 Nicole Fluhr, '"Queer Reverence": Aubrey Beardsley's Venus and Tannhäuser', *Cahiers Victoriens et Édouardiens*, 90 (2019). Online first. https://doi.org/10.4000/cve.6482.

127 Ian Fletcher, 'Inventions for the left hand: Beardsley in verse and prose', in Robert Langenfeld (ed.), *Reconsidering Aubrey Beardsley* (Ann Arbor: UMI Research Press, 1989), pp. 227–66, at p. 240.

128 George Y. Trail, 'Beardsley's *Venus and Tannhäuser*: two versions', *English Literature in Transition, 1880–1920*, 18:1 (1975), 16–23, at 22.

129 Beardsley and Glassco, *Under the Hill*, p. 76.

130 *Ibid.*, pp. 83, 84–5.

131 *Ibid.*, pp. 88–9.

132 Trail discusses the two versions in his previously cited article, 'Beardsley's *Venus and Tannhäuser*: two versions'.

133 *Ibid.*, 22.

134 Linda C. Dowling, '*Venus and Tannhäuser*: Beardsley's satire of decadence', *Journal of Narrative Technique*, 8:1 (1978), 26–41, quote at 35.

135 Allison Pease, *Modernism, Mass Culture, and the Aesthetics of Obscenity* (Cambridge: Cambridge University Press, 2000), p. 34.

136 *Ibid.*, p. 95. Ellipsis in original.

137 Dowling, '*Venus and Tannhäuser*', 37.

138 Michelson, *Speaking the Unspeakable*, p. 72.

139 Letter from Lawrence Durrell to Richard Aldington [August? 1959], in MacNiven and Moore, *Literary Lifelines*, p. 101.

140 Lawrence Durrell to Henry Miller, 5 September 1949, in MacNiven, *Durrell–Miller Letters*, p. 232.

141 *Ibid.*, p. 233.

142 *Ibid.*, p. 232. Emphasis in original.

143 Alexander Trocchi, *White Thighs* (North Hollywood: Brandon House, 1967), p. 120. First published as Frances Lengel [Alexander Trocchi], *White Thighs* (Paris: The Olympia Press, 1955).

144 Alexander Trocchi, *Thongs*, introduction by Robert Creeley (North Hollywood: Brandon House, 1967), pp. 52–3. First published as Carmencita de las Lunas [Alexander Trocchi], *Thongs* (Paris: Olympia Press, 1956).

145 *Ibid.*, p. 170. Ellipsis in original.

146 Burroughs, *Naked Lunch*, p. 79. Ellipses in original. For reference to the pornographic sections, see William S. Burroughs to Allen Ginsberg, [late

July 1959], in William S. Burroughs, *The Letters of William S. Burroughs, 1945–1959*, ed. Oliver Harris (New York: Viking, 1993), p. 418.

147   'Boston trial of *Naked Lunch*', 41.

148   Anonymous [Jean Cocteau], *The White Paper*, with a preface and illustrations by Jean Cocteau (Paris: The Olympia Press, 1957) [translated by Austryn Wainhouse], p. 12.

149   *Ibid.*, p. 13.

150   *Ibid.*, pp. 44–5.

151   *Ibid.*, p. 50.

152   *Ibid.*, pp. 50–1.

153   *Ibid.*, p. 58.

154   *Ibid.*, p. 65.

155   Jean Genet, *The Thief's Journal*, foreword by Jean-Paul Sartre, trans. Bernard Frechtman (Paris: The Olympia Press, 1959), p. 18, first published under the Collection Merlin imprint in 1954; Jean Genet, *Our Lady of the Flowers*, trans. Bernard Frechtman (Paris: The Olympia Press, 1957), pp. 24, 25. The books are No. 78 and No. 36, respectively, in the Traveller's Companion Series.

156   Genet, *Thief's Journal*, pp. 22–5.

157   *Ibid.*, p. 207.

158   *Ibid.*, p. 20.

159   *Ibid.*, p. 147.

160   *Ibid.*, p. 215.

161   *Ibid.*, p. 208.

162   Genet, *Our Lady of the Flowers*, p. 19.

163   *Ibid.*, p. 69.

164   Elizabeth Stephens, *Queer Writing: Homoeroticism in Jean Genet's Fiction* (Basingstoke: Palgrave Macmillan, 2009), p. 99.

165   Genet, *Our Lady of the Flowers*, p. 47.

166   *Ibid.*, p. 91.

167   *Ibid.*, p. 43.

168   SCRC, Austryn Wainhouse Papers, Correspondence, Box 6, Richard Seaver: Austryn Wainhouse to Richard Seaver, 8 February 1958.

169   Pierre Angélique [Georges Bataille], *The Naked Beast at Heaven's Gate*, trans. Audiart [Austryn Wainhouse], with a preface by Georges Bataille (Paris: The Olympia Press, 1956), p. 30. Ellipses in original.

170   Patrick Ffrench, 'Bataille's literary writings', in Mark Hewson and Marcus Coelen (eds), *Georges Bataille: Key Concepts* (London: Routledge, 2015), pp. 189–200, at p. 190.

171   Michelson, *Speaking the Unspeakable*, p. 148.

172 Georges Bataille, *Story of the Eye: By Lord Auch*, trans. Joachim Neugroschal, with essays by Susan Sontag and Roland Barthes (London: Penguin Books, 2013), pp. 9, 67. First published in translated form as Pierre Angélique, *A Tale of Satisfied Desire* [*L'Histoire de l'oeil*], trans. Audiart [Austryn Wainhouse] (Paris: The Olympia Press, 1953).

173 Bataille, *Story of the Eye*, p. 51.

174 *Ibid.*, p. 42.

175 Roland Barthes, 'The Metaphor of the Eye', in Bataille, *Story of the Eye*, pp. 119–26, at p. 126.

176 Sontag, 'The pornographic imagination', p. 346.

177 Vladimir Nabokov, 'Lolita and Mr. Girodias', *Evergreen Review*, 11:45 (1967), 37–41, at 40.

178 Sontag, 'The pornographic imagination', pp. 321, 330.

179 Geoffrey Wagner, 'The end of the "porno" – or, no more Traveling Companions?', *Sewanee Review*, 75:2 (1967), 364–76, at 375.

180 Kate Millett, 'Henry Miller', in her *Sexual Politics* (London: Virago, 1981), pp. 294–313, at pp. 309, 313. First published in 1969.

Conclusion

1 Maurice Girodias, 'Pornologist on Olympus – a memoir', *Playboy*, 8:4 (April 1961), 56, 68, 145–8, quote at 148.

2 Maurice Girodias, 'Advance through obscenity', *Times Literary Supplement*, 6 August 1964, pp. 708–9, at p. 708.

3 *Ibid.*

4 *Ibid.*

5 *Ibid.*

6 *Ibid.*

7 *Ibid.*, p. 709.

8 John de St. Jorre, *Venus Bound: The Erotic Voyage of the Olympia Press and Its Writers* (New York: Random House, 1994), pp. 84–5, quote at p. 84.

9 *Ibid.*, p. 85.

10 Special Collections Research Center, Syracuse University Libraries, Grove Press Records, Olympia Reader Files: Philip Oxman to Richard Seaver, 28 January, 1965.

11 Gregory Stephenson, 'Tête-à-tête with the Frog Prince: conversations with Maurice Girodias', in his *Points of Intersection* (Thy, Denmark: Eyecorner Press, 2018), pp. 114–34, at p. 127.

12 Girodias, 'Pornologist on Olympus'.

13 Maurice Girodias, *The Frog Prince: An Autobiography* (New York: Crown, 1980), p. 2.

14 Stephenson, 'Tête-à-tête with the Frog Prince', p. 129.

15 Chris Forster, *Filthy Material: Modernism and the Media of Obscenity* (New York: Oxford University Press, 2018), pp. 181, 191.

16 Terry Southern, Richard Seaver and Alexander Trocchi (eds), *Writers in Revolt: An Anthology* (New York: Berkeley Publishing Corporation, 1965). First published in 1963. The quote comes from the book's cover.

17 Loren Glass, *Rebel Publisher: Grove Press and the Revolution of the Word* (New York: Seven Stories Press, 2018), p. 20.

18 S. E. Gontarski, 'Introduction: the life and times of Grove Press', in S. E. Gontarski (ed.), *The Grove Press Reader, 1951–2001* (New York: Grove Press, 2001), pp. xi–xxvii, quote at p. xiii.

19 Maurice Girodias to Samuel Beckett, 17 September 1986, in Barney Rosset, *Dear Mr. Beckett: The Samuel Beckett File*, ed. Louis Oppenheim (Tuxedo Park: Opus, 2017), pp. 351–60, quotes at pp. 355, 358.

20 *Ibid.*, p. 359.

21 The links between Beckett, Grove and the Merlinois (and Girodias) can be traced in Beckett's correspondence for the period 1952–56: George Craig, Martha Dow Fehsenfeld, Daniel Gunn and Lois More Overbeck (eds), *The Letters of Samuel Beckett, Volume 2: 1941–1956* (Cambridge: Cambridge University Press, 2011), especially pp. 356, 384–8, 397–8, 512–13, 607–8.

22 Amy Wyngaard, 'The end of pornography: *The Story of O*', *MLN*, 130:4 (2015), 980–97, at 982.

23 Sabine d'Estrée, 'Translator's note', in Pauline Réage, *Story of O* (New York: Grove Press, 1965), pp. ix–xiii, at p. xii; Wyngaard, 'End of pornography', 986; Richard Seaver, *The Tender Hour of Twilight*, ed. Jeannette Seaver (New York: Farrar, Straus and Giroux, 2012), p. 362.

24 Rosset, *Dear Mr. Beckett*, p. 358.

25 Austryn Wainhouse, 'On translating Sade', *Evergreen Review*, 10:42 (1966), 50–6 and 87, quote at 87.

26 Bruce Abbott [Robert Sewall], *The Sign of the Scorpion* (New York: Grove Press, 1970); L. Erectus Mentulus [Gershon Legman], *The Oxford Professor Returns* (New York: Grove Press, 1971); Gershon Legman, 'Introduction', in Anonymous, *My Secret Life: Abridged but Unexpurgated* (New York: Grove Press, 1966), pp. 15–57. See Glass, *Rebel Publisher*, p. 140, for the sales figures for *My Secret Life*.

Index

Note: the authors rather than the titles of literary works are listed in the index.

Ablemann, Paul 76, 78
Abrams, Barbara 183
Abrams, Sam 158, 159, 183, 194
Ackerley, J. R. 78
Admiral, Virginia 39, 40, 44, 50
Aldington, Richard 20–2, 199, 213
Amelinckx, Frans 108
Amory, Richard (Richard Love) 162
Angélique, Pierre (George Bataille)
    82
anonymity 3, 81–2, 99, 203, 204,
    207, 208
    see also pseudonyms
Apollinaire, Guillaume 67, 94, 99,
    105–6, 107, 108–9, 110, 111,
    112, 113, 114, 115, 116, 117,
    118–19, 147
Ashby, Richard 166
Atchenson, Louis 160
Atwood, Margaret 129
Auden, Rene (Uta West) 166–7
Audiart (Austryn Wainhouse) 68,
    84, 97

Aury, Dominique 82, 87, 137–42,
    195–6, 203, 224, 225
avant-garde literature 2, 3, 4, 24–5,
    67, 77, 101, 153, 162, 182,
    187, 211, 220, 221, 224

Babou, Henri 4, 6, 9, 21
Bald, Wambly 29–30
Banis, Victor 162
Barker, George 40, 55
Barnes, Djuna 23
Baron, Willie (Baird Bryant) 84,
    124–5
Barr, Cecil (Jack Kahane) 4, 7–9
Barthes, Roland 219
Bataille, Diane 82, 87, 130–1
Bataille, George 67, 68–9, 72, 82,
    92, 156, 176, 218–19, 220
BDSM 9, 131, 140, 145, 208
    see also whipping
Beach, Sylvia 6–7, 13, 17, 20, 23, 188
Beardsley, Aubrey 28, 84, 98, 126,
    188, 204, 208–13

Beckett, Samuel 2, 34, 66, 67–8, 72, 75, 76, 146, 148, 182, 199, 221, 224, 225
Beiles, Sinclair 84
Bell, Daniel 93
Bellmer, Hans 72
Beplate, Justin 67
Berger, John 64
Bernet, Michael 189–91
Bernofsky, Susan 199
Bowles, Patrick 64, 67–8
Bradley, William 23, 31
Brandon House 121, 156, 157, 184, 185
Brennan, Karen 193
Brophy, Brigid 74
Broughton, James 66
Bruce, Lenny 90
Bryant, Baird 68, 80, 81, 84, 88, 124–5, 222, 223
Bryant, Denny 82, 88
Burgess, Anthony 15, 203
Burroughs, William 2, 66, 72, 73, 77–8, 93, 154, 155, 158, 163, 177, 180, 182, 201–2, 203, 214–15, 220, 221, 222, 224, 225
Burroughs, William Jr 174, 179–80
Busby, Brian 126–7

Calder, John 81, 149, 185, 203, 223
Campbell, James 65
Carter, Angela 105, 107, 119
Carter, Angela M., 137
Casavini, Pieralessandro (Austryn Wainhouse) 68, 84, 97
Casement, Roger 89, 154, 155, 224

censorship 1, 4, 5, 11–12, 14, 21, 25, 26, 70, 90, 91–6, 100–1, 154, 188, 154, 155, 201–3, 210, 220, 221–2, 225
Chelsea Hotel 157
Chester, Alfred 86–7, 142–3, 222
Child, Sally 150
Childs, J. Rives 53
Cleland, John 91, 97, 100, 102, 103–4, 111–12, 118, 188, 201, 222
Cocteau, Jean 68, 171, 215–16
Coleman, John 82
Collier, Peter 157, 160–1, 184
Colligan, Colette 63, 99, 196
Connolly, Cyril 13–14
Corso, Gregory 77, 90
Cousins, Sheila 26–8
Craig, Alec 5
Crannach, Henry (Marilyn Meeske) 86, 90, 133
Crosby, Caresse 39, 50
Curtis, Jackie 183

Daimler, Harriet (Iris Owens) 87, 113, 133, 150, 199
Darnton, Robert 100, 103, 118
Darrich, Sybah (Richard Ashby) 166
de Fariente, Beauregard 97, 102, 103, 111, 118
Deforges, Régine 138
Delany, Samuel 183, 185
de las Lunas, Carmencita (Alexander Trocchi) 85, 149, 222
del Piombo, Akbar (Norman Rubington) 85, 144–6, 153, 222
Desmond, Robert (Robert Desmond Thompson) 84, 123–4

Desnos, Robert 101
de St. Jorre, John 75, 80, 86, 89, 122, 123, 138, 223
d'Estrée, Sabine (Richard Seaver) 225
di Prima, Diane 160, 161, 167, 174
dirty books 1, 2, 4, 63, 72, 85, 86, 121–52 passim, 158, 162, 164, 165, 166, 168, 169, 171, 183, 188, 190, 191, 194, 198, 206, 219, 223, 224
Donleavy, J. P. 2, 66, 72, 74–5, 82, 88, 95, 182, 221
Douthit, Peter 160, 178
Dowling, Linda 211–12
Drake, Hamilton (Mason Hoffenberg) 84, 152
Drake, Winifred (Denny Bryant) 82, 88
Duhème, Jacqueline 198
Duncan, Robert 39, 40, 41
Durrell, Lawrence 2, 4, 5, 66, 72, 182, 199–201, 213, 221, 224

erotic classics 97–120 passim
Essex House Press 163, 185
Ewart, Gavin 14
exaggeration (in pornography) 46, 111–12, 118, 193, 195, 212

Ferguson, Robert 55
Ferrone, John 47, 56, 60, 61, 133–4
Ffrench, Patrick 218
Fishman, Melvin 158
fisting 109
Fitch, Noël Riley 50, 55
Fletcher, Ian 210
Ford, Charles Henri 2, 5, 23–5, 29, 72, 77

Forster, Chris 11, 223–4
Fraenkel, Michael 81
Frappier-Mazur, Lucienne 115, 118
Freide, Donald 136
Fremont-Smith, Eliot 182, 195
French Ministry of the Interior 94–5
Frogé, Gaït 63, 80

Gall, Michel 79–80, 82–3
Genet, Jean 2, 66, 72, 75, 93, 154, 182, 199, 216–18, 221, 222, 224, 225
Gertzman, Jay 163
Ginsberg, Allen 73, 180
Girodias, Maurice 2, 4, 6, 9, 34, 62–96 passim, 97, 99, 100, 101, 118, 120, 121, 124, 126, 130, 131, 137, 142, 143, 145, 146, 147, 148, 150, 153–86 passim, 188–91, 194, 199, 204, 205, 207, 213, 219, 221–6 passim
Glass, Loren 224
Glassco, John 84, 92, 98, 126–9, 204, 208, 210–11, 213, 222, 224
Gontarski, S. E. 224
Goulemot, Jean Marie 105, 112, 114, 116, 118
Greene, Graham 27, 76
Greenleaf Press 162, 184
Greta X (John Millington-Ward) 85
Grimm, Benjamin (Spencer Lambert) 159, 164–5
Grove Press 34, 62, 77, 82, 83, 93, 95, 120, 138, 154–7, 159, 180, 184, 185, 186, 188, 195–6, 202, 203, 220, 224–5
Gysin, Brion 78, 90

Hall, Radclyffe 2, 5, 188
Hammer, Stephen (John Coleman) 82
Hanley, James 14–16, 94
Harrell, Margaret 157–8
Harris, Frank 16–20, 78–9, 94, 188, 224
Hellier, Odile 139
Herron, Paul 54
Himes, Chester 73–4, 182
Hoffenberg, Mason 80, 84, 152, 222
Home Office 93–5
Homer & Associates (Michel Gall) 82–3
homoeroticism 14, 24, 40, 89, 98–9, 143, 162, 177, 215–18
Hornwood, Harvey 159, 174
Howard, George 54
Howard, Gerald 151
humour 7, 36, 88, 108–9, 116–18, 144, 145, 146–8, 151, 174, 194, 223
Hunt, Lynn 100, 118

incest 110–11, 114, 131, 165

Jackson, Roger 53
James, Norah 6, 9–11
Jay, Victor (Victor Banis) 162
Johnson, Roy Melisander 35–61 passim, 134, 135, 192–3, 221
Jones, Henry (John Coleman) 82
Joyce, James 6–7, 15, 63, 74, 177, 188, 199, 200, 212
Juengel, Scott 104

Kahane, Jack 2, 4–34 passim, 63, 78, 148, 188, 189, 200, 221, 222

Kamboureli, Smaro 134, 137
Kasak, Richard 207
Kearney, Patrick 64, 72, 83, 86, 91, 92, 159, 184
Kemp, Earl 162, 184
Kerouac, Jack 167
Kenton, Maxwell (Mason Hoffenberg and Terry Southern) 84
Kimball, George 162, 183
Kinsey Institute 48, 51, 56
Klein, K. K (Robert Turner) 162–3
Klinkowitz, Jerome 182
Kronhausen, Eberhard 49, 79, 144
Kronhausen, Phyllis 49, 79, 144

Ladenson, Elisabeth 25, 201, 220
Lambert, Spencer 159, 164–5
Lancer Press 156, 185
Larkin, Philip 13
Lawrence, D. H. 5, 63, 77, 176, 188, 199, 222
Lawrence, T. E. 15–16
Laughlin, James 34
Le Brun, Annie 119
Legman, Gershon 1, 35–61 passim, 62, 83, 121, 225
Lengel, Frances (Alexander Trocchi) 85, 204, 207
Lesse, Ruth (John Millington-Ward) 85
Lewys, Peter (Pierre Louÿs) 99, 105, 107, 109, 110, 111, 112, 113, 114–15, 118, 119
literature vs pornography 2, 4, 6, 9, 34, 65, 67, 69, 71, 72, 76, 100, 140, 142, 151, 152, 153, 174, 175, 182, 183, 187–200 passim, 221–5

Lodge, David 203
Logue, Christopher 64, 66, 69, 71, 81, 82, 83, 123, 222
Lougee, Jane 65, 69, 80, 87, 222
Louÿs, Pierre 67, 99, 105, 107, 109, 110, 111, 112, 113, 114–15, 118, 119, 147
Love, Richard 162
Lowenfels, Walter 81, 180
Luboviski, Milton 53–4

McCaffery, Larry 181
Mahon, Alyce 70, 101, 119, 139, 140
Mailer, Norman 177, 215
Major, Clarence 180–3
Malzberg, Barry 166, 174, 178–9, 182
Mansfield, June *see* June Miller
Marcus, Steven 106, 125, 126, 130, 146, 188, 190, 210
Mardaan, Ataullah 88
Martin, Ed (Edgar A.) 80, 153, 220
Martin, Jay 50
Masquerade Books 204, 207, 213
masturbation 103, 107, 117, 118, 127, 142, 144, 145, 152, 160, 173, 179, 189, 190, 194, 210, 211
Matthews, Ronald 26
Meeske, Marilyn 71–2, 80, 86, 87–8, 90, 96, 133, 144, 151–2, 159–60, 222
Merlin collective 64, 65, 66, 67, 68, 69, 71, 159, 225
Merlin periodical 64, 65, 67, 70, 71, 82, 87, 225
Michelson, Peter 114, 119–20, 193–5, 212, 218
Miller, Edmund 137

Miller, Henry 1–2, 4–5, 7, 12, 29–30, 32, 33, 34, 35–61 passim, 66, 70, 72, 78, 94, 121, 122, 135, 148, 154, 155, 168, 173, 180, 181, 182, 188, 199–201, 202–3, 213, 219, 220, 221, 222, 224, 225
Miller, June 30, 32, 43
Millett, Kate 220
modernism 2, 3, 5, 15, 20, 23, 24–5, 34, 63, 137, 196, 200, 219, 220, 223
Mole, Oscar (Alexander Trocchi) 99
Moline, Marlene 160, 172–4
Monty Python 164
Musset, Alfred 97, 103, 106, 110
My Secret Life 37, 46, 47, 225

Nabokov, Vladimir 2, 67, 72, 75–6, 82, 95, 148, 154, 168, 179, 196, 199, 219, 221, 222
Neagoe, Peter 11–12, 29
Nesbit, Malcolm (Alfred Chester) 86–7, 142–3
Newman, Frank (Sam Abrams) 159, 183, 194
Nin, Anaïs 2, 5, 7, 30–4, 35–61 passim, 80, 121, 133–7, 139, 142, 147–8, 191–3, 219–20, 221
Norberg, Kathryn 105
Norden, Marika (Mirjam Vogt) 28

Obelisk Press 2, 4–34 passim, 36, 63, 64, 78, 79, 94, 188, 199, 213, 219, 221, 223–4
O'Connor, Philip 76
Olympia magazine 87, 89–90

Olympia Press 2, 62–96 passim, 97, 98, 99, 100, 102, 103, 105, 107, 109, 111, 115, 121, 122, 123, 125, 127, 131, 133, 143, 144, 146, 148, 150, 152, 153–86 passim, 188–91, 194, 197, 199, 203, 204, 205, 206, 207, 211, 213, 218, 219, 220, 223–4, 225
O'Neil, Peter 122
oral sex 19–20, 46, 49, 54, 58–9, 61, 78, 105, 107, 110, 114, 115, 125, 131, 136, 140, 166, 176, 194, 201, 207–8, 209, 214, 217
orgasm 19, 44, 55, 58, 102, 103, 104, 112, 114, 125–6, 127, 128, 129, 136, 145, 146, 147, 165, 173, 176, 202
orgies 42, 103, 107–8, 111, 113, 153, 166, 168, 177
Owens, Iris 2, 72, 80, 81, 87, 89, 90, 96, 113, 121, 133, 147, 150–1, 152, 199, 222, 223
Oxman, Philip 82, 129–30, 223

paedophilia 80, 119, 165
Palin, Michael 164
Patchen, Kenneth 40
Paulhan, Jean 138, 139, 141
Pauvert, Jean-Jacques 70, 92, 137, 225
Peachum, Thomas (Philip Oxman) 82, 129–30
Pearson, Angela (John Millington-Ward) 85–6
Pearson, Neil 4, 5, 28, 29
Pease, Allison 212
Pekinpah, Deneen 160, 171–2
Penguin Press 220
Perez, Faustino (Mason Hoffenberg) 84

Perkins, Michael 169, 172, 176, 194
Perlès, Alfred 7–8, 148
Phillips, John 67, 105, 117–19, 140, 142, 191, 195
philosophy 72, 100, 102, 120, 125, 136, 148–9, 176, 195
Platt, Charles 163–4
polymorphous sexuality 24, 98, 114, 120, 165, 177
pornographic effect 115–16
pornotopia 106, 125, 126, 130, 146, 190, 210
Potter, Rachel 200
Powell, Anna 137
pseudonyms 4, 6, 28, 35, 81–9, 99, 121, 122, 123, 131, 138, 153, 162, 165, 166, 172, 178, 180, 182, 188, 194, 222, 225

Queneau, Raymond 72, 197–9, 220

Rabbit, Peter (Peter Douthit) 160, 178
Rabe, Claire 87, 90
Ramparts magazine 157, 159, 184
rape 8, 19, 27, 41, 54, 81, 93, 106, 111, 114, 123, 124, 130, 131, 132, 140, 150, 160, 165, 170, 190, 194, 218
Raskin, Lyn 160
Réage, Pauline (Dominique Aury, Anne Desclos) 67, 82, 137–42, 195–6, 203, 224, 225
Reed, Ishmael 181
Rembar, Charles 201
Restif de La Bretonne, Nicholas-Edme 68, 97, 107–8, 111, 115, 116
Richard-Allerdyce, Diane 193

Richardson, Humphrey (Michel Gall) 79–80, 82
Robinson, William 99
Rosset, Barney 34, 62, 83, 95, 154–7, 186, 203, 224–5
Roth, Samuel 16–17, 18, 37, 59, 210
Rubington, Norman 80–1, 85, 90–1, 144–6, 147, 153, 154, 222, 223
Rudahl, Sharon 167–71, 174
Ruder, Barnet 35, 36, 38–47 passim, 52, 53, 70, 192, 200

Sabor, Peter 104
Sade, Marquis de 34, 68, 69–71, 72, 87, 94, 97–120 passim, 138, 140, 155–6, 165, 171, 173, 185, 188, 224, 225
Sativa, Mary (Sharon Rudahl) 167–71
Scheiner, Clifford 48, 59
Schmidt, Judith 93, 154
Scott, Andrew Murray 73, 185
Seaver, Richard 64, 65, 67, 99, 155–6, 185, 203, 218, 222, 224, 225
Seftali, Leila (Marlene Moline) 172–4
Sellers, Peter 158
Sewall, Robert 35–6, 47–52, 54, 55, 225
sexual revolution (1960s) 3, 153–86 passim, 220, 222, 223, 224, 226
Shaw, Bernard 16
Shaw, Charlotte 16
Sherwood, James 87–8, 146
Singer, Norman 160–1, 163

Singleton-Gates, Peter 88, 89
Smith, Wallace 25–6, 188
Smithers, Leonard 208, 211
sodomy 15, 22, 49, 98, 103, 105, 108–9, 111, 112, 113, 114, 127, 130, 131, 133, 140, 143, 144, 167, 173, 194, 215
Sohmers, Harriet 86–7, 142
Solanas, Valerie 157, 174, 186
Sontag, Susan 87, 118, 141–2, 195, 219, 220
Southern, Terry 73, 84, 143–4, 147, 221, 224
Sparrow, John 89
Spencer, Sharon 31
Stein, Gertrude 23
Steintrager, James 110, 120
Stephens, Elizabeth 217
Stephenson, Gregory 142, 223
Stevenson, John 80, 81, 84–5, 93, 122–3, 125–6, 222
Stonier, George Walter 27
Suárez, Juan 24–5
Suck magazine 158–9
surrealism 24, 33, 40, 70, 77, 146, 171–2, 201

Talsman, William (James M. Smith) 83
Tavel, Roland 177–8
Teleny 69, 98–9
Templeton, Edith 131–3, 142, 220
Thoma, Richard 28–30, 78
Thomas, Édith 141
Thompson, Hunter S. 157, 162
Thompson, Robert Desmond 84, 123–4
Tice, Clara 37, 47

Townsend, Larry 162
Toynbee, Philip 76
Trail, George 210, 211
translation (of erotic material) 34,
	64, 65, 67, 68–71, 86–7, 88,
	95, 97, 99–100, 120, 121,
	155–6, 158, 185, 197, 199,
	218, 225
Trocchi, Alexander 2, 64, 65, 66,
	67, 69, 73, 79, 81, 85, 99, 121,
	148–50, 151, 185, 204–7,
	212–14, 222, 224
tropes (pornographic) 130, 133,
	134, 143, 169–70, 193, 194,
	201, 209
Turner, Robert 162–3
Tyler, Parker 2, 5, 23–5, 29, 72,
	77

underage sex 16–17, 20, 86, 108,
	110, 111, 113, 114, 119,
	127–9, 130, 131, 162, 163,
	164, 166, 170, 194
	see also paedophilia
Underwood, Miles (John Glassco)
	84, 92, 222

van Heller, Marcus (John Stevenson)
	80, 81, 84–5, 93, 122–3,
	125–6, 222
Vassi, Marco 174, 175–7
Vicarion, Count Palmiro
	(Christopher Logue) 83, 123,
	222
Vidal, Gore 37–8
violence 15, 41, 45, 57, 58, 80, 106,
	114, 119–20, 133, 149–50,
	181, 182, 206–7
	see also rape

Vogt, Mirjam 28
Von Soda, Bernhardt (Robert Waltz)
	83, 126
voyeurism 50, 105–6, 129–30, 143,
	147–8, 193

Wagner, Geoffrey 220
Wainhouse, Austryn 63, 64, 65, 66,
	68–71, 72, 80, 81, 84, 92, 97,
	155–6, 218, 222, 224, 225
Wainhouse, Muffie (Mary) 78, 80,
	81, 88
Walbrook, Louise (Edith
	Templeton) 131–3, 142, 220
Wallace, Irving 187–90
Waltz, Robert 83, 126
Warhol, Andy 174, 178, 183, 186
West, Uta 166–7
whipping 38, 49, 74, 81, 82, 85,
	108, 111, 122, 127–9, 130–1,
	140, 164, 176, 195, 208, 211
Wilde, Oscar 99
Willett, John 203
Williams, Gerald 158, 185–6
Williams, Tennessee 34, 77
Wilson, Edmund 70, 115, 196
Wolfe, Bernard 39, 41–2
women (and pornography
	production) 3, 42, 86–9, 121,
	130–42, 147–8, 150–2, 153,
	159–60, 161, 166–74, 222,
	225
	see also Nin, Anaïs
Wood, Clement 16–17, 37
Worms, Miriam 75, 77, 80–1, 87,
	96
Wu Wu Meng (Sinclair Beiles) 84
Wyngaard, Amy S. 70–1, 225